Colección Támesis

SERIE A: MONOGRAFÍAS, 280

POETRY AND LOSS

THE WORK OF EUGENIO MONTEJO

In a study which covers the entirety of Montejo's career as poet and essayist, this book examines how the work of this seminal Venezuelan writer explores and deals with the experiences of loss in the twentieth century. Focusing on the broad areas of temporal and spatial loss, the analysis underlines the different levels on which such experiences are located in Montejo's writing, from the personal to the national, from the continental to the wider ontological, all filtered through the poet's own lived experience of growing up and writing in Venezuela. It explores how the poetic act emerges throughout as the potential means by which such experiences can be expressed and through which such loss can be reversed and, henceforth, avoided.

This represents the first book-length study in English of Montejo's work and the first monograph in any language to offer a sustained thematic analysis of his entire output. In the process, it serves to bring out from the academic shadows one of the most important and commanding poetic voices to emerge from Latin America in the last fifty years.

NICHOLAS ROBERTS lectures in Hispanic Studies at the University of Durham.

NICHOLAS ROBERTS

POETRY AND LOSS

THE WORK OF EUGENIO MONTEJO

TAMESIS

First published 2009 by Tamesis, Woodbridge

ISBN 978-1-85566-193-6

Tamesis is an imprint of Boydell & Brewer Ltd
PO Box 9, Woodbridge, Suffolk IP12 3DF, UK
and of Boydell & Brewer Inc.
668 Mt Hope Avenue, Rochester, NY 14620, USA
website: www.boydellandbrewer.com

A CIP catalogue record for this book is available
from the British Library

The publisher has no responsibility for the continued existence or accuracy
of URLs for external or third-party internet websites referred to in this
book, and does not guarantee that any content on such websites is,
or will remain, accurate or appropriate

This publication is printed on acid-free paper

Printed in Great Britain by
CPI Antony Rowe Ltd, Chippenham and Eastbourne

CONTENTS

For my parents

ACKNOWLEDGEMENTS

I should like to thank Luis Rebaza-Soraluz, Catherine Boyle, Julian Weiss, Chris Perriam, and Jason Wilson for their help, patience, and academic and scholarly insights, which proved invaluable on so many occasions over the course of my research. For its financial support, I should like to thank the Arts and Humanities Research Council. My thanks must also go to Eugenio Montejo himself, whom I was fortunate enough to meet in 2002 and then correspond with on a regular basis. His help in providing illuminating details about his work and in facilitating the obtaining of the more elusive texts was invaluable, and surpassed only by my gratitude to him for revealing that beneath the many books piled on my desk there was a warm and generous human being. It is, thus, both academically and personally, a cause of great sadness that he passed away before I had the chance to present him with this completed study of his literary production.

For her unswerving love and support I must also declare myself indebted to Heiddy Roberts. She has helped me in more ways than she can ever know to get through both the writing of this book and the various trials and tribulations that occurred during that period. Likewise, I should like to thank my parents for their support, not just during the writing of this book, but over the last thirty-three years. It is their constant encouragement during this time which has given me the confidence to pursue my goals in life, both academic and otherwise. My thanks also go to Dr Sarah Partridge, Lorraine, and Lesley, without whom this book and much more would not have been.

Finally, I must also thank Gabriela for helping me to understand what life is really about.

ABBREVIATIONS AND BIBLIOGRAPHICAL NOTE

Whilst I have used the Author–Date system throughout for references, the following abbreviations are used for Montejo's principal poetry and essay collections. First editions have been prioritised wherever possible. The exceptions are: *Alfabeto del mundo*, where the first edition is not obtainable; *El taller blanco*, whose first edition lacks several essays from subsequent editions; *El cuaderno de Blas Coll*, where previous editions were successively expanded in subsequent editions; and *Adiós al siglo XX*, whose first edition lacks many poems found in the second (1997) and subsequent editions. I have not been able to obtain the further-expanded fourth edition (2004) of this book. I have not used anthologised/amended versions of poems, unless otherwise stated. Where editions other than those detailed here are referenced, the Author-Date system has been used. For full bibliographical details, see Bibliography.

Eugenio Montejo

Poetry

Humano paraíso (1959)	*HP*
Élegos (1967)	*É*
Muerte y memoria (1972)	*MM*
Algunas palabras (1976)	*AP*
Terredad (1978)	*T*
Trópico absoluto (1982)	*TA*
Alfabeto del mundo (1988 [1986])	*AM*
Adiós al siglo XX (1997 [1992])	*AS*
Partitura de la cigarra (1999)	*PC*
Papiros amorosos (2002)	*PA*
Fábula del escriba (2006)	*FE*

Essays

La ventana oblicua (1974)	*VO*
El taller blanco (1996 [1983])	*TB*

Heteronymic works

El cuaderno de Blas Coll y dos calígrafos de Puerto Malo (2007a [1981])	BC
Guitarra del horizonte (1991), Sergio Sandoval	GH
El hacha de seda (1995), Tomás Linden	HS
Chamario (2004), Eduardo Polo	CH
La caza del relámpago (2006), Lino Cervantes	CR

Extracts from *GH* appear with the permission of Alfadil.
Extracts from *PC*, *PA*, and *FE* appear with the permission of Pre-Textos.
Extracts from *AM* appear with the permission of El Fondo de Cultura Económica: D.R. © (1988) FONDO DE CULTURA ECONÓMICA Carretera Picacho-Ajusco 227, C.P. 14738, México, D.F.

Every effort has been made to contact the original publishers of Montejo's other works where long citations are used, and any omissions will be gladly remedied in the next edition of this book, if the necessary information is provided. My profound thanks to Aymara Montejo for giving me her blessing with respect to the use of all citations from her late husband's work.

Introduction: Locating Montejo

Traditions and modernity

Within the tradition of modern Venezuelan poetry, Eugenio Montejo (1938–2008), *nom de plume* of Eugenio Hernández Álvarez, is a central figure. Recent years have witnessed an increasing recognition, both within and beyond the confines of his homeland, of his importance in Venezuela's literary history, and have seen the rapid growth of his reputation as one of the most notable individual literary voices to emerge not just from Venezuela but from Latin America generally in the twentieth century. Such recognition culminated in his being awarded the Premio Internacional Octavio Paz de Poesía y Ensayo 2004. Despite this prominence, Montejo's work has received little critical or academic appraisal, in particular outside of Venezuela itself.[1] It is, in part, this relative dearth of scholarly study which led to the genesis of the present book, whose aim is to explore how Montejo responds both individually and poetically to (his) place and time. It represents, to my knowledge, the first book-length study in English of Montejo's work and the first monograph in any language to offer a sustained thematic analysis of his entire output.[2]

At the heart of Montejo's significance as an individual Venezuelan literary figure lies his positioning within wider national and international poetic lineages, and in his profuse essayistic production and the many interviews that he gave during his lifetime, Montejo consistently underscored the importance of understanding the traditions within which one writes, traditions which play a determinant role in moulding the individual poetic voice. In Montejo's case, this voice bears witness to a particular conjoining of national (as well as wider Latin American) and European poetic traditions, whose resonances are fundamental in determining both the style and the thematic concerns of

---

[1] Only three articles in English, for example, have been published: Roberts (2004; 2007) and Gomes (2004).

[2] The only other book-length publications are: Medina Figueredo (1997), which covers Montejo's poetry from *Élegos* (1967) to *Adiós al siglo XX* (1997 [1992]), generally working poem by poem and chronologically through the collections; and Chirinos (2005), which reads more as a history of Romanticism than a monograph on Montejo, dedicating only about a quarter of its pages to an analysis of three of Montejo's collections (*Alfabeto del mundo* (1988 [1986]), *Adiós al siglo XX*, and *Partitura de la cigarra* (1999)).

the poet, and which are, hence, no less indispensable to our own appreciation of his writing.

Montejo's place within Venezuela's national tradition involves the recognition of two focal points in the poetic tradition of the country, both of which were discussed several times by Montejo: the *generación del 18* and the *generación del 58*.[3] The former comprises a group of Venezuelan intellectuals who lived their formative years under the dictatorship of Juan Vicente Gómez (1908–35). Writing from 1918 onwards, they represent a transitional movement, breaking what Nelson Osorio T. terms 'el estancamiento Modernista' (1985: 123) and paving the way for the emergence of the Venezuelan avantgarde, otherwise known as the *movimiento del 28*, in which several members of the *generación del 18* went on to participate.[4] The group includes such figures as José Antonio Ramos Sucre, Luis Enrique Mármol, Andrés Eloy Blanco, and Fernando Paz Castillo, and its importance for both Montejo and Venezuelan poetry cannot be overemphasised.

In his 1979 prologue to an anthology of Paz Castillo's poetry, Montejo declares the group to be 'de tan determinante gravitación en nuestras letras' (1979: 8), going on to describe the poets which make up the group as the very foundations upon which any and every Venezuelan poet since builds:

> [Estos poetas] integran lo que llegará a ser el primer intento coherente por establecer un clima de modernidad literaria tal como hoy lo concebimos. Por eso quienes más tarde se sumen al empeño de reactualizar nuestras artes, lo harán sobre todo a partir del avance que ellos anticiparon proyectándose así hasta el presente, con aportes inéditos, la gestión renovadora de los hombres del 18. (8)

And some twenty years later, he states unambiguously that he considers them the founders of 'la poesía moderna en Venezuela' (López Ortega 1999: 8).

---

3   See, for example, Montejo (1979: 8–13) for comments on the *generación del 18* and comments made in interview on both *generaciones* in López Ortega (1999: 8–11). These two *generaciones* are not, of course, the only poetic movements of significance in twentieth-century Venezuelan poetry. The *generación* or *movimiento del 28*, for example, was both an important anti-Gómez student movement and a pivotal poetic movement in Venezuela centred around the publication of the journal *Válvula* in 1928 and headed by figures such as Miguel Otero Silva, Jóvito Villalba, and Rómulo Betancourt (see Osorio T. (1985: 89–109; 143–80)). Likewise, the increasingly urban poetics begun by the *generación del 58* led to the emergence in the early eighties of groups such as *Guaire* and *Tráfico*, headed by figures such as Rafael Arráiz Lucca, Armando Rojas Guardia, and Yolanda Pantin (see Gackstetter Nichols (2000)). Montejo himself, however, focuses predominantly on the *generación del 18* and the *generación del 58*.

4   For a more thorough introduction to the *generación del 18* see Castellanos (1966). There is also a short, though informative, essay entitled 'La transición y los poetas del 18' by Nelson Osorio T. (1985: 121–5).

What stands out in Montejo's 1979 description of these poets is the focus on the act of *renovación* and *(re)actualización*: the group's primary importance lies in bringing Venezuelan poetics up to date. This characteristic of the *generación del 18* has frequently been commented on by critics: Juan Liscano points to their work being 'una poesía de ruptura violenta o parcial con el lenguaje estereotipado imperante' (1973: 20), and Nelson Osorio T. signals their role in 'colocar a la literatura venezolana en una hora más ajustada con la que marcan los relojes del continente y el mundo' (1985: 123). For Montejo, likewise, the global situation and understanding of these poets is important: coinciding with the end of the First World War, 'la acción de este grupo notable se inserta [...] en un movimiento más vasto, el cual reúne sus *coetáneos* [de Fernando Paz Castillo] entre hombres de varios países que guardan una sintonía similar ante los hechos que les corresponde vivir' (1979: 9). And yet elsewhere Montejo sees the importance of the *generación del 18* as lying not so much in an *actualización* in continental or universal terms, as in the fact that it was one which responded to the needs and conditions of the time in the Venezuela of Gómez:

> En plena dictadura [...] estos muchachos de apariencia distraída oponen a la teoría del 'gendarme necesario' asumida por la inteligencia de la época la de la 'palabra necesaria'. Ellos desafían el hecho de no tener una vida holgada ni mucho menos y van haciendo una poesía que hoy nos honra.[5]
> (López Ortega 1999: 8)

Put simply, in his comments on the *generación del 18* Montejo reveals his understanding of modern Venezuelan poetics as built upon a model of *(re)actualización*, where the poetic act becomes '[e]l empeño de reactualizar nuestras artes' (1979: 8) in accordance with the national experience of the time. This understanding of twentieth-century Venezuelan poetry may go some way to explaining the tendency for its classification in terms of 'generations': the tradition founded by the *generación del 18* is one of the periodic re-generation of existing poetics in order constantly to align it with the new social and political realities experienced by the people and poets. In short, it is an approach to twentieth-century Venezuelan poetry which looks to identify the determining moments of the lived experience of the nation with its determining poetic moments, or movements, each of which renovates the inherited poetics.

In this respect, it is not surprising that the second landmark movement in Venezuelan poetry to which Montejo frequently alludes is another 'genera-

---

[5] The concept of the *gendarme necesario* originates in Vallenilla Lanz (1961 [1919]). It refers to the argued need for a *caudillo* in order to maintain public order and was used specifically to justify the Gómez regime.

tion' marked by an abrupt change in the political, as well as the social and economic, character of the country.[6] The *generación del 58* comes at the point when Venezuela was both beginning its incursion into democracy following the regime of Marcos Pérez Jiménez (1952–58) and also undergoing a period of radical transition from an agrarian country to an increasingly industrial one dominated by oil.[7] With these democratic and industrial times came a corresponding need for a new *poética actualizada*, what Ángel Rama describes as a 'reconsideración de los sistemas expresivos heredados de los mayores [...] postulando una urgente modernización para dotar a las obras de su buscada capacidad comunicativa y de posibilitar la apropiación amplia de la realidad del período' (1987: 15). It is within this generation that Montejo finds himself, a generation writing from 1958 onwards and throughout the sixties, and which includes such figures as Rafael Cadenas, Ramón Palomares, Francisco Pérez Perdomo, and Juan Calzadilla, often working within poetic groups such as *Sardio, El Techo de la Ballena*, and *Tabla Redonda*.[8]

Given the combination of the wildly different nature of the sociopolitical situation in the two periods and what Montejo identifies as the need to *reactualizar* the country's poetics accordingly, these two literary movements represent, in Montejo's words, 'dos extremos, dos polos entre los que median cuarenta años' (López Ortega 1999: 9). And, indeed, the differences between the poetry and approach of the members of the two generations are marked. For the *generación del 18*, for example, as Montejo notes, 'el paisaje es una preocupación fundamental' (10), whereas 'la generación del 58 que escribe a cuarenta años de la generación del 18 se define, naturalmente, por lo urbano' (11). It is a contrast played out within Montejo's work itself, as I shall examine in chapter 3.

Yet these differences also run alongside and work towards a common goal. Contained within the concept of *reactualización* found in both movements there lies, for Montejo, a predominant concern for a poetics which reflects and represents the nation in a more 'authentic' way. In the case of the *generación del 18*, their lyricism and distinct preoccupation with the Venezuelan *paisaje* formed the basis for a reimposition of the autochthonous. In a decidedly anti-decadent poetics, they attempted to 'liquidar el modernismo en Venezuela y equilibrar los valores autóctonos (nativismo) [...] [y]

6   Chirinos describes the *Viernes* movement (c.1935–41) and the *generación del 42* as, similarly, having 'la intención de actualizar nuestras artes' (2005: 66).

7   For an overview of the changes experienced during this period, and the particular importance of the year 1958, see Ewell (1984: 94–154). Montejo's witnessing of these changes is referred to in Rodríguez Silva (2005a: 9).

8   See Ángel Rama's prologue to *Antología de 'El Techo de la Ballena'* (1987) for an informative discussion of the emergence of the poets (and artists) of these groups and this *generación*. Rama draws attention to the need for 'la renovación literaria contemporánea de Venezuela' (11) which characterised the group/journal *El Techo de la Ballena* in particular.

revalorizar los elementos propios de la nacionalidad en la búsqueda de un mensaje propio que asumiera lo nacional' (Carrera 1997). Both the dictatorial regime of Gómez and the prevailing literary (Modernist) climate of the beginning of the century were seen as suffocating the nation, repressing its 'authentic' being. The reaction against this by the poets of the *generación del 18* was, as Montejo pointed out, to reclaim the poetic description of the land itself, transforming it from what he terms a literary, that is, by implication, a shrouded or 'inauthentic', presentation, into one which was more 'authentic', more *criolla*:

> Se dice que ellos nacionalizaron el paisaje porque antes [...] el paisaje era un paisaje literario. Un poema brasileño se preguntaba que qué importancia tenía que el ruiseñor no cantara aquí si cantaban otros pájaros. Si tú recorres la poesía venezolana del siglo XIX te vas a encontrar con ruiseñores (aunque la paraulata sabanera blanca sea también un ruiseñor, eso no hay que decirlo). Pero para la generación del 18 fue una preocupación seria la búsqueda expresiva en torno al paisaje nuestro [...]. En un poema Paz Castillo dice: 'Cuando Jiménez dice chopo, cuando Machado dice olmo, yo digo urape'. Ahí se ve la lucha del poeta por introducir con la mayor naturalidad espiritual posible una palabra como urape.
>
> (López Ortega 1999: 10)

As the reference to the nightingale and the Spanish poets Juan Ramón Jiménez and Antonio Machado shows, the prevailing literary models in Venezuela were, in Montejo's understanding, 'inauthentic' in the sense that they were identifiable not as Venezuelan but as distinctly European (Spanish).[9] The *generación del 18*, then, were attempting to reassert a poetics and a language of and for Venezuela, understood by Montejo as, by implication, a poetics and a language which would not be *literarios*, but somehow natural, 'authentic'. Within this context, the importance of Montejo's notion of the *palabra necesaria*, referred to above in interview with López Ortega, becomes apparent. Extending his discussion of the term in his acceptance speech for the Premio Nacional de Literatura in 1998 (2006b: 291–4) and in the 2004 essay 'La balada del insomnio venezolano' (2006b: 263–72), Montejo lays bare that the groundwork laid by the *generación del 18* was not just that of the *(re)actualización* of the poetic word in Venezuela, but that of an attendant specific engagement by the Venezuelan poet with the language and being of the Venezuelan people, whereby his/her role was to realign and 're-authenticate' these two elements. In both these pieces, the identification

---

[9]   On this association of Modernism with Europe, Gerald Martin has noted that 'in Latin America writers almost unconsciously identified Naturalism with American concepts and Modernism with European forms' (1989: 5).

of the term with a specifically Venezuelan context, implied by its contrast to the *gendarme necesario*, is reiterated, and, likewise, there is the sense that the (poetic) word in question is one which is to speak for and bring together the nation as a whole, as Montejo underscores in his description of Leoncio Martínez's 1920 poem 'Balada del preso insomne', where 'va a reunirse [...], *avivado por el alma colectiva*, un hallazgo de lo que debemos llamar la "palabra necesaria", vale decir, una concreción del verbo más verdadero *a los ojos de todos*' (2006b: 263–4, italics mine). The role of the poet as both reflecting and speaking for the people of Venezuela is a theme which, as we shall see, marks much of Montejo's poetics, and the centrality of (national) language and being to the poetic project in Venezuela is brought to the fore in Montejo's affirmation that, in the Venezuelan poetic tradition, 'la aspiración a una vida digna principia por la vigilancia de la palabra que la nombra, y por la consecuente identificación entre vida y palabra' (2006b: 294). These words speak not just of the *generación del 18*, then, but of Montejo's under-lying philosophy of the role and aims of poetry, set squarely here within the context of Venezuela. Furthermore, both in emphasising the need to be atten-tive to the way in which language is used and in the subsequent alignment of language with the (ontological well-)being of the people, they also attest to a distinctly (in this case, late) Heideggerean mode of thought within Montejo's work,[10] to which I shall refer at several points in this study.

Returning, for now, to the specificities of Montejo's depiction of the *gener-ación del 18*, we might note that the question of how any poetic presentation of the Venezuelan *paisaje* could ever not be *literario* is left hanging, as is the implied problematic notion of the 'authentic' or 'natural'. These themes will be taken up in chapters 3 and 4, where Montejo's own attempts at such a recasting of language and *paisaje* are explored.

The questionableness of a poetics which is not literary is further enhanced by the evident identification of the nationalisation of the *paisaje* and the imposition of indigenous terms for its flora and fauna with arguably the most famous Venezuelan poem of the nineteenth century, Andrés Bello's 'Silva a la Agricultura de la Zona Tórrida' (1985: 40–9). What is more, the engagement with this earlier poet also anticipates one of the primary characteristics of the *generación del 58*'s attempts to create a renewed national poetics to counter the petite bourgeoisie's dominance of Venezuelan culture and society (Rama 1987: 12), namely the fact that their own search for and use of new poetic forms runs alongside a renewed interest in the country's poetic tradition, and, in particular, the poetry of key members of the *generación del 18*, notably Ramos Sucre, whose work began to receive its first critical appraisal from

---

[10] See Pattison (2000: 173–5) for an overview of these aspects of Heidegger's thought.

1958 onwards.[11] This interest reflects both the debt owed by the later generation to the earlier poets as they seek to repeat their move of *actualización*
and also a parallel, underlying concern for the rescuing of a sense of national
poetic tradition. And it is here that the ambiguous nature of the concern for
'the national' becomes clear. The model set down by the *generación del 18* is
one of *renovación*, of rejection of the existing poetics and a move towards one
which might address the concerns and nature of the nation of the time. And,
indeed, both *generaciones* point towards new poetic horizons, in the case
of the *generación del 18*, the avant-garde, and in the case of the *generación
del 58*, an appropriation of a heterogeneous range of often anarchic styles,
languages, and rhythms (Lasarte 1991: 5–6; Rama 1987: 11). Yet, together
with this diachronic view of a changing nation, there is a concomitant desire
to assert a synchronic concept of 'the nation' and a national poetic tradition,
as indicated by their interest in central figures of the country's past poetics.[12]
And it is precisely in this tension between the need to *actualizar* and the
affirmation of a past national poetic tradition that Montejo locates modern
(twentieth-century) poetry in general, stating in a 1987 interview with Rafael
Arráiz Lucca that 'la modernidad es la relectura de una tradición bajo formas
nuevas, hasta entonces desconocidas' (1987: 4). Indeed, it also serves to
define Montejo's own poetic production. López Ortega, for instance, refers to
the latter as 'un punto donde la tradición se recoge y transforma, un espacio
que es origen pero también desembocadura' (2005: 16), and, more recently,
Miguel Gomes has talked of the 'imposibilidad de clasificarlo como inno-
vador de vocación o tradicionalista empedernido' (2007: 16).

More broadly, we are left with the question of where Montejo himself is
positioned within the genealogy of *generaciones* and movements of modern
Venezuelan poetry. In his essay 'Nueva aproximación a Ramos Sucre' (*TB*),
first published in 1981, Montejo referred to himself as a member of the
generación del 58 (29), as he did in interview in 2001 with Francisco José
Cruz (2006: 372). But Montejo also underlined the complexity of his relationship with the movement, acknowledging that he was 'muy perplejo frente
a la situación social de entonces' (López Ortega 1999: 9), as a result only
publishing his first 'libr[o] definitiv[o]' (9), *Élegos*, in 1967, thus locating him

---

[11] See Lasarte (1991: 6). This is also alluded to by Montejo in his essay 'Nueva aproximación a Ramos Sucre' (*TB*, 29–39, p. 29).

[12] This understanding of national tradition resonates with Hobsbawm's *The Invention of
Tradition* (1983) and the 'contrast between the constant change and innovation of the modern
world and the attempt to structure at least some parts of the social life within it as unchanging
and invariant' (2). The result is not just an invented or created (poetic, national) tradition, but,
as Benedict Anderson pointed out in *Imagined Communities* (1991), the realisation that (a
sense of) nation, both of a particular time and synchronically uniting all times, constitutes an
imagined or posited community (6–7).

'en la cola de la generación del 58' (9). What is more, Montejo highlighted a notable poetic and creative distance between himself and this *generación*:

> ¿Cómo me situé ante ellos? Los vi con gran amor, con gran cariño, pero también sentí distancia con la perspectiva creadora. El surrealismo, tomado como lo tomaron algunos, me pareció que no era un terreno fértil. Pero tampoco lo negué rotundamente; quería más bien que el tiempo verificara las cosas. (9)

Indeed, more than with the *generación del 58*, Montejo emphasised on occasion his links with the poetic tradition of Valencia, Venezuela's third city, in which he spent much of his upbringing and youth, and which was, at least during this time, a semi-rural location. Here, together with poets such as Teófilo Tortolero and Reynaldo Pérez So, he made up the so-called *Grupo de Valencia*, founding the journal *Poesía* in 1971.

Given these diverse factors, influences, and movements, it is difficult to identify Montejo with any one group or tendency in particular. Throughout this study, the concerns of the *generación del 58* found in Montejo's work will be apparent: the move into a Venezuela characterised by increasing urbanisation and industrialisation and how this is handled poetically and personally; the interest in the rediscovery or unearthing of past poetic traditions and figures in Venezuela, not just of the *generación del 18*, but of pivotal intervening figures such as Vicente Gerbasi and Juan Sánchez Peláez; and the sense of a need to reinvent a national poetics are all present in Montejo's writing. But, as Montejo himself indicated, both the way in which he responds to the poetic and social situation in which he finds himself and the themes and techniques which characterise his work are not solely guided by the *generación del 58*, nor by any other poetic group. Indeed, whilst his membership of the more 'rural' *Grupo de Valencia* can be seen to inform, as we shall discover, his approach to the increasing urbanisation of Venezuela, it is as an individual poet working within wider traditions that Montejo most often presents himself, rather than as a member of a specific school or movement.[13]

The effect of this positionality is, on the one hand, to point up the extent to which Montejo's concern for an overall sense of nation and national poetic tradition comes to be seen as the search for a national *meta*tradition, observing

---

[13] Even as regards his membership of the *Grupo de Valencia*, the extent to which Montejo downplayed any sense of a common or unified cause is noticeable. He stated, for instance, that 'éramos un grupo de amigos; no teníamos metas comunes como no fuesen la de aupar publicaciones y trabajar en conjunto [...]. No tuvimos una agenda de principios para seguirlos' (López Ortega 1999: 7). The only thing Montejo did describe them as having in common was a posture against Neruda's 'tono de poesía social' (7) and, as with the wider *generación del 58*, 'el estar pendiente uno del otro ante el país de entonces, ante el nacimiento de la democracia' (7).

and bringing together the diverse elements of the Venezuelan traditions of which he is a part. But it also leaves us with the dilemma of how we are to locate and understand the individuality of Montejo. Key, in this respect, are Montejo's early essays, collected, for the most part, in *La ventana oblicua* (1974). These writings, centred around specific poets and poetry in general, act as signposts to the influences and tendencies which make up Montejo's particular poetic approach and identity. Moreover, it is in these pivotal essays that the primary thematic threads and concerns of Montejo's work, what I have referred to in my title as 'poetry and loss', are made apparent, as I shall discuss shortly.

Whilst prominent Venezuelan figures such as Ramos Sucre and Sánchez Peláez do appear as the subject of individual essays in *La ventana oblicua*,[14] as well as of later essays,[15] underlining the importance of the national poetic heritage, we see, above all, a broader contextualisation of Montejo's literary apprenticeship and interests in these works. There is, for example, a sense of the interest in Oriental philosophy and poetics which makes itself felt in much of Montejo's writing, emerging in the essay 'I Ching, el libro de las mutaciones' (*VO*, 101–9), and, earlier still, in the Taoist ruminations of 'Textos para una meditación sobre lo poético' (1966), a text published in the same year as Rafael Cadenas's collection *Falsas maniobras* (1966), itself imbued with a sustained engagement with Zen Buddhism.[16] Similarly, an awareness of the wider Latin American context within which both he and Venezuelan poetics in general are situated is hinted at early on by essays on Drummond de Andrade (Brazil) and César Dávila Andrade (Ecuador) in *La ventana oblicua* and by pieces such as the short introduction to César Vallejo's work published in 1971.[17] Indeed, the question of these broader Latin American influences and concerns was addressed more directly by Montejo in later years, drawing attention to the presence of poets such as Carlos Pellicer, Eliseo Diego, Vallejo, and Octavio Paz in his poetic sensibilities.[18]

[14] See 'Aproximación a Ramos Sucre' (*VO*, 67–84) and 'La aventura surrealista de Juan Sánchez Peláez' (*VO*, 151–60). Montejo's first published article on the work of Ramos Sucre, 'El laúd del visionario' (1969), appeared some three years before 'Aproximación a Ramos Sucre' was written (1972).

[15] See 'Nueva aproximación a Ramos Sucre' (*TB*, 29–39) and 'Adiós a Juan Sánchez Peláez' (2006b: 279–83).

[16] Taosim is also an overt concern throughout the heteronymic work *Guitarra del horizonte* (1991) and is mentioned explicitly in the title poem of Montejo's *Partitura de la cigarra* (*PC*, 53).

[17] See, respectively: 'Poesía y vitalidad en Drummond de Andrade' (*VO*, 93–100); 'La fortaleza fulminada' (*VO*, 85–91); and Vallejo (1971: 9–11).

[18] Montejo discusses the influence of poets such as Vallejo and Pellicer in the interviews: Araujo (2004); Martins (1998); and Rodríguez Marcos (2002), as well as dedicating an essay to Pellicer in *El taller blanco* ('En torno al primer Pellicer', *TB*, 17–28). Diego is discussed in 'Recuerdo de Eliseo Diego' (2006b: 253–6) and Paz is shown to be a particularly significant

Several critics have also underlined Montejo's debt to such Latin American figures,[19] and I shall be drawing out some of the most salient resonances with poets such as Paz and Vallejo during the course of this study.

Despite the clearly important role played by these wider Latin American currents, it is nevertheless striking that it is, to a large extent, European traditions that make up the primary subject matter of the essays of *La ventana oblicua*. Twelve of the nineteen essays in the collection are dedicated to European figures or literatures: the Grail legend; Novalis; Arthur Rimbaud; Paul Valéry; Antonio Machado; Gottfried Benn; Giuseppe Ungaretti; Joë Bousquet; Jean Cassou; Luis Cernuda; Salvador Espriu; and, hovering between the Latin American and the European, though always writing in French, Jules Supervielle. This preponderance of European poetic models in his thought and formation is reiterated by Montejo himself in many interviews,[20] and its significance cannot be underestimated, pointing towards a conjunction which remains at the heart of Montejo's poetics throughout his career. In short, whilst, as my focus on the Venezuelan context of his work has reflected, Montejo frequently emphasised the importance of his specifically Venezuelan poetic influences (2006b: 300) and, more generally, of the need to appreciate the nature of the homeland of any artist in an evaluation of his/her work,[21] it is at the intersection of the concerns of a modern (late twentieth-century) Venezuelan poetics and those of a diverse range of European poets and movements that Montejo's work finds its heart. Moreover, this dual concern underlines the way in which a national poetics in Latin America is inextricably caught up with European poetic and philosophical traditions. To take the particularly pertinent examples of the two *generaciones* on which Montejo focused, the *generación del 18*, whilst working against European poetic models and terms, were, nonetheless, strongly influenced by Bergsonian thought;[22] and, as Rama has noted, in the *generación del 58* 'se registra una rápida y muchas veces superficial o indiscriminada apropiación de los valores europeos' (1987: 17). It is a further problematisation of 'the national' which is never far from the surface of Montejo's work, as shall be evident throughout this study.

Perhaps the most important tie which links Montejo to European shores in his poetic training and reading is also the most obvious of the ties which link

figure in Montejo's poetic reading and background in 'En la muerte de Octavio Paz' (2006b: 285–7) and in his acceptance speech for the Premio Octavio Paz (2006b: 299–309).

    [19] Among critics to draw particular attention to Montejo's Vallejian traits is Ferrari (1988: 15).

    [20] See, for example, López Ortega (1999: 7–8; 9–10; 12–13) and Gutiérrez (2002).

    [21] See 'El horizonte espacial del Orinoco en las obras de Jesús Soto y Alirio Palacios' (2006b: 329–43).

    [22] See Montejo (1979: 10).

Latin America in general to Europe and, specifically, Spain, namely that of a common language. Once again for Montejo it is a question of acknowledging the traditions within which, as poet, one finds oneself, in this case that of the language in which one writes:

> Desde el principio traté de situarme ante las nuevas corrientes sin sacrificar el diálogo con la tradición poética de nuestra lengua. Siempre procuré identificar en la nueva palabra poética algún eco de las voces antiguas, las voces que conforman su magnífica tradición. (Cruz 2006: 372–3)

Within that tradition, Montejo finds himself drawn in particular to the 'veta lírica [que] procede del Romancero o de más lejos, pasa por algunos anónimos populares y se concreta más hermosamente en Manrique y Fray Luis de León [y] luego [...] Quevedo' (373), and, we might add, which leads to the Romantic verse of poets such as Machado, about whom Montejo wrote and commented a great deal, and Lorca's *Romancero gitano* (1928).[23] Yet, whilst appreciating this Spanish heritage, Montejo underlines that this was a tradition which was transposed into Latin America as part of the *tradición culta*, in that 'las filiaciones también pueden rastrearse en la relectura que de estos creadores se ha hecho en Hispanoamérica. Se puede reconocer, por ejemplo, lo que hay de Quevedo en Vallejo o lo que hay de Quevedo en Borges' (López Ortega 1999: 8), a transposition in which it is important to note 'la búsqueda de una entonación específicamente latinoamericana' (Cruz 2006: 373). Bringing this lineage still closer to home, Montejo also underscores the continuation of the *Romancero* tradition within the *tradición popular* of Venezuela and, more generally, Latin America, referring to the *Romancero* as 'ese canto que se repite y que hoy lo encontramos acá tanto en la copla llanera [de Venezuela] como en toda hispanoamérica' (López Ortega 1999: 7).[24] Such a tracing of the *Romancero* lineage from medieval Spain to the modern Venezuelan folk tradition reflects the importance for Montejo both of the Peninsular heritage of the Spanish language and its poetic traditions and, as we saw in relation to the *generación del 18*, of the need to affirm both the Latin American and, in particular, the Venezuelan modulations of that (poetic) language. This is made particularly evident in his acceptance speech for the Premio Nacional de Literatura, where the evident pride in belonging to the Spanish linguistic tradition is foregrounded in Montejo's stressing that

---

[23] Montejo frequently underscored the importance of this Spanish lineage: see, for example, López Ortega (1999: 8) and Araujo (2004). Chirinos has focused on the relevance of Machado and Lorca in understanding Montejo's Spanish debts and influences (2005: 76–84; 106–12).

[24] The *copla llanera* is a traditional Venezuelan lyric form comprising four octosyllabic lines. It is the form used by Montejo's heteronym Sergio Sandoval in the collection *Guitarra del horizonte* (1991).

it is 'nuestra lengua, la misma lengua que cuando la hablamos delante de otras gentes [...] hace possible que sin vacilación se nos identifique como venezolanos' (2006b: 291).

Tracing the Orphic

Amidst the numerous references to the *Romancero*, European Romanticism, and twentieth-century figures such as Cernuda and Ungaretti, the most central and recurrent European poetic strand in Montejo's work is a classical one: the myth of Orpheus. At regular intervals in Montejo's production, the presence and importance of Orpheus is rendered explicit, specifically in the poems 'Orfeo' from *Muerte y memoria* (1972), 'Arqueologías' from *Terredad* (1978), 'En esta ciudad' from *Trópico absoluto* (1982), 'Orfeo revisitado' from *Alfabeto del mundo* (1988 [1986]), 'Partitura de la cigarra' from *Partitura de la cigarra* (1999), and 'Máscaras de Orfeo' from *Fábula del escriba* (2006a), with the first of these, 'Orfeo', constituting one of the most determining poems of Montejo's *œuvre*. Aside from these explicit instances, Orpheus is also an implied presence, in particular in Montejo's early essays on the Grail legend and German Romantics such as Novalis and Rilke.[25]

A discussion of Montejo's adaptation of the myth in the poem 'Orfeo' is central to any understanding of the essential concerns and thematics of his work, as several critics have recognised.[26] But it is important first to examine the basic topoi with which any engagement with the Orphic myth necessarily enters into dialogue, not least, in Montejo's case, because of the continued resonance of these topoi throughout his corpus.

One of the most important characteristics of the mythical figure of Orpheus in European literature is as an analogy that serves to expose the contradictory positions and pulls of any poet in any time and place. In the successive retellings and reengagements with the myth of Orpheus, from Virgil and Ovid to Milton and Rilke,[27] several key paradoxes emerge: the ability of poetry to triumph over death, an affirmation prioritised in the Ovidian version, and yet also the failure of poetry and the poet before death; the Orphic song as both a revitalising song which moves and unites the animate and the inanimate, and yet also as a song of mourning, of lamenting a loss which it could not reverse,

---

[25] In particular, see 'Desde el ciclo de la tabla redonda' (*VO*, 135–42) and 'Novalis, el fuego ante la noche' (*VO*, 27–38). Montejo refers to Rilke in 'Textos para una meditación sobre lo poético' (1966).

[26] Among the critical works to draw attention to the figure of Orpheus in Montejo's poetics are Balza (1983), Rivera (1986), Iribarren Borges (1987), and Medina Figueredo (1997).

[27] Among recent recastings of the myth, the trilogy of Orphic films by Jean Cocteau is one of the most famous, comprising *Le sang d'un poète* (1930), *Orphée* (1950), and *Le testament d'Orphée* (1959). Montejo himself shows an awareness of Cocteau in referring to him twice in 'Fragmentario' (*TB*, 238; 239).

as is emphasised in Milton's *Lycidas* (1983 [1638]);[28] the power of poetry as both immanent and yet also transcendent, a contradiction between whose polarities Rilke's *Sonnets to Orpheus* (1992 [1922]) in particular shift.[29]

Throughout Montejo's work these basic contradictory positions and characteristics of the poet and poetry are never far from the surface. Moreover, Montejo also engages with a further – and more fundamental – poetic questioning found within the figure of Orpheus. As Charles Segal has noted, one of the central oscillations in the character of Orpheus, both as poet and as a religious figure, is between his Apolline and his Dionysiac heritage (1993: 9). As Nietzsche famously discussed in *The Birth of Tragedy* (2000: 1–144), the figure of Apollo represents form, structure and rationality, and that of Dionysus ecstasy, unbridled emotion, and instinct. And the conflicting presence of these two within the figure of Orpheus is felt throughout the discussion in Montejo's essays of the *poeta nascitur non fit* debate, a discussion that extends more than twenty years from the essays of *La ventana oblicua* (1974) to those of *El taller blanco* (1996). In the former, Montejo brings this question to the fore in writing on the German Romantics. In 'Novalis: el fuego ante la noche' (*VO*, 27–38), Montejo takes a somewhat critical view of the importance given to systematic thought, theory, and 'la especulación científica' (31) by figures such as the Schlegel brothers, Fichte, and Schelling, describing Hölderlin as a notable exception to this rule, even if such a theoretical schooling was inevitably to be found in the poet:

> Cierto que [Hölderlin] escapará al rigor teórico por no sabemos cuál gracia angélica que le demarca otros cometidos [...]. Él será, con todo, el menos atrapado en los rigores intelectivos, el menos tentado por aquellas formas que los otros acometen como un mandato generacional. (31)

As the tone of this passage suggests, Montejo leans towards the characteristic which is most commonly associated with Romanticism in general, namely the assertion of emotion and intuition over rationalism. In this vein, in the essay 'Sobre la prosa de Machado' (*VO*, 125–34), Montejo describes Machado as a 'refutador de la poesía intelectual y de la llamada *estética de la construcción*, por más que, como lúcidamente advirtiera Gottfried Benn, el arte moderno tienda hacia una "cerebración progresiva"' (133). Yet Montejo also dedicates considerable attention in *La ventana oblicua* to discussing precisely those poets who emphasise the importance of intellect, form, and control, not least Benn himself, for whom 'el poema es [...] un *hacer*, una

---

[28] Where helpful, original publication dates (in original language where appropriate) have been included with references. All original publication dates are in the Bibliography.

[29] For a good overview of these central contradictions and the way in which they are played out in different renderings of the Orphic myth, see Segal (1993: 1–35).

operación volitiva que refuerza la experiencia y que se nutre en el dificilísimo combate librado a cada instante para conquistar formas nítidas de expresión' (*VO*, 45). Likewise, Montejo refers to Valéry's 'brillantez formal' (21) before commenting on how Valéry 'def[iende] [...] el poema que *se hace* [...] frente al poema que *nace*' (23).[30] Indeed, what is striking throughout these early essays by Montejo is the extent to which, alongside the laudatory descriptions of a Romantic rejection of 'los rigores intelectivos' (31), he stresses the importance of the technique and technical prowess of the poets about whom he writes, as, in a decidedly Modernist manner, he depicts the task of the poet as that of a craftsman, not least in his description of Ramos Sucre as a poet who 'se det[iene] en el oficio e intent[a] por sobre todo recrear una especie de gema arduamente trabajada' (77), an image echoed in his reference to the Brazilian Modernist poet Drummond de Andrade's 'humilde artesanía ante cada vocablo' (97). Moreover, critics have frequently commented on the sustained concern for poetic construction in Montejo's own work. Guillermo Sucre, for instance, describes Montejo's 'pasión constructiva y el casi perfecto control sobre el desarrollo del poema, que excluye lo divagatorio y deshilvanado' (1985: 309), and it is notable that Montejo's first published collection *Humano paraíso* (1959) was a collection of sonnets, a strict and measured poetic form.

The discussion of the two sides of the *se hace/nace* debate continues into the piece entitled 'Fragmentario' in the later *El taller blanco* (*TB*, 229–43), first published in 1983. This 'essay' is in fact a series of fragments, as the title suggests, concerned primarily with expressing Montejo's thoughts on poetry and the poetic act.[31] Here Montejo sides firmly with intuition, inspiration, and emotion, declaring in the very first fragment that:

> Aprender a sentir: esta sola tentativa, que no es nada pequeña, formaría mejor al joven poeta que todo el aprendizaje perseguido a través del conocimiento literario, las reglas, modas, etc. [...] [E]l sentimiento mismo, cuando es legítimo, procrea su forma o la posibilidad de inventarla.
>
> (229–30)[32]

---

[30] Many of the figures on both sides of the *se hace/nace* debate referred to by Montejo engage with the myth of Orpheus, Valéry in his poem 'Orfée' (1957: 76) and Benn in his poem 'Orpheus' Tod' (1986: 182–3), precisely in the period in which he had turned from the Dionysiac to the Apolline (see Ridley (1996)). On the other side of the debate, Goethe, to whom Montejo refers in 'Fragmentario' (*TB*, 241–2), likewise turns to the Orpheus myth in *Faust* (1956: 133).

[31] The nature and title of 'Fragmentario' recalls Novalis's *Fragmente* (1929 [1798]). The connection is especially acute given the number of fragments of Montejo's piece which display Romantic sensibilities and tendencies. For a detailed, if rather too single-minded, analysis of Montejo as a Romantic poet, see Chirinos (2005).

[32] This rejection of the intellect and rationality is also found in the first of Montejo's heteronymic works *El cuaderno de Blas Coll* (2007a [1981]), a collection of fragments concerning

Nevertheless, later fragments also emphasise the importance of the controlled, formal construction of the poem, to be drawn up in a distinctly methodical manner:

> La intuición de la forma llega a hacerse tan necesaria como el mismo hálito inicial que les da vida. Tal vez lo más útil sea [...] esbozar un tratamiento desde diversas direcciones formales hasta conseguir la medida justa. (233–4)

The shifting ways in which Montejo presents the two sides of this debate as to how the poet is to work and how poetry is to be written reflect the unresolved tension between the Apolline and the Dionysiac which has built up in the Orpheus myth in the course of its successive retellings and adaptations. Despite this tension, however, what Montejo seeks in the fragments cited here appears as an harmonious coexistence of the two strands. This can be seen in the particular attention he gives to Novalis in his discussion of emotion versus rationality in the German Romantics, depicting him as the 'mezcla perfecta de pensador y soñador, de poeta y filósofo' (*VO*, 31), and as 'ese yo superior por rescatar' (30). Moreover, it is in markedly Orphic terms that Montejo portrays this 'yo superior', describing Novalis's poetics as 'el acercamiento fiel a la noche, a las entrañas profundas de la tierra, en una "astrología a la inversa"' (34). In short, rather than as a site of continuing tension, Montejo posits Orpheus, or an Orphic figure, as a locus where the contradictions of the poet are somehow in harmony. And it is within the context of this ongoing (Orphic) debate that we must locate Montejo's predominant concern for harmony in his own praxis, stated most explicitly in his declaration that 'tiendo siempre a la búsqueda de un equilibrio y me desvivo por lograr tanto como puedo la armonía' (Gutiérrez 2002). It is a concern which we have already seen to underpin his engagement with the topoi of nation, national poetics, and (poetic) language.

Of course, despite the presence of the Dionysiac/Apolline tensions, the idea of harmony is nevertheless central in many portrayals of Orpheus. As Segal points out in his analysis of the myth, from the earliest stories of Orpheus there is 'the notion [...] of the basic interrelatedness of all parts of the world. The magic of the poet's song makes visible and communicable that hidden harmony' (1993: 28). Yet there is the caveat that, in particular from

---

primarily language and philosophy. Montejo's heteronym Blas Coll is quoted as stating that 'la lógica sirve a la realidad tanto como la geometría a las nubes. De llegar a mostrarse a través de formas rígidas y predeterminadas, qué poco encanto ofrecerían a la contemplación las cambiantes formas de un nubario matinal' (*BC*, 50). Further adding to the Romantic connection, this view is reminiscent of Keats's lament in *Lamia* (1990: 41 (lines 229–38)) of the deleterious effect of scientific investigation and understanding on one's appreciation of the world's beauty.

the time of the Romantics onwards, Orpheus and his harmonious song appear as absent and remote, as a cipher for precisely the lack of what we might term the *poeta superior*. Whilst this is found within certain engagements with the myth in antiquity, the prime example of such a use of Orpheus is that of Rilke.[33] Commenting on sonnet 1.26 from *Sonnets to Orpheus*, Segal notes that:

> the poet's defeat and triumph become symbols of modern man's loss and attempted recovery of the spirit of song in a world of alienation, violence, depersonalized and demythicized life. [...] Orpheus, the 'lost god', is a 'trace' of some larger entity or mystery that we must pursue and recover. (1993: 5)

And it is within this Rilkean tradition that Montejo's own presentation of the myth in the poem 'Orfeo' (*MM*) is located, focusing on the loss or absence of Orpheus and his abilities from the world of the twentieth century, emphasised in the revision made to line 11 in all subsequent publications of the poem, indicated here in square brackets:

> Orfeo, lo que de él queda (si queda),
> lo que aún puede cantar en la tierra,
> ¿a qué piedra, a cuál animal enternece?
> Orfeo en la noche, en esta noche   4
> (su lira, su grabador, su cassette),
> ¿para quién mira, ausculta las estrellas?
> Orfeo, lo que en él sueña (si sueña),
> la palabra de tanto destino,   8
> ¿quién la recibe ahora de rodillas?
>
> Solo, con su perfil en mármol, pasa
> por entre siglos [por nuestro siglo] tronchado y derruido
> bajo la estatua rota de una fábula.   12
> Viene a cantar (si canta) a nuestra puerta,
> a todas las puertas. Aquí se queda,
> aquí planta su casa y paga su condena
> porque nosotros somos el Infierno.   16
>   (*MM*, 19)

The initial impact of the poem comes from its questioning of the abilities attributed to Orpheus in the mythic accounts. Montejo's Orpheus is one whose powers are waning: the stones and the animals, precisely what the classical myth depicts as being charmed by the Orphic song, are no longer

---

33 Segal (1993: 6) refers to the classical example of such a portrayal of the Orphic myth found in the writings of Antipater of Sidon.

susceptible to its enchantment (line 3). But it soon becomes clear that what is at stake is a combination both of this weakened Orpheus and of the attitude and being of people in the modern world. This is initially implied by the poem's questioning of whether there is anyone for whom Orpheus can work as astronomer, presaging their life (line 6), and anyone to whom he can offer a transcendent poetic Word (line 9), and continues, in a more explicit vein, in the second strophe. Here, Montejo portrays a broken, lifeless Orpheus separated from the world into which he desires to come; he is camped outside it, which is to say outside us, where we are depicted as 'el Infierno' (line 16). In effect, then, twentieth-century humankind has become the Underworld into which Orpheus seeks to descend (with the implication being that the Eurydice he desires to retrieve is located within ourselves). This image at once highlights Orpheus's diminishing powers, as he is figured as now unable to cross the boundaries of life and death and enter the world-as-underworld, yet also underlines that modern humanity, as the new keeper of hell's gates, is denying him even the possibility of such an entry. As well as addressing the broken powers of Orpheus, then, this poem questions whether there is anyone even interested in hearing him anymore. Put simply, Montejo is asking whether there is any place left in the modern world for Orpheus, and, by implication, for both the classical and privileged lyric poet of old and poetry *per se*.

Perhaps the most striking aspect of Montejo's 'Orfeo', however, emerges from the use of parentheses, which raise the question of whether Orpheus exists at all. The three short parentheses '(si queda)', '(si sueña)', and '(si canta)' serve to heighten the level of uncertainty in the poet's mind as to quite what is left of Orpheus. In the case of the first two affirmations questioned ('Orfeo, lo que de él queda' (line 1); 'Orfeo, lo que en él sueña' (line 7)) we see the poet casting doubt on both the existence of even a remnant of Orpheus and the idea of poetic inspiration still functioning respectively. This is continued in the third affirmation ('Viene a cantar' (line 13)) which shows both the possibility of Orpheus offering himself to be accepted once more by the world and even the very idea of an Orphic song ('(si canta)') to be in doubt. Alongside the depiction of waning Orphic powers and a world which rejects Orpheus and his song, then, Montejo's poem questions the notion of there even being an Orpheus and an Orphic song to reject in the twentieth century.

Mythic, sacred, and poetic loss

Whilst 'Orfeo' most obviously depicts the effects of this blend of the loss, weakening, and rejection of the Orphic, it is also central in pointing towards the causes that Montejo sees as lying behind this *mengua*. For instance, the poem tells of an Orpheus faded and destroyed by and in the twentieth century, present only under the guise of 'la estatua rota de una fábula' (line 12), a turn of phrase which echoes the 'Estatua rota' of Paz's 'Himno entre ruinas' (1988: 304), only here devoid of the affirmative context provided by the sunlight in that poem. But it is a line which also captures eloquently the dismissive and disbelieving attitude towards myth which Montejo sees in the twentieth century, brought down from its revered position in the classical, medieval, and Romantic periods. This is particularly evident in the essay 'Desde el ciclo de la tabla redonda' (*VO*, 135–42), written in 1971, a year before the publication of 'Orfeo', where Montejo discusses how the modern reader can no longer read the stories of the Grail legend with the necessary belief, experiencing ' "esa amargura de leer sin creer" ' (141) now that 'nuestras exploraciones se acometen [...] por vías analíticas reñidas con toda forma de misterio' (141). By implication, then, the myth of Orpheus is subject to the same fate of simply not being believed in anymore.

I shall return in due course to this question of the mythic. But we must first turn our attention to how, alongside this focus on the concept of myth in modernity, 'Orfeo' also points up the question of the religious in its appeal to a Eucharistic image (line 9). The effect of this line within this pivotal poem is to emphasise the importance of Orpheus's religious, in addition to his poetic, identity and heritage. This consists of two parallel strands: firstly, and as Segal has signalled, the identity of Orpheus as a 'lost god', and, secondly, his role as an intermediary between the gods and humankind. Moreover, the identification of the poet *per se* as just such a high priest figure is found throughout Montejo's writing, with Montejo saying of Jean Cassou, for example, that he would almost call him 'el sacerdote' (*VO*, 182), and, later, describing the 'conmovedora voz de sacerdotisa' (*TB*, 114) of the Venezuelan poet Ana Enriqueta Terán. The terms invoked here of lost gods and of the (absent Orphic) poet as a 'vate trasmisor de potestades ocultas' (*VO*, 45), as originally described in Plato's *Ion*, clearly underscore the debt of heritage to Rilke and Hölderlin, poets whom Montejo had read. But they also accentuate the alignment with Heideggerean thought, both through the common interest in Rilke and Hölderlin and in the specific envisioning of the poet as, as Heidegger put it, 'stand[ing] [...] between gods and men' (1968a: 312) in a time when 'not only have the gods and the god fled, but the divine radiance has become extinguished' (2001: 89).

Concomitant with this presentation of the poet as divine mediator, it is notable that Montejo also frequently identifies the poetic figure with that of the alchemist, most explicitly in the poem 'El esclavo' (*T*), where, with Jungian echoes, he describes the poet as 'el alquimista' who changes 'en oro el barro humano' (*T*, 33). If the poet is an intermediary of the divine, then his additional depiction as an alchemist discloses that he is to be seen both as the *conveyor* of the divine and as the *producer* of the experiencing of that sacredness in the world.[34]

The combination of the poetic and the religious in the figure of Orpheus and the poet *per se* indicates the nature of the lack that Montejo perceives in the modern era. For Montejo, 'nuestro siglo' is one characterised by the loss of religious faith and the attendant loss of an experiencing of the world and life as imbued with the sacred. This is summed up in the 1969 essay 'Tornillos viejos en la máquina del poema' (*VO*, 59–66) where Montejo describes the modern poet as writing:

> 'después de los dioses' […] después que lo divino ya no encarna una presencia dentro de lo cotidiano; la nostalgia de ese pasado en que lo sobrenatural imponía de un modo tan fuerte su sello sobre los hombres, los días, las cosas, todo ello bastaría para explicarnos el sentido de desolación radical que domina la poética de los últimos tiempos. (61)

The echoes of a Hölderlinian discourse – amongst other Romantic poets – are once more keenly felt, but that Montejo is referring specifically to the end of the nineteenth and beginning of the twentieth century here is clear not just from the later reference to 'nuestro siglo' in the revised version of 'Orfeo', but from the preponderant concern for this period of incipient modernity and its poets in the essays of *La ventana oblicua*. The loss of religious faith and of faith in the existence of gods which marked this period, centred around and symbolised by the work of Darwin, Marx, and Nietzsche, has led, for Montejo, to a 'mengua religiosa' (*VO*, 61) which not only leaves the world an impoverished place and humanity ontologically lacking ('el barro humano' (*T*, 33)), but, as 'Orfeo' lays bare, leaves the poet unable to do his job as intermediary and alchemist in giving expression to and enabling people to see the sacredness in things. For Montejo, this offers a stark contrast between the possibilities for the poets of 'premodernity' and for those of the modern era, at once underlining that the Romantic poetic tradition of alienation and desolation is to be seen as a precursor to, but not a part of the same phenomenon as, the manifestation of those concerns as experienced in the twentieth century:

> Los supuestos religiosos que de un modo tan natural alimentaron las sociedades precedentes, se ven sustituidos por una celebración de la máquina, elevada inconscientemente a categoría sagrada. Todavía a Hoelderlin [*sic*]

---

[34] See Fabricus (1976) for a discussion of the connection between alchemy and the experiencing of the divine in the world, as seen in the medieval *opus alchymium*, which presents alchemy as a 'mystical system for man's salvation of his soul and ultimate reunion with his divine source' (5).

le fue posible vivir entre los dioses, habitar ese clima de poesía que hizo
posible el *Hiperión*. (*VO*, 62)

Furthermore, in referring to a time where a belief in gods was still possible
as one of a 'clima de poesía', Montejo further reinforces the idea of the
concomitance of the poetic and the religious.[35] In short, the absence in
'Orfeo' of Orpheus as both god and (authentic) poet in the twentieth century
reflects the fact that, for Montejo, citing Ungaretti, in this era 'la poesía "ha
cesado de ser la palabra de Dios"' (*VO*, 145). That is, with the loss of the
gods and religious belief comes the loss of a divine or perceived 'authentic'
poetics.

As indicated in the quotation above, alongside the loss of religious and,
hence, poetic belief, Montejo's characterisation of the bereft modern era also
focuses on its industrial nature, what he refers to as the 'celebración de la
máquina' (*VO*, 62). For Montejo, the change in landscape, lifestyle, and the
relationship of humankind with nature brought by the onset of industrialisation is also key in understanding the problem for poets and poetry. With the
frenetic pace of modern life, and alluding specifically to the second half of
the twentieth century, Montejo affirms in the essay 'Poesía en un tiempo sin
poesía' (*TB*, 9–15), citing Ungaretti once more, that ' "ya no existe la posibilidad de la contemplación y, por consiguiente, de la expresión de la poesía"'
(12). Once again, the Heideggerean resonances are clear, with Montejo
referring explicitly to the German philosopher here (13). Moreover, further
echoing Heidegger, the concomitant loss of contact with nature brought
about by increased industrialisation and urbanisation is felt as a constant
source of poetic lamentation by Montejo, and is inextricably tied up with the
lack of the divine found and experienced in the modern world.[36] This is stated
unambiguously in the earlier 'Tornillos viejos en la máquina del poema',
where Montejo declares that 'la distancia a que nos situamos de lo sagrado
corresponde, en el mundo práctico, a una lejanía cada vez más acentuada de
la naturaleza. El contacto con lo natural nos llega tamizado, cubierto, trastor-
nado' (*VO*, 62). Anticipating his engagement with the Orphic myth, Montejo
depicts this loss of an ontological harmony with nature as inseparable from

---

[35] This is also implied by Montejo's later essay 'Poesía en un tiempo sin poesía' (*TB*,
9–15), which concerns poetry in the twentieth century, and whose title thus implicitly links
'premodernity' not just with the presence of religion, but with that of poetry.

[36] The ontologically deleterious effects of the separation from nature are addressed in,
for example, Heidegger (1977). Montejo's emphasis is, more than Heidegger's, on this loss
of contact with nature, a loss tied more overtly to urbanisation than to technology in most of
Montejo's work. Chapter 3 explores this aspect of his *œuvre*.

the loss of the divine. It is an Orphic harmony which Montejo persistently attempts to rediscover, as I shall explore in chapters 3 and 4.

As should be evident by now, the latent presence of the Orphic, or, rather, of the absence of Orpheus, in Montejo's work underscores the centrality of the figure of the poet in his exploration of the poetic and ontological paucity that he identifies with the twentieth century. We have already seen how the loss of religious faith problematises the intermediary and alchemic role of the poet as supposed high priest of such sacredness. But Montejo goes further, presenting the lyric poetic figure in the post-industrial age as utterly fragmented. Underlining the lost Romantic image of the poet as the 'yo transcendental' (*VO*, 30) or 'mezcla perfecta de pensador y soñador' (31) in 1972's 'Novalis: El fuego ante la noche', Montejo describes, in the 1973 essay 'Poesía y vitalidad en Drummond de Andrade' (*VO*, 93–100), how 'a la deificación romántica del individuo como vértice mítico de la creación, se ha opuesto el monólogo quebrado del yo lírico moderno' (99).

Nowhere is this fragmentation made more overt than in the emergence of heteronymic writing, again in the period comprising the end of the nineteenth and beginning of the twentieth century. It is, moreover, a central part of Montejo's own writing, both early and late. In 'Sobre la prosa de Machado' from *La ventana oblicua* and 'Los emisarios de la escritura oblicua' (*TB*, 181–92) from *El taller blanco*, as well as in numerous interviews throughout his career, Montejo talks about and discusses this literary phenomenon, which saw figures such as Antonio Machado, Paul Valéry, Gottfried Benn, Valery Larbaud, and, most famously, Fernando Pessoa engage – independently of one another in the case of Machado and Pessoa at least – in the creation of separate authorial identities through whom they would write alongside their own orthonymic production. As Montejo notes, the emergence of what he terms 'escritura oblicua' (*TB*, 183) (to talk in more general terms rather than specifically the case of Pessoa, who coined the term 'heteronyms') occurred at the beginning of the twentieth century alongside several other notable revolutions in the fields of human knowledge and artistic endeavour, all of which appear interlinked: 'El nacimiento del cine mudo, del arte moderno, el descubrimiento de la relatividad, el nacimiento del psicoanálisis, están seguramente gravitando y mezclándose con este fenómeno' (Dagnino 1997). Certainly, the emergence of Freud's theories of the self and Einstein's theories of relativity fit in with the notion of a breakdown in ideas of solidity, univocality, and certainty, a breakdown in which the splitting of the quasi-divine, central figure of the lyric poet partakes. Furthermore, as Montejo underlines, asserting his understanding of art and poetry as intricately bound up with each other, the emergence of *la escritura oblicua* is mirrored in art by that of cubism, which, likewise, is concerned with a radical splitting up of the self into many constituent facets, what Montejo terms the 'poli

yo' (López Ortega 1999: 13).[37] The importance of *la escritura oblicua* in
Montejo's work, and hence the strength of the link tying him to this turn-of-
the-century period with all its social and poetic concerns and upheavals, is
seen in the fact that such writing forms an integral part of his own production. His main heteronym is Blas Coll, a bizarre character living in a small
town on the Venezuelan coast who owns a printing press and who 'tiene la
tentativa y la chifladura de modificar el idioma' (López Ortega 1999: 13).
Part philosopher, part linguistician, Blas Coll has a number of *contertulios*,
his 'colígrafos' as Montejo refers to them (13), including Sergio Sandoval,
Tomás Linden, Eduardo Polo, Lino Cervantes, and Jorge Silvestre. All of
these *colígrafos* are heteronyms of Montejo who have published works either
separately or as *addenda* to other works by Montejo: *Guitarra del horizonte*
(Sandoval 1991); *El hacha de seda* (Linden 1995, expanded in Montejo
2007a); *Chamario* (Polo 2004); *La caza del relámpago (treinta coligramas)*
(Cervantes 2006); and various poems by Jorge Silvestre providing epilogues
of sorts to Montejo's last three orthonymic collections *Partitura de la cigarra*
(1999), *Papiros amorosos* (2002), and *Fábula del escriba* (2006a). In the case
of Blas Coll himself, *El cuaderno de Blas Coll* is not strictly speaking Coll's
own work, but a transcription of fragments from his *cuaderno*, given to us
and commented on by Montejo, as editor, and to which new(ly discovered/
transcribed) fragments were added regularly.[38]

Put simply, this conscious engagement with heteronymic writing underlines that, for all his latent nostalgia for the Orphic poetic figure, and a time
when the world was thus imbued with the sacred and the poetic, Montejo
cannot – and does not – simply place himself outside of the time in which he
was born and writes. As with the writing of a national Venezuelan poetics,
then, Montejo appears caught between the desire for a return to a perceived
'Orphic age' and a desire to write of, in, and for the times in which he finds
himself.

Language in the twentieth century

In drawing attention to the importance of the times in which Montejo writes,
it is necessary to point up that, if Montejo is (self-)identifiably a twentieth-

---

[37] Montejo specifically aligns *la escritura oblicua* with cubism both in this interview
(López Ortega 1999: 13) and in 'Sobre la prosa de Machado' (*VO*, 131).

[38] *El cuaderno de Blas Coll* was first published in 1981 and subsequently revised and
expanded in 1983, 1998, 2005, and 2006. The most recent edition is from 2007. Montejo once
stated that the idea for the character Blas Coll dated back to the late 1960s (López Ortega
1999: 13). This, coupled with the consistent writing of heteronymic works and rewriting of *El
cuaderno de Blas Coll* throughout the latter half of Montejo's career in particular, demonstrates
the extent to which it is an axial element of his work and thought.

century poet concerned with and focusing on the poetic, religious, and attendant ontological loss which he perceives as beginning at the turn of the century, he is, more specifically, doing so from within the second half of that century. In 'Poesía en un tiempo sin poesía', Montejo stresses the increased and near-total conversion of rural and semi-rural towns and cities into modern urban centres in this period, a concern central to his own experiences in the increasingly urbanised Venezuela, as I shall examine in chapter 3, leading him to conclude that this half-century is 'el más huero en espacio vital para la poesía' (*TB*, 15). But, over and above the problems of being in the industrial and technological era, writing in the late twentieth century is also riven by and cannot escape from the linguistic and ontological theories of the period, characterised by a deep problematisation of language – the very tool of poetry – whose origins can be traced back to Augustine and medieval times.[39] And it is in considering this more philosophical context that we begin to unravel the inherent problematics within and against which Montejo's writing is situated.

Montejo's first major collection of poetry, *Élegos*, was published in 1967, the same year as Jacques Derrida's three foundational works: *La Voix et le phénomène*, *L'écriture et la différence*, and *De la grammatologie*, and the latter's theories provide a highly fruitful lens through which to study Montejo's work, one that I shall be employing at various points in this study. Aside from sharing the same intellectual climate and times as Derrida and post-structuralist thought in general, Montejo's work lends itself particularly to such theoretical scrutiny in its engagement with and (apparent) faith in the sort of idealising of and pining for modes of expression and eras that we have seen in his essays and in the poem 'Orfeo'. Specifically, his focus on an Orphic poetic language and a clear division between the 'modern' and the 'premodern' in terms of poetry, belief, relationship with nature, and ontology presents itself as precisely the sort of binary undercut by deconstruction.

Key in this regard is line 5 of 'Orfeo', referring to the tools of Orphic production: '(su lira, su grabador, su cassette)'. At first glance, this line would seem to detail the move of Orpheus from classical and medieval times into the age of modernity, once again aligned with the twentieth century in the specific focus on the tape recorder.[40] Initially depicting him singing with a lyre, the line suggests this instrument has been replaced by the tape recorder and the cassette: Orpheus is no longer singing with his instrument but mechanised and automatised, recorded and played back on one of the machines of modernity. It is a fate clearly viewed with dismay by Montejo, and resonates

---

[39] For the problematisation of language, notably the notion of 'fallen language', in medieval times, see Jager (1993).

[40] The Danish inventor Valdemar Poulsen first demonstrated his Telegraphone, the precursor to the modern tape recorder, in 1900.

strongly with Walter Benjamin's approach to certain aspects of the topos in 'The Work of Art in the Age of Mechanical Reproduction' (1992 [1936]).

And yet, in reading this line, it is important to consider what each of these three tools – the lyre, the tape recorder, and the cassette – symbolises individually for the notion of poetic production, beyond a simplistic opposition between the premodern and the modern.[41] In this respect, the lyre represents an oral poetic production, performed, sung, and recited in person; the tape recorder marks the possibility of the performance being recorded; and the cassette completes the progression, standing for the possibility contained within the act of recording, namely that of repeating the performance. The significance of this progression, however, only becomes clear when we see that the line does not have to be read as a compendium of changes in the nature of the poetic act through time. Rather, this asyndetic line opens itself up to the possibility of a conflationary reading of the three terms, each seen as synonymous with and inseparable from the other two. In short, I am proposing that all three describe the same thing: the inherent nature of the Orphic poetic act, both past and present. What is at stake here, then, is a reevaluation of the very primacy and (poetic and ontological) superiority of the premodern, or what we might term the perceived 'Orphic age'.

An understanding of what this means for both the Orphic act and Montejo's poetics can be found by looking at how this line – and the reading of it I am proposing – engages with Derridean thought. In *Résistances de la psychanalyse* (1996), picking up on Heidegger's mistrust of modern technology, a characteristic of the German philosopher with which Montejo was sympathetic (*TB*, 12–13), Derrida specifically describes the way in which tape recording and playback is rejected by Lacan, as he talks of the latter's 'disqualification (elle aussi d'esprit très heideggerien dans son rapport à la technique) du "*record*", du "*recording*", de l'enregistrement et de l'archive méchanique comme "aliénante"' (1996: 76). For Lacan, the mode of communication of record/playback is one of alienation, which stands in contrast to the full presence of the spoken word. Citing Lacan, Derrida goes on:

> 'Mais la retransmission même de son discours [du sujet psychanalytique] enregistré, fût-elle faite par la bouche de son médecin, ne peut, de lui parvenir sous cette forme aliénée, avoir les mêmes effets que l'interlocution psychanalytique' – qui devrait donc être directe, de vive voix, immédiate, etc. Donc 'la parole pleine' qui 'se définit par son identité à ce dont elle parle'. (76)

In short, what is desired, and prized, is '[la] parole sans interposition technique, sans dispositif de répétition archivante, sans itérabilité essentielle'

---

[41] See, for example, Rivera (1986: 40) for such a reading.

(76–7). The tape recorder and cassette are seen as flawed because they are the tools of iterability, a loss of the notion of a unique and fully present performance. In Montejo's case, and in the case of 'Orfeo', the *parole pleine*, or performance, at stake is the poetry sung by Orpheus, or the Orphic poet, with his lyre. But Derrida's point in his description of Lacan's views of the tape recorder is, as he frequently argued, that such iterability is a characteristic of language *per se*, including the performative speech of Orpheus here. It is the means by which language, or meaning, is made possible, in that a word – spoken, written, or, here, recorded on a tape recorder – must contain the capacity to be repeated in other contexts and at other times in order to function as language.[42] In my conflationary reading of the three terms 'lira', 'grabador', and 'cassette', then, Montejo's poem draws attention to the fact that the Orphic performance prior to twentieth-century modernity is, in fact, shot through with the same capacity for repetition: the notion that this 'natural' lyric production is somehow fully present is thus undermined even as it is affirmed.

Beyond the division superficially set up between modern (twentieth-century) mechanical reproduction and the premodern, or Orphic, lyre, the tape recorder and cassette of 'Orfeo' also bring into play, as I have suggested, the more basic dichotomy of orality and writing, in that they act, more generally, as symbols of writing down (the poetic performance) and the possibility of (re)reading (it) respectively. This, of course, is the fundamental dichotomy which Derrida works to collapse, arguing that the traits imputed to writing, that is, those of alienation, iterability, and a concomitant lack of full presence, are prior to, or, rather, already contained within, all language, including the spoken word.[43] Hence Derrida's far wider understanding and use of the term *écriture* to denote (the function and nature of) language *per se*. Moreover, just such a hierarchisation of orality and writing is also brought out explicitly in 'Tornillos viejos en la máquina del poema', an essay whose problematic discussion can be seen as the lengthier version of all that came to be distilled in line 5 of 'Orfeo' just a few years later. Lamenting 'el sentido perentorio de lo escrito' (*VO*, 63), Montejo sees in the future a chance to recover the 'reino de la oralidad' (64), before closing the essay by reiterating several times just what he envisages this move (back) into orality meaning for language and, specifically, for the language of poetry, in terms which leave little doubt as to his view on the writing/orality divide:

[42] Derrida develops this discussion of iterability fully in 'Signature Événement Contexte' (1972a: 365–93).

[43] See Derrida's discussion of Rousseau and the prioritising of speech over writing in *De la grammatologie* (1967c: 203–34).

Pero la comunicación del pensamiento, el análisis, las doctrinas, las vari-
adas formas del arte, quizás han de volver al reino del habla y la palabra
retomará una gravedad perdida ha mucho tiempo. La realidad no será
así evocada a través del signo, sino en su fábula directa, en sus nítidos
contornos que posibilitan la verificación y el conocimiento. [...] En el reencuentro de la palabra como verbo que verifica el ser, puede gestarse quizá
un universo de propiedades sagradas que devuelva una nueva esperanza en
estos tiempos diluvianos. (65)

Chiming with 'Orfeo', this return to orality is implicitly aligned with a return
to the poet working, in Orphic fashion, as a divinely inspired, harmonious
figure, a mediator between humans and the gods, as Montejo ends by stating
that 'tal vez la era mítica del poeta, el universo de su armonía estelar, esté
pronto a llegar bajo nuevas formas del mismo principio, en el retorno de sus
dioses tutelares' (65). Orality, poetry as a religious Word, ontological authenticity, and the sacredness of the universe are all brought together in these
passages, which resonate strongly with Heidegger's reading of Hölderlin,
who 'in the act of establishing the essence of poetry, first determines a new
time. It is the time of the gods that have fled *and* of the god that is coming'
(1968a: 313).

Yet this essay also brings the problematics of Montejo's recourse to this
divide into sharp relief, and enables us better to understand the inherent contradictions of his presentation of the 'modern' and the (Orphic) 'premodern' in
general. The valorisation of the oral over the written represents the culmination of the essay's discussion of the problems of language transmission for
poetry. Anticipating the levels of reading we have seen in line 5 of 'Orfeo', it
begins by identifying the 'sentimiento de desolación' (*VO*, 62) of poets in the
late twentieth century as an effect of 'la ascensión de los medios audiovis-
uales y un sentido de practicidad que invade todas las zonas del pensamiento'
(62), which, together with the speed of modern life, are leading the modern
poet to feel that his language is disappearing from him, destined for erasure,
in that 'al inclinarnos sobre la página tenemos la sensación de llenarla de
líneas condenadas a desaparecer en breve plazo' (63). But Montejo then shifts
his focus from modern audiovisual technology to the emergence of writing,
culminating in the invention of the printing press, as he cites the communica-
tions theorist Herbert Marshall McLuhan who 've en la actual era alfabética,
que llega a su apoteosis con la invención de la imprenta, la explicación de
todos los males de nuestra época: escisión entre poder y moral, ciencia y
arte, corazón y espíritu' (64). In short, from the divisional portrayal of poetics
and ontology into pre- and post-the-end-of-the-nineteenth century, Montejo's
own text now works to shift this division further back: the problem is not the
emergence of the industrial and technological age at this historical juncture,
but the emergence and development of writing and, in particular, the printing

press. Of course, this must then lead to a reexamination of Montejo's claims for poets who were writing prior to the twentieth century, both in this essay, where he talks of Hölderlin's 'vivir entre los dioses' (62), and elsewhere. The supposedly 'Orphic' poets, writing in a time when such 'sacred' lyric poetry was still possible, were, after all, scarcely oral poets, but poets working in and through writing, and publishing with the aid of the printing press.

Furthermore, in moving the division back to that of speech and writing, Montejo does not just effect a deconstruction of the divide between pre- and post-the-end-of-the-nineteenth century. Rather, the essay lays bare that any such division and any such period of 'Orphic poetry' is both elusive and illusory, as is suggested by the fact that the descriptions of twentieth-century poetics and being which we have been looking at in this essay and in the later 'Poesía en un tiempo sin poesía', in spite of being set up in opposition to a previous time, could in fact be taken accurately to describe earlier periods, in particular that of early Romanticism. In valorising orality over the writing of these 'tiempos diluvianos' (VO, 65), Montejo is, in effect, repeating a hier-archisation which dates back to medieval times, where the Fall of language represented in Genesis was considered to correspond to the transition from orality to literacy.[44] Far from a simple parallel, this concept of orality as compared with literacy thus points to a crucial aligning of 'Orphic' orality with a mythical, prelapsarian time, an irrecuperable time that, historically, never was, as we are reminded of the modern world's lack of belief in these (religious) myths.

In typical deconstructionist style, however, it is within the terms of the essay itself that we find the most significant undermining of the affirmation of an authentic and sacred poetry and being in orality. Hanging over the closing sentiments of the piece is the declaration found near the beginning of the essay that 'toda *lengua* lleva en sí una condición perecedera' (VO, 63, italics mine), disclosing that, even in orality, full presence is impossible, since orality is itself driven by the same fundamental processes as both writing and audio recording. Indeed, the very title of the essay points to the inescapability not just of the problematics imputed to the post-industrial world we inhabit, but to the notion of production, recording, and repetition inscribed *a priori* into poetry.

What both 'Orfeo' and 'Tornillos viejos en la máquina del poema' show, then, is the effect (and presence) of deconstructionist, and, more widely, post-structuralist thought in a poetics which sets up a simplistic divide between orality and writing, and between discrete past and present eras. Despite his emphasis elsewhere on the national, Montejo also stressed that, for him, a poet belongs to his time more than to the place from where he comes. In

---

[44] See Jager (1993: 61–75).

interview in 2002, for instance, he responded to a question regarding this idea by saying that:

> Es una idea de Yeats, que decía que uno pertenece más a su tiempo que a su país. [...] Yo tengo menos que ver con un venezolano del siglo pasado que con alguien de otro país pero con las preocupaciones de hoy.
>
> (Rodríguez Marcos 2002)[45]

And in the time in which Montejo is writing, it is the faith in language and the dream of logocentricity, in addition to the faith in gods, which are being dismantled. Moreover, this represents, as we have seen in these two central Montejian pieces, not just a break between what was and now is. Rather, the modern questioning of language and concomitant deconstruction of apparently discrete binary terms impacts on the past too, undermining the notion that a fully present language, and, thus, a fully Orphic poetics, ever was. Poetry and our contact with nature, both symbolised in the figure and power of Orpheus, are lost not just because of a loss of the sacred in the mechanised and technologised present, but because we now see that, at least from a theoretical standpoint, they were always mediated through language, and language is always alienating, *perecedero*.[46] As a poet of the late twentieth century, then, this is what Montejo's desire for a 'return' to an Orphic poetics and 'authentic' ontology must struggle against, as I shall examine in chapters 1 and 2 of this study in particular.

Towards a poetic future

Aside from the ramifications of 'Orfeo' and 'Tornillos viejos en la máquina del poema', Montejo's work certainly exhibits an awareness of the ineluctable problematics of language. This is evident in his first collection *Humano paraíso*, where, in almost every poem, the presence of the word 'o' is striking: 'vida o canción' (*HP*, 12) in 'Tú que duermes la lluvia'; 'mejilla o pétalo' (*HP*, 3) in 'Canción para besar una mujer', for example.[47] Nothing can

---

[45] Just two years later, however, Montejo had modified this stance, saying that 'debo decir que ya no repito literalmente la frase de Yeats. Ahora digo simplemente que uno pertenece a su propio destino, es decir, a su propio naufragio' (Campo 2004).

[46] As Brownlee has noted, this idea of language as alienating emerges in philosophical and literary discourse from twelfth-century nominalist roots (1990: 3). Brownlee focuses on the particular case of the Spanish *novela sentimental* of the fifteenth century, where linguistic alienation is a principal thematic.

[47] This use of 'o' may well reflect the influence of the Spanish poet Vicente Aleixandre (see, for example, *La destrucción o el amor* (1935)), whose Romantic traits are outlined by Chirinos (2005: 85–6).

ever simply be named or defined; there is always a sense of what is being described exceeding the limits of any signifier. Indeed, this is the impression given by the self-negating formulations in several poems from Montejo's late collections, perhaps most notably in 'Los ausentes' ('con un trago o ninguno, pero con un trago' (*PC*, 29)). Yet, despite this, Montejo's work maintains a continual focus on the potential of poetry somehow both to reverse and henceforth to combat the perceived loss of an Orphic poetics and ontological fullness. In short, in counterpoint to the doubt and theoretical ramifications of the parentheses in 'Orfeo', there is a persistent optimism and determination to see a way beyond such questioning problematics, and, hence, the indirect piecing together of a challenge to a Derridean viewpoint.

At the heart of Montejo's optimism lies his repeated assertion of the role of poetry as a religion, filling the void left behind by the former gods and religions (and chiming with a distinctly Modernist view of poetry), to the extent that the line 'la poesía es la última religión que nos queda' (Szinetar 2005: 96, interview dates from 1982), derived from Wallace Stevens, became a staple of his interviews from at least 1979 onwards.[48] It may be that Montejo shared Ungaretti's view, which he quotes, that poetry ' "ha cesado de ser la palabra de Dios" ' (*VO*, 145), but, from this, he saw poetry emerging as its own religion, as its own Word, rather than that of a distant God: 'el reencuentro de la palabra como verbo que verifica el ser' (*VO*, 65).

Central to this view of poetry is the idea that the poet should hold firm not to a belief in gods, but to a valorisation of myth and the mythic, a move signalled by the foregrounding in Montejo's poetics of the mythic Orpheus. In the essay 'Ungaretti: entre la inocencia y la memoria' (*VO*, 143–9), for example, Montejo talks of the Italian poet's call for the today's poet to rejoin 'los mitos esenciales que unen a los hombres' (145), at once hinting at the humanist element of Montejo's own work, with its concern for the being and unification of the whole of humankind. Likewise, he signals the importance of the mythic in an artistic representation of the world in several later texts, with regard to both the artist (2006b: 318–20) and the poet (Posadas 2002: 309–10).

There are several reasons for Montejo's championing this poetic counter-current of a continuing faith in myth, not least that it distinguishes the sacredness, which Montejo seeks to recover, from a concept of religiosity based (purely) on (the existence of) gods. In interview with Arráiz Lucca, for instance, he is keen to underline that 'cuando me refiero al arte y a su arraigo religioso no estoy pensando, claro está, en un sentido cristiano solamente, sino en el más amplio y antiguo de la palabra' (1987: 4). Furthermore, this move away from identifying Christianity with the religiosity that he desires is

---

48 See, for instance, Arráiz Lucca (1987: 4).

evident in (his depiction of) several of the poets on whom he writes. Writing
on Cernuda, Montejo talks of how Philip Silver, in his book *Luis Cernuda:
el poeta en su leyenda* (1995), 'nos advierte que en su tiempo, dentro de
España, "nadie fue tan preciso como Cernuda en su crítica al cristianismo"'
and that 'en esa misma perspectiva sitúa su evocación del paganismo prec-
ristiano, el cual aparecía a los ojos del poeta más lleno de auténtica vida'
(*VO*, 170), before linking this with the concept of *poetic* religiosity in his
reference to Cernuda's 'ejemplar dedicación de su vida a la revelación de la
poesía' (172). Similarly, in Drummond de Andrade he sees an elevation of 'lo
humano en su marchita inmediatez a una especie de religión de lo cotidiano'
(*VO*, 100). This latter statement in particular also provides an indication of
what Montejo understands by the idea of 'the religious' as a concept with
which a twentieth-century poetics, imbued with a faith in the mythic, can
engage and towards which it can aim. Central here is the idea of a religious
reverence towards the world, a sense of what Montejo frequently referred to
as 'el misterio' which lies behind all things,[49] and a vision which chimes with
Paz's depiction of the poet as seeing the 'luz [...] | que brilla en cada hoja,
en cada piedra' ('La vida sencilla', 1988: 148) and in particular, and possibly
by way of Paz's essays in *El arco y la lira*,[50] with Heidegger's understanding
of poetry as 'a means of [...] letting beings appear in their being, *as* what
they *are*' (Pattison 2000: 161), achieved by 'preserv[ing] the[ir] mystery as
mystery' (Heidegger 2000: 43), that is, by refusing to submit that mystery
– or sacredness – to rational understanding or the sort of reification found
in traditional Judaeo-Christian dogma. Indeed, this is exactly the contrast
Montejo sets up when discussing the work of the Venezuelan artist Alirio
Palacios, who 'opone a la racionalidad predominante su universo chamánico,
sus míticas figuras de la magia deltaica' (2006b: 324).

   In essence, what we see here is both Montejo's acknowledgement of the
twentieth-century (Judaeo-Christian) godless framework within which he is
working, and also his suggestion that this does not necessarily mean a loss
of (an appreciation of) the sacred once one accepts the idea of a 'religion'
based not on historical narratives or reified deities, but on mythic histo-
ries, mythic gods, and a concomitant sense of (the) mystery (of things), all
understood *as such*. Indeed, such an assertion of the possibility of the sacred
entering into and being seen in the world and poetry without a belief in gods
is found in his description of earlier times where 'en ese clima esencial no
precisamos siquiera ser creyentes: la creencia emana, por decirlo así, de las
cosas mismas. La poesía es allí esa gravitación que el misterio da a toda
forma visible' (*VO*, 61). These are important lines, for they also disclose

---

   [49] See, for example, Lozano Tovar (2007: 26) and Posadas (2002: 306–7).
   [50] Montejo refers to his assiduous reading of this book in his acceptance speech for the
Premio Octavio Paz (2006b: 303).

how Montejo's discourse of myth and *misterio* fits into his repeated affirmation of poetry as being the last remaining religion. They underscore that the *misterio*, the mythic sacredness, is unknown, imperceptible, and, in effect, non-existent prior to its revelation by and through poetry *as* an (unknowable) *misterio*, that is, not as something that can be grasped or located temporally or spatially. Poetry, that is, – as religion – must bring into existence, or create, its own myth(ic sacredness), its own foundation. Tellingly, this is exactly the implication of the final aphoristic fragment of 'Fragmentario', published in the first edition of *El taller blanco* (1983). Here, we are told that 'el poema es una oración dicha a un Dios que sólo existe mientras dura la oración' (*TB*, 243). It is a tenet clearly central to Montejo's thought as he was to repeat it frequently throughout the rest of his career (stressing at one point that it is a type of prayer 'muy distante del político ritualismo de las iglesias' (Cruz 2006: 377)). Echoing Paz's notion that 'la palabra poética se pasa de la autoridad divina. La imagen se sustenta en sí misma' (1967: 137), it is an idea that talks overtly of the poem as creating and sustaining its own religiosity and its own 'beyond', or God, which does not exist in any meaningful sense outside of the poem, and which, within the poem, is experienced as a mystery to which one is opened up, recalling Heidegger's concept of the 'Open which poetry lets happen [...] [where] the Open brings beings to shine and ring out' (2001: 70). Thus when Montejo later formulates this idea in terms of poetry as 'un diálogo con el misterio' (Bracho 2006: 363), we see that it is the poetic dialogue itself that opens up and brings into (poetic, mythic) existence the sacred interlocutor.

This conception of the *misterio* or transcendent 'beyond' as a mythic production of the language of the poem also ties in with the theoretical limits and questioning of language which I have identified with the time of Montejo's writing. In the essay 'La structure, le signe et le jeu dans le discours des sciences humaines', for example, Derrida talks of how 'le foyer ou la source [du mythe] sont toujours des ombres ou des virtualités insaisissables, inactualisables et d'abord inexistantes. Tout commence par la structure, la configuration ou la relation' (1967b: 419). In short, language produces myth, which is, thus, nothing outside of the structure and relationships of language, what Derrida terms *différance*. In contrast to Derrida, however, for Montejo this is not a sign of the frustrating inability of language to get beyond itself and its workings, the play of language and meaning. Rather, the production in language of something ungraspable and whose 'meaning' cannot be fixed or defined is to be valorised as the transcending of the need for such meaning. A key to this challenge to a Derridean perspective lies in the priority given by Montejo to the musicality and voice of orality, not because this is any more capable of a full 'presenc(ing)' of meaning, but because the music and voice of poetic language is beyond and not directly related to signification. This is most eloquently put in Montejo's acceptance speech for the Premio

Octavio Paz, where he underlines the connection between magic/myth, the enigmatic *misterio*, and the musicality and orality of poetry, and, in so doing, transmits an understanding of orality which is not simply caught in the problematic writing/voice duality that I earlier identified in 'Tornillos viejos en la máquina del poema':

> la antigua noción de magia verbal [...] que ha logrado sobrevivir al asedio racionalista, viene a recordarnos que la escritura de un texto lírico nace acompañada de una porción de enigma inseparable de la voz que la recorre. (2006b: 307)

In reiterating the importance of the vocal and lyrical nature of poetic expression, Montejo also implicitly reminds us here of Orpheus once more. Only now we are better able to grasp the importance of the triune nature of this persona, as god, poet, and myth, in that this essential combination of all three identifications underlies Montejo's concept of poetry as religion: in appearing as both cause (the Orphic poet writing the poem) and effect (the production *in the poem* of a mysterious sacredness in the world) of such a poetics, Orpheus's mythic nature is underscored, as the figure as used by Montejo refuses to be bound by or understood through a mode of thought and 'religiosity' tied either to the causality of linear time and history or to rational comprehension.

There is, however, one further way in which Montejo's valorisation of myth and what he sometimes terms 'pagan' religiosity is of particular importance. For in using this discourse of myth and *misterio* Montejo effects a move away not just from the Judaeo-Christian tradition, but, concomitantly and interrelatedly, from Europe towards America, suggesting that it is the latter rather than the Old Continent which provides a more promising locale for a poetics based on a preponderant concern for a belief in myth and magic. Such a line of thinking is made explicit in conversation with Floriano Martins in 1990, as he underlines the attempted engagement with a distinctly American tone in his writing:

> A busca do tom americano [...] relaciona-se com a formulação mítica do pensamento poético. A magia do mito como história verdadeira constitui um elemento fundamental da arte de nosso continente. À missão atribuída ao poeta por Mallarmé, de purificar as palavras da tribo, missão honrosa e nobre por si mesma, temos que acrescentar outra, menos divulgada porém muito nossa, posto que provém dos pré-colombianos. Eles definiam o poeta como aquele que, ao falar, faz com que as coisas se ponham de pé. Este último é impossível sem a força mítica da palavra. (1998: 250)[51]

---

[51] This interview was originally published in 1990 in the *Suplemento Literário Minas Gerais*, 1139 (20 February 1990). A Spanish translation is available in Montejo (2006b: 351–6).

The 'pré-colombianos' referred to here are the Nahuas, and the saying attributed to them here was repeated several times subsequently by Montejo, marking out the importance of this Indigenous American concept of the poet.[52] Significantly, this idea of the poet as one who 'al hablar hace ponerse de pie a las cosas' (Montejo 2006b: 307) is itself reminiscent both of the power of Orpheus to move nature and of Heidegger's notion of the poet as revealing things in their essence: 'the unconcealedness of beings' (2001: 48). Yet it is the American formulation and location of such a concept – in contrast to a European concept of poetry (Mallarmé) – that Montejo foregrounds. In short, we see here how Montejo's engagement with European traditions and thought, in terms philosophical (Heidegger), poetic (Hölderin, Rilke, Cernuda, Machado), and mytho-religious (Orpheus), fuses with and leads back to the American/Venezuelan focus with which I began, and which I have observed to be evident elsewhere in Montejo's work. Two elements are at stake here. Firstly, there is the simple fact that, as a Latin American poet, Montejo seeks, as he states here, a Latin American tone to his work. Secondly, and recalling Carpentier's development of the *real maravilloso*,[53] Montejo is effectively declaring that what he sees as the necessary faith in myth and magic – elements which are absent in such explicit terms from the thought and heritage of Heidegger and the poetics of Hölderlin, Cernuda, *et al.* – is present in the (poetic) heritage and locale of America. He may tap into European traditions, then, but the discourse and underlying approach-to-the-world by which he does so are distinctly autochthonous. Thus, when he identifies the poet as a 'purificador, pero también mago', adding that 'Y este último sentido, *el de la magia y el mito*, puede estar un poquito olvidado y es deber nuestro rescatarlo' (Posadas 2002: 310, italics mine), he is speaking both of a *general* idea of the role of the poet, as evidenced by his engagement with the European traditions which feed into his concept of poetry and the sacred, and yet also of the specific duty of American poets, 'que trabajamos y hemos nacido acá' (Posadas 2002: 310).

That said, we should not overlook the fact that what Montejo stresses here is the dual engagement which it befalls a poet of the Americas to undertake: the need to be both *purificador* and *mago*, attentive to the European as well as the American legacy under which (s)he is writing. Moreover, both sides of this equation are brought to bear on Montejo's most affirmatory depiction of how such an 'authentic' or 'religious' poetics might be achieved (beyond the mere claims of its possibility), namely in a Symbolist approach. An indication of the latter's importance for Montejo is evident from his conception of the texts of the Grail cycle, whose 'lenguaje habla al intelecto a través del

---

[52] See, for example, Posadas (2002: 309).
[53] See Carpentier (1967).

símbolo como obra de revelación' (*VO*, 141), a process of revelation which, citing Mallarmé, Montejo discloses as being linked with the idea of language as creating a (non-reified) myth, in that it is a question of 'sugerir' rather than 'nombrar un objeto' (*VO*, 82) in order to reveal it more wholly. As is implied by his recourse to Mallarmé, Montejo here, in contrast to his later statements cited above, exhibits a far less pessimistic view than Carpentier of the possibilities of such a mythic poetics in Europe, apparently identifying the French poets of the *savoir caché* as a prime example of what he aims for in his own work: the alchemic ability to poeticise the world and our relation to it (and hence our being), quoting Pierre Delisle's statement regarding the work of these poets where '"en las vastas regiones del universo poético moderno, las cosas de la tierra, un guijarro, un árbol, revisten el trazo solemne y misterioso de las cosas de la religión. Todo objeto se torna sagrado"' ('La fortaleza fulminada', *VO*, 90).

Nevertheless, Montejo underlines that any such Symbolist writing requires, perforce, the development of a certain symbology. In 'Aproximación a Ramos Sucre', for example, Montejo writes of how 'para habitar el espacio que una mitología del progreso nos ha tornado insoportable, es preciso forjarse una simbología a través de la cual lo cotidiano cribe su aspereza' (*VO*, 81–2). And it is here that the shift towards American traditions makes itself felt, not least because Montejo's 'cotidiano' is that of America, of Venezuela. Returning to Martins' interview, we see Montejo once more reminding us of his debt to the poetics of *actualización* of the *generación del 18*, pointing to the need both to preserve tradition and to bring that tradition up to date, as he talks specifically of the symbology of pre-Colombine America:

> Creio que o legado de símbolos e presenças arcaicas, que junto com outros formam as raízes de nossa tradição, para conservar sua perene vigência terão de ser reformulados a partir da experiência concreta de cada criador e das relações com os dados de seu tempo. (1998: 250)

In effect, Montejo here prioritises a reengagement with the symbology of these traditions in modern Latin American poetry. Moreover, such a move towards an American(ised) symbolic tradition is also found in Montejo's later essay on Simon Bolívar's educator, the Venezuelan Simón Rodríguez, where Montejo affirms Rodríguez's anticipation of several typographical traits of European Symbolist poets such as Mallarmé and Apollinaire, effectively shifting the focus away from Symbolism as simply a European phenomenon ('El tipógrafo de nuestra utopía', *TB*, 71–84: see pp. 78–80).

And yet all the while Montejo demonstrates an understanding of the ineluctable presence of the European in any such reformulation. Indeed, not only is the reformulation of American symbols inseparable from 'os dados de seu tempo' (Martins 1998: 250), both nationally and more widely, but, as Montejo recognised, any poetics of and for Latin America must inevitably take into account the opposing process, whereby a European religious symbology – of exactly the Judaeo-Christian tradition we have seen him to lean away from in several essays and interviews – has come to be reframed within an American context:

> En cada uno de nosotros [...] perviven los rituales más o menos desatendidos del catolicismo criollo, los altares caseros, en fin, toda la serie de comportamientos venidos de Europa y adaptados a los trópicos. No basta una simple declaración externa para librarnos de estas prácticas que han modelado nuestro modo de sentir y juzgar. ('Fragmentario', *TB*, 235)

Thus, in the course of this study, we shall see how Montejo repeatedly engages with the (European) Judaeo-Christian tradition as he works towards the poetic construction of his own personal and national symbology, an engagement implied, furthermore, by the Judaeo-Christian tones of his gloss on Mallarmé's call to 'purificar las palabras del tribu' – part of the American poet's role – as being to 'devolver las palabras a su estado de *pureza genésica*' (2006b: 307, italics mine). In short, whilst he may at times prioritise the American and more specifically Venezuelan legacy of his poetics and being, and at times focus on the European, in striving towards an 'authentic' poetics and ontology as a Venezuelan poet, Montejo finds himself constantly working at this fusion of the two.[54]

This, then, is the backdrop in terms of thought, aims, and philosophy against which I shall set this study of Montejo's work. In addressing both poetry and being, Montejo draws in the national, the regional/continental, the European, and more widely, the human, and my reading of his corpus will be attuned to all of these levels of engagement. On the one hand, leading on from the diverse modes and contextualisations of loss that I have outlined, my aim is to examine how Montejo's poetics explores and deals with the traditions and experiences of loss in the twentieth century in relation to the Venezuela in which the poet grew up and wrote. But, as Montejo's conception of the religious and, concomitantly, ontological possibilities of poetry underscore, there is also an attendant belief in the potentiality of poetry to overcome such loss. Thus, I shall also examine how Montejo develops and addresses

---

[54] This duality is pervasive in Montejo's biography as well: he spent periods living in both Paris and Lisbon, and he came from a family originating in the Canary Islands. Little wonder, then, that Montejo declared that 'un poeta que siento con más identidad ahora es el franco-uruguayo Jules Supervielle' (Araujo 2004), a poet pulled between both sides of the Atlantic, and on whom Montejo wrote in 'Supervielle: lamento y trovas de la muerte' (*VO*, 53–8).

the need for an authentic or 'Orphic' poetics and ontology on the personal and the national level in Venezuela, to be brought about, ultimately, by a Venezuelan Orphic figure, whilst also being alert to the more general role of poetry in addressing and offering a solution to the wider ontological and poetic *malaise* of the world as a whole. At the same time, I shall analyse to what extent Montejo's claims and hopes for poetry nevertheless come up against some of the theoretical pitfalls discussed above, underscoring the difficulties of turning potentiality into actuality.

The following study focuses more heavily on the first half of Montejo's output, up to and including *Alfabeto del mundo* (1988), primarily since it is in these collections that the basic thematic and symbolic threads of Montejo's writing as a whole are set up. That said, later works are also discussed in some detail, but my aim has generally been to examine how the poetic strands from the earlier collections are continued and developed, rather than to undertake an analysis of the later work as a 'block' of poetic production in its own right. I should also add that, with the exception of the towering figure of Blas Coll, I have made relatively limited detailed reference to Montejo's heteronymic writing. These figures will be addressed in a subsequent work.

Chapters 1 and 2 deal with different temporal aspects of loss. I begin by examining how, in his earlier poetic works, Montejo presents his own experiences of the loss effected by time's passing from his childhood onwards and attempts to invoke a reversal and a combating of this loss through his poetry. From this discussion, I shall argue that it is language itself which emerges as the principal stumbling block to an overcoming of what is perceived as temporal loss. In chapter 2, I proceed to address how memory is posited as a potential way of achieving this recuperation of what is past, demonstrating how Montejo's own presentation works to deconstruct this affirmation, as memory is shown to work as and through language. Finally, I examine the development of snow as a leitmotiv for the poetic potential in Montejo's work, and suggest it is here that the most complex and theoretically significant approach to the (linguistic) question of loss over time as experienced in Venezuela is to be found.

Moving on to a more sustained examination of the middle period of Montejo's production, chapters 3 and 4 turn, broadly, to the question of place. In chapter 3, I focus on how Montejo presents the ontological and poetic night in which the world finds itself as symptomatic of an increasingly urbanised reality. I examine Montejo's understanding of both the poet and humankind in general as, thus, alienated from a harmonious relationship, or oneness, with nature, and explore the theoretical and ethical questions raised by Montejo's positing of a 'natural' poetic language as a way to reengage with nature and retrieve a lost ontological authenticity. Chapter 4 then takes up these lines of enquiry and examines how they fit in with and are altered by the particularities of the Venezuelan sense of alienation and exile as experienced by the poet. I end by looking at where, finally, this leaves Montejo's quest to construct a poetics which might be an authentic home for himself as an 'Orphic poet' and for the wider nation (and beyond) in and for which he writes.

1

Childhood, Cycles of Loss, and Poetic Responses

Setting the scene

In his first two major collections of poetry, *Élegos* (1967) and *Muerte y memoria* (1972),[1] Eugenio Montejo presents us with the foundations of what will become his poetic universe. Much like the actual universe, these early poetic building blocks constitute not so much a stage which will be left behind, buried under the subsequent pages of poetry, as one which grows by expansion, the symbols, concerns, and topoi becoming more complex and intertwined, but the essential matter out of which all is, ultimately, formed remaining the same.

As their titles indicate, these early collections are bound up with death and mourning, and, in line with these central thematics, Montejo sets up two distinct spaces and times in these works: the childhood and youthful past of the poetic *yo* and the present of the poet and his poetry as it looks back on and surveys that past, this dialectic being particularly prevalent in *Élegos*. The first lines of the first poem of this collection, 'En los bosques de mi antigua casa', introduce us to this schema and set out the scene on which the rest of the collection will build, as we are told how 'En los bosques de mi antigua casa | oigo el jazz de los muertos' (*É*, 5). The poetic *yo* remembers those who are now dead, hearing their music in his mind, which in turn adds to the sombre ambience. But it is the backdrop to this music and this remembrance that anchors both these lines and the collection as a whole. They indicate the setting of the past which is described and mourned in *Élegos* as being the rural house of the poetic *yo*'s childhood, hinting, in the process, at the Valle-jian debt to be found in Montejo's early poetry, here chiming with Vallejo's 'Canciones de hogar' in particular.[2] This *casa* represents the central location

---

[1]   Montejo's first collection of poetry, the often-ignored *Humano paraíso*, stands apart from the majority of his work in terms of poetic form and subject matter. Montejo himself commented in personal correspondence that 'pronto advertí que todo aquello [*Humano paraíso* and the influences behind it] nada tenía que ver con mi sensibilidad, que era una caprichosa forma de plantearme mis comienzos' (13 September 2005). Unfortunately, time and space do not permit me to rescue this work here from its status as a bibliographical curiosity.

[2]   Américo Ferrari notes that, in addition to the final section 'Canciones de hogar' of Vallejo's *Los heraldos negros* (1988: 3–120, pp. 108–15), the insistence on 'la casa y el

in seven of the twenty-one poems that make up *Élegos*, and within it and around it Montejo constructs the full space of the past homestead.

The rural location of this homestead is emphasised by a focus on the presence of trees both in the *bosques* of the opening poem and throughout the collection. 'Acacias' stands as a prime example, with the trees of its title placed in a wind-swept, rural *paisaje*, linked to the 'antigua casa' in its description as itself being 'antiguo':

> Estremecidas como naves
> acacias emergidas de un paisaje antiguo
> y no obstante batidas en su fuego
> bajo la negra luz de atardecida
> yo miro yo asisto
> a este mínimo esplendor tan denso. (*É*, 31)

The scene is dark and lugubrious, the metaphor of the ships being blown to and fro in a storm emphasising the elements out onto which the poet is looking, as well as hinting at the Romantic sensibilities which prove constant in Montejo's work. And yet the acacias are captivating and magical even in the darkness, as Montejo gives this rural location an aura of splendour and mystery.

Further conveying this setting's rural nature is the frequent mention of animals, including the dog which belonged to the poetic *yo* 'en mi año séptimo' ('Mi perro ateo mi perro de talento obsesivo', *É*, 8), and which is linked forever with this period of infancy ('enrazado de infancia y tiovivo' (8)). But the specifically rural character of the animals of this early collection emerges in relation to the *casa* itself, with the house being supplemented by a stable in the opening 'En los bosques de mi antigua casa', before being fused with a horse in the pivotal 'De quién es esta casa que está caída', where the poet talks of its 'puerta con ojos de caballo | y flancos secos en la brida muerta | de su aldaba' (*É*, 12). Moreover, Montejo employs the same technique in 'Mi casa clueca en el invierno', this time depicting the house as a hen:

> Mi casa clueca en el invierno
> mi casa corva en su potencia animal
> tía de unos huevos ya sin nacer
> gravita su mudez empolla aquel tacto doméstico
> con que escarba en la tierra para nosotros. (*É*, 15)

---

hogar' (Ferrari 1988: 15) in *Élegos* echoes a similar focus in several poems from *Trilce* (1988: 159–272).

Here, then, the house is not just described in terms which fuse it with a country animal, but becomes a living being which forms, gestates, and cares for those who emerge from it, that is, the poetic *yo* and his family.

Underlining the persistence of certain thematic threads and leitmotivs in this early collection, a similar image to that of 'Mi casa clueca en el invierno' is also found two poems later in 'Mi ayer es una bizca tía', where Montejo begins with a statement defining in explicit terms the past of the poetic *yo* being set out before us:

> Mi ayer es una bizca tía
> y una casa emplumada donde los muertos
> hacen café. (*É*, 17)

The house appears as central and, once again, with a veiled reference to the previous 'mother hen' identification. Likewise, the dead people of the house from 'En los bosques de mi antigua casa' are once more present in the remembrance of the poet. Significantly, however, they are also linked with the preparation (and, by implication, drinking) of coffee, a process which recurs persistently in both *Élegos* and *Muerte y memoria*. In 'Otra lluvia' (*MM*), for example, Montejo presents an image of the poetic *yo* as a child returning home with other children, possible siblings, to 'Quienes a nuestra vuelta hacían café | y nos secaban' (*MM*, 30), and in 'En los bosques de mi antigua casa' (*É*), immediately after referring to the music of the dead, Montejo describes how 'Arde en las pailas ese momento de café | donde todo se muda' (*É*, 5). The making and sharing of coffee emerges from these two collections, then, as an integral part of this past, rural home scene, constituting what I shall term a 'communional rite', that is, a ritual and familial moment of rural domesticity which grants a sense of community to those who share in it.[3]

The presence of the 'coffee moment' also signals the importance of the family *per se* in Montejo's construction of the past homestead, and Montejo populates these early poems with numerous family members. Aside from the 'bizca tía', who is named further on as Aunt Adela (*É*, 17), the figure of the poetic *yo*'s father is a constant presence in the two collections, providing the central focus of poems such as 'Mi padre regresa y duerme' and 'Había una vez un padre y yo era su hijo' from *Élegos*, and 'Levitación' and 'Caballo real' from *Muerte y memoria*, and thus recalling, once more, Vallejo's 'Canciones del hogar'.[4] Beyond this, there are the nameless 'muertos' from this past

---

3 Gutiérrez Plaza, in an article which offers, amongst other things, a useful gloss of the central symbols in Montejo's work, has also commented on his use of coffee as 'un elemento que evoca una suerte de rito ancestral' (1994: 552).

4 Montejo's 'Mi padre regresa y duerme' (*É*), for example, incrementally echoes Vallejo's 'Los pasos lejanos', which begins 'Mi padre duerme' (1988: 110).

home, as well as the figures of the mother, sister, and brother in the poem
'Elegía a la muerte de mi hermano Ricardo' (*É*), with many of these family
figures resurfacing some twenty years later in the poem 'Álbum de familia'
from *Alfabeto del mundo* (1988).

The distinctly personal nature of Montejo's poetics and of his construction of the homely scene of the past is underlined in this insistence upon the
familial. But it also reveals how far the past scene that Montejo lays before
us has autobiographical bases. Montejo himself lived the first few years of
his life in Caracas, a city which was, at that time (late 1930s/early 1940s),
a long way from the bustling metropolis of the end of the twentieth century.
Following this, most of his childhood and youth was spent in the provincial
cities of Valencia and Maracay, cities which, during this period (1940s and
1950s), were relatively small and rural, or semi-rural, in nature, much like the
scene described in these early collections.[5] And in interview in 1982, he laid
bare that the preoccupation with death in *Élegos* and *Muerte y memoria* was
due to his experiences whilst writing these poems. On the one hand, there
was his sentimental adherence to the political *guerrilleros* of the 1960s in
Venezuela, where 'tantos y tantos murieron de los que yo vi' (Szinetar 2005:
101) (and we might add that the political climate of repression during the
Pérez Jiménez dictatorship (1952–8) no doubt contributed to a similar awareness of death in this earlier period).[6] But Montejo also points in this interview
to the death of his brother Ricardo in 1961, when Montejo was in his early
twenties, that is, at the very end of this period of youth. The importance of
this event underscores that it is in the family names and concerns that the
most explicit autobiographical identifications are to be found, with the most
striking of these being the references to Ricardo, who is the subject of the
elegiac 'Elegía a la muerte de mi hermano Ricardo':

> Mi hermano el Rey Ricardo murió una mañana
> en un hospital de ciudad, víctima
> de su corazón que trajo a la vida
> fatales dolencias de familia. (*É*, 23)

---

[5]   See Chirinos (2005: 58–9) for the reasons why this was the nature of Venezuela's cities
as a whole in this period. The fact that rapid growth came to Valencia, for example, only
towards the end of the 1950s is evident from State censuses (see Instituto de Investigaciones
Económicas y Sociales, Universidad de Los Andes (2008)). It should be noted that there is
some confusion as to where Montejo spent his childhood years. Most sources, including interviews with Montejo himself, speak of Valencia, though without specifying exactly when the
author was living here. Other sources close to Montejo have referred, in private correspondence, to Maracay as the locale where much of his childhood was spent. What is important for
the present discussion, however, is that both cities were to a large extent rural or semi-rural in
nature during the period in question.

[6]   For more on the largely rural guerrilla movement of the 1960s in Venezuela, see Guevara
et al. (1997: 217–25).

Aside from its stark, bare descriptions telling of child mortality, the poem underlines the centrality and solidity of the family unit in Montejo's depiction of the past. It also points once more to the Vallejian concerns and tone found in Montejo's verse, dialoguing with Vallejo's poems 'A mi hermano muerto ...' (1988: 148) and 'A mi hermano Miguel' (1988: 111), which, likewise, concern the death of a brother whilst still young. (Indeed, the overall emphasis in *Élegos* on what appears as a distinctly personal nostalgia focused around infancy has distinctly Vallejian antecedents.[7]) Montejo here portrays the family coming together in the face of this tragedy, united around the central figure of the mother,[8] as we are told that 'Todos lo amamos, mi madre más que todos, | y en su vientre nos reunimos en un llanto compacto' (*É*, 25). It is an image of the family enclosed within the womb of the mother which echoes both the description of the house as a mother hen in 'Mi casa clueca en el invierno' and the opening lines of the poem 'Oscura madre de mis élegos', also from *Élegos*:

> Oscura madre de mis élegos
> tú que gravitas tú que antecedes
> calma central en el vacío de la casa. (*É*, 6)

In the enjoining of these three poems, then, the rural, the mother (familial), and the central space of the *casa* are fused, as Montejo both strengthens the familial, nurturing, and communional nature of the past rural homestead which he creates in this early poetry, and, in 'Oscura madre de mis élegos', explicitly affirms it as the inspirational origin of these poems.

Yet, despite the seemingly positive attributes conferred on the homestead scene, far from a joyous affirmation of the past being laid before us, the poetry of both *Élegos* and *Muerte y memoria* is, as the titles suggest, laden with sadness and melancholy: the past childhood homestead being described is presented in and from the time of the poetry's writing, where this past and all that is associated with it is now gone. It is presented, that is, primarily as absent, as dead. The house, for example, is mentioned only in terms which underscore its collapse over the years, as the poet progressively heightens the extent of the loss: from the opening poem 'En los bosques de mi antigua casa', where the poet surveys the ruins of his past home, suggesting a building

---

[7] See, for example, Mariátegui on Vallejo's 'nostalgia de ausencia' (1979: 204). In Vallejo's case, in particular in the poems of 'Canciones de hogar' from *Los heraldos negros*, the poet places himself in the figure of the child of the past, a technique which, for the most part, contrasts with Montejo's positioning of the poetic voice as the adult remembering.

[8] Once again, the echoes of Vallejo's 'A mi hermano Miguel' make themselves felt, with the mother appearing here as a similarly central presence.

half-standing as 'cae luz entre las piedras' (*É*, 5), we are then told, in 'Gira todo vivir por mi reloj ya calvo' that 'cae sol a las piedras ausentes' (*É*, 9), implying that the stonework has in fact disappeared completely. Finally, we are informed that all that remains is 'un poco de polvo invencible | sobre la arcada' ('Un poco de polvo invencible', *É*, 36), the atomised condition of the house reflecting the fate of this period of infancy and youth as a whole, where all that is left are 'restos de infancia | hacinada en lo hondo del ser [que] levantan cenizas de estupor' ('Había una vez un padre y yo era su hijo', *É*, 26).

Similarly, the persistent references to life, both animals and vegetation, are tied in with an overriding preponderance with their being now decrepit or dead. The trees in 'Tosen viejos los árboles de invierno' (*É*) are old and surrounded by a scene of cold, barren deathliness ('sobre los blancos pavorreales de la muerte | donde la lluvia habla latín' (*É*, 14)). And in the case of the rural animals we are repeatedly made aware of their present condition, the image of the *casa* as a hen, for example, being tempered by the placing of this animated description firmly into the past, in contrast to the dead ruins of the present, a contrast emphasised by the anaphora of the lines:

> De quién *es* esta casa que está caída
> de quién *eran* sus alas atormentadas. (*É*, 12, italics mine)

This presentation of animal life continues into *Muerte y memoria*, where the same technique of comparison between past and present is used to particularly striking effect. In 'Regreso', 'A una bicicleta', and 'Bancos en una iglesia de montaña', Montejo takes, respectively, a chair, a bicycle, and church pews, and shows the poet, in each case, comparing the inanimate object in front of him with an animate object from the past of which the modern object serves as a sad reminder. The chair is linked with the 'lejano árbol' which its wood once was, its current form aligned with the death not just of the tree, but of the whole environment: the cattle which grazed beneath it and the birds who lived in it:

> Un instante la silla ha regresado
> a su lejano árbol
> con sus verdes tatuajes ya secos.
>
> Sus pájaros están dispersos, muertos,
> y la manada del rugoso cuero
> yace plegada bajo las tachuelas. ('Regreso', *MM*, 13)

In 'A una bicicleta' and 'Bancos en una iglesia de montaña' the effect is more subtle, but no less deathly. As with the house in *Élegos*, the objects here are analogically described as animals, a horse in the case of the bicycle and a flock of sheep in the case of the church pews. But both alignments are undermined by an emphasis upon the temporal difference between the objects and the animals with which they are apparently fused. The bicycle, imagined as returning to the stable of the poet's rural homestead, does so to:

> comerse mis pastos oscuros
> y devorar mi sangre
> con resoplidos de una antigua amistad. ('A una bicicleta', *MM*, 16)

The now-lost friendship shared with the horse of before is glimpsed in the bicycle as it eats away the dark pastures of the poet's past home. Similarly, the description of the pews as sheep is undercut by a series of questions which lay bare the difference between the wooden benches and the rural animals:

> Los bancos están hincados en una tropa
> de animales mansos, ¿pero de qué se alimentan?
> El hocico inclinado y sin hierba,
> claveteadas orejas bajo un son de maitines,
> recuerdan el sermón de la sierra en sus tablas,
> ¿pero cómo tendrán lana este invierno?
>> ('Bancos en una iglesia de montaña', *MM*, 15)

Like the bicycle, the pews are also closely linked with death: whereas the image of sheep in a Christian context implies people being guided by the shepherd of life, here Montejo asks '¿Y a dónde los arrea el pastor de la muerte[?]' (15).

Across these two early collections, then, Montejo unfolds an alive, rural past, and sets up a contrast with a 'dead' present, in which the rustic and the natural have been supplanted by inanimate beings. To this extent, Montejo's early work displays a strong pastoral element, an identification suggested, moreover, both in the presentation of the poems of the first collection as elegies and in the specific use of the Greek term *élegos*, thus sending us back not just to the Romantic elegies of Shelley and Arnold, but to the world of the pastoral elegies of poets such as Theocritus. And, as befits the elegiac nature of the poems of *Élegos*, the awareness of and focus on the present, dead condition of the *casa* and the rural nature of the homestead is also reflected in the references to the people of this past space. As we have seen in the opening lines of both 'En los bosques de mi antigua casa' and 'Mi ayer es una bizca tía', the people from the past are described *en masse* simply as 'los muertos'. Further still, *Élegos* as a whole is dominated by the poem most overtly preoccupied with such a theme, 'Elegía a la muerte de mi hermano Ricardo', the longest in the *poemario*.

The inescapable presence of death and loss in both *Élegos* and *Muerte y memoria*, where nothing from the past homestead can be recounted or spoken

of without reference to its present condition,[9] is sustained poetically by the
ubiquitousness of images and sounds of mourning. The tears and weeping of
'Elegía a la muerte de mi hermano Ricardo' are mirrored by similar references to flowing water, either tears once more, such as the 'lágrimas' in 'Mi
padre regresa y duerme' (É, 16), or in the constant presence of rain, with 'la
persistencia de la lluvia | que cae con los años' referred to in 'Las ventanas'
(MM, 18) acting as an accurate description of the persistence of its falling
in Montejo's poems.[10] And both collections contain frequent references to
music and sounds of lament. In 'Salida' from *Muerte y memoria* the poet
imagines his own dead body being carried in a procession 'con lamento de
corno o de fagot | al monótono croar de los sapos ...' (MM, 23), tapping into
images from several poems from the earlier *Élegos* including 'Octubre en el
lamento de mis árboles', where Montejo firmly establishes the presence of
instruments and music of mourning in his verse:

> Octubre en el lamento de mis árboles   1
> vuelve al oboe que eriza las cortinas
> cuando sopla mi vida aniversarios
> ya llueve lo que soy en lo que fui   4
> [...]
> otra luna de sangre sepulta   9
> en su coro mis muertos
> otro golpe baldío y se cierra la tapa.
> No soy lo que he nacido y Libra me lleva.   12
>   (É, 18)

Indeed, this poem, whose colloquial tone and sentence rhythms recall Vallejo's 'Fue domingo en las claras orejas de mi burro' (1988: 343), in many
ways serves to define these two early collections. The ambience created by
the mournful oboe and choir acts as a backdrop to repeated images of the
change, death, and absence that come with the passing of time. The inexorable move into death and loss effected by the latter is here applied to the
poet himself, as his life blows by in successive birthdays, a journey into
death, as the reference to Pluto's chariot Libra discloses. The result is that
the poet of the present acts ineluctably as a sign of the loss of the poet of
the past (line 12). Moreover, the former, identified as itself being the falling
rain of lament, engulfs and overrides any image of the poet of the past (line
4). In short, Montejo articulates here the core of what might be termed the

---

9   This element is reminiscent of Quevedo's 'Miré los muros de la patria mía' (1995: 30–1).

10   In these early collections rain is present in 'Octubre en el lamento de mis árboles', 'Mi
casa clueca en el invierno', 'Había una vez un padre y yo era su hijo', 'Mayo', and 'Un poco de
polvo invencible' from *Élegos*, and 'Otra lluvia', 'Retornos', and 'Las ventanas' from *Muerte
y memoria*.

'poetics of loss' that he constructs in these works, namely the impossibility of conceiving of the past in a way which escapes the loss and death of that past in the present of the poem. As the image of the blood-moon with its deathly choir underlines (lines 9–11), the act of mourning, with which the present is inevitably synonymous, serves as a tomb in which the past is sealed.

Cycles and circles

In 'Fatales sapos de mis élegos' (É) the contrast between, on the one hand, the deathly and elegiac nature of the present and the poems and, on the other, the now-dead past, is particularly evident, with the past being identified more generally as the infancy of the poetic *yo*:

> La infancia duerme como sierpe
> en su fasto de anillos mal atados
> se comba por el ocio de ser
> gravita en ese punto inocente que me dobla
> nimbado a la piedad de lo que fui
> y anúdase en elipsis cuando sopla
> aquel fagot en el pantano íngrimo
> muda como quien teme una revelación
> y no despierta. (*É*, 20)

As in the later 'Salida' (*MM*), the sound of the bassoon tells of death, as the snake of infancy coils up tightly ('anúdase en elipsis') and remains asleep. However, the dominant image here is the persistent mention of circles and cycles: 'anillos', 'se comba', 'gravita', 'nimbado', with such images also being conspicuous in several other poems from *Élegos*. Particularly notable is the repeated use of the verbs *gravitar* and *girar*, not least in 'Gira todo vivir por mi reloj ya calvo', whose opening lines reveal the reason for these recurrent references to circles and cycles. The poem begins: 'Gira todo vivir por mi reloj ya calvo | el expósito ayer entre las hojas amarillas' (*É*, 9). The passing of time which both causes and marks the loss described by Montejo in this early poetry is viewed, then, as cyclical. tied in here not just to the circular movements of the clock's hands, but, in the reference to the autumnal leaves, to the wider yearly cycle. Indeed, throughout Montejo's work there is frequent allusion to *la redondez del tiempo*, a notion introduced specifically in the poem 'Retornos' in *Muerte y memoria*, where Montejo makes clear its decidedly negative sense, describing how 'el tiempo es redondo y atormenta' (*MM*, 10). Within this recourse to the annual temporal cycle, there is, nevertheless, a certain optimism and affirmation. This is particularly evident in the later poem 'Setiembre' from *Terredad* (1978), where the loss of everything mourned by Montejo in *Élegos* and beyond is countered in the

image of the allegorical September gathering up the leaves once more and
in the reference to the continuing radiance of the sun, which stands in sharp
contrast to the 'luna de sangre' (*É*, 18) from 'Octubre en el lamento de mis
árboles':

> Mira setiembre: nada se ha perdido
> con fiarnos de las hojas.
> La juventud vino y se fue, los árboles no se movieron.
> El hermano al morir te quemó en llanto
> pero el sol continúa.
> La casa fue derrumbada, no su recuerdo.
> Mira setiembre con su pala al hombro
> cómo arrastra hojas secas. (*T*, 19)

But the affirmatory tone of this later poem does not represent a total shift
in Montejo's poetry from pessimism to optimism in the portrayal and understanding of (the cycle of) time. Whilst certainly revealing an underlying desire
for a more positive poetics of time, it is the focus on September here which is
significant. For one, it ties this poem to the same time of year as 'Octubre en
el lamento de mis árboles' (*É*), the very poem to which, I have suggested, it
stands in contrast, signalling these months as the point in the yearly cycle on
which Montejo concentrates. Furthermore, just as his engagement with the
pastoral is indicative of a distinctly European (poetic) tradition in his depiction of the past, so too is the European significance of this time of the year
paramount in Montejo's verse. Whilst in Venezuela September and October
are warm, sultry months in the middle of the rainy season, in Montejo's
poetics they come to signify the autumn, as in Europe and European literary
tradition. This is implied in the lamented gradual move towards the winter
of one's life in 'Octubre en el lamento de mis árboles' and in the *hojarasca*
of 'Setiembre', with the disparity between the Venezuelan location and the
European seasons being alluded to in the much later 'Al retorno' in *Partitura
de la cigarra*, where the poet begins by musing: 'No sé si entonces era otoño
| el apócrifo otoño de estos trópicos' (*PC*, 25).

In fact, Montejo's poetry repeatedly makes the autumnal present through a
persistent return to the image of (dead) leaves, highlighting that, rather than
emphasising springtime, the time of rebirth, Montejo's engagement with the
topos of the yearly cycle is centred around the moment in the cycle at which
loss and death take place. In addition to 'Gira todo vivir por mi reloj ya
calvo' (*É*) and 'Setiembre' (*T*), this is the case, for instance, in the later 'En
las hojas' (*AM*), where we find a stark reference to the autumnal *hojarasca*
as Montejo rewrites the optimism of 'Setiembre':

> Aunque también temblando se equivoquen
> y rueden en inútil hojarasca

llenas de nervaduras ilegibles,
siempre quedarán otras para mí, para el viento.
El árbol sabe que el futuro es un vicio. (*AM*, 165)

The dead leaves here do act as a sign of the constant renewal of time, but a renewal and a repetition of loss, with the affirmation of the future found in the trees, leaves, and sun of 'Setiembre' dramatically recast as a vice, essentially a cruel (self-)deception.[11] Furthermore, the reference to the 'nervaduras ilegibles' of the leaves underlines the relevance of the double meaning of the *hojas* of the title here, suggesting that these lines also act as a commentary on the writing of poetry: rather than renewing that which it seeks to present, poetry serves merely to mark its loss – elegies indeed – with the poems themselves destined for the same fate.

This representation of time as a cycle of loss is not, however, limited solely to the annual cycle. It also characterises Montejo's appeal to the daily rotation. Once more, this circular movement does harbour a certain optimism for the poet and is, at times, affirmed, primarily in celebration of the life that it affords us. This is most notable in the later love poem 'La tierra giró para acercarnos' (*AM*), which talks of the earth's rotation bringing with it 'tanto amor, tanto milagro' (*AM*, 201). Yet, as with the yearly cycle, it is not only that without which we would not be, but, as Montejo discloses in his following orthonymic collection, *Adiós al siglo XX* (1997), that which marks the movement of life into loss, as the poet watches on, helpless to halt its circular and incessant course:

> Dios me movió los días uno tras otro,
> dio vueltas con sus soles hasta paralizarme
> como un gallo ante un círculo de tiza.
> [...]
> Fue Dios el que movió todos mis días,
> la redondez de Dios que no da tregua. ('El inocente', *AS*, 16)

Furthermore, in depicting what has, up to this point in his poetics, been the roundness of time as that of God, Montejo underlines to what extent time appears in his poetry as being synonymous with the divine giver and the taker away of life.

Such an alignment with the figure of the divine is also found, though more subtly, in the earlier poem 'Otoño' (*MM*), which brings together both

---

[11] The image of the *hojarasca*, linked to a negative understanding of the cyclical passing of time, is echoed in several other later poems including 'Al retorno' (*PC*) and 'Las sillas' (*AS*), where Montejo refers to the way in which 'sigue el tiempo cayendo gota a gota | en polvo y niebla y lluvia y hojarasca' (*AS*, 67).

the yearly and the daily temporal cycles. In this poem, both cycles contribute
to the construction of a sense of the falling away into absence which time
effects, as Montejo begins by positioning the poet and reader in what I shall
term the 'death moment' of each cycle, that is, autumn and dusk respectively.
In so doing, he portrays the poet and humankind in general as locked into an
inescapable fall into death and absence:

> Otoño, con cada sol caemos, caigo,
> con cada ocaso lento
> guardo las viejas hojas de otros años. (*MM*, 28)

The poet, lamenting this fall and desiring to retain what has been lost previously, then calls out to the autumn for the second time, the typographical
pause adding to a feeling of prayer-like lamentation and making the connection between the autumn and a divinity more explicit:

> Otoño,
> a esta vuelta la tierra
> se va lejos, distante,
> y en el puente ¡tan tarde!
> oigo mi antigua voz entre las aguas. (28)

As in 'El inocente' (*AS*), the Will of the Autumn-God being invoked is that
time and the loss it brings about should continue, as the lines here persist with
images of distancing, the earth continuing its rotation, and the past, possibly
childhood, voice of the poet ('antigua voz', cf. 'antigua casa' (*É*, 5)) flowing
away on the waters of time.

These lines also provide a further liminal locus to add to those of dusk
and autumn, although this time in the spatial form of the 'puente', an addition to the pastoral environment. It is a reference taken up again in the fourth
stanza, where it comes to be seen more clearly as, as with dusk and autumn,
the moment of the movement from life to death:

> En el puente mi olvido, mi sangre,
> o mañana en las manos del árbol,
> en otro viento, en otras cartas. (*MM*, 28)

The poet locates himself on the bridge, at the intersection of his death (his
oblivion) and his life (his blood), and on the point of being turned into letters
written on the wind by the tree's now leafless branches. Indeed, this latter
image is particularly important in the development of the poem's imagery,
with Montejo here building upon the previous stanza in which he describes
how, the leaves now fallen, 'la rama escribe en el viento desnudo' (28) and
wonders '¿a qué ojos se abrirán estas cartas?' (28). For Montejo, the tree

represents life, and the leaves falling from it the individual lives which are now ending, as the opening lines of the poem suggest. Playing with the double meaning of the term, as he will do later in 'Setiembre' (*T*), Montejo describes these *hojas* being replaced by those of the letters written on the air in a bleak metaphor for death, a metaphor which, in its focus on writing and *hojas*, also points towards an alignment of being and language which I shall explore in chapter 2.

The key element of this image for my present discussion, however, is found in the preceding lines, which focus on how 'En el fondo del árbol | madura el hacha de algún dios amargo' (*MM*, 28). Taking the tree as symbolic of life, we see how within life itself there is an axe. What this axe represents becomes clear some twenty-three years later in Montejo's heteronymic work *El hacha de seda* (Linden 1995), where the 'hacha' of the title is revealed to be 'el tiempo como silenciosa e infinita dimensión devoradora de todo' (*HS*, 11). Time, then, as in 'La tierra giró para acercarnos' (*AM*), is both the heart of life, that which enables it ('en el fondo del árbol'), and also that which marks its destructive and withering qualities, leading to the end of the individual examples (leaves) of the abstract entity which is life (tree).[12] Inevitably, then, 'Otoño' ends with the atomised poet figured as communing with his lost relatives, now, like them, dead:

> Ahora de lo amarillo,
> cuando la tierra cae y derivamos
> flotando entre los aires,
> con mis muertos fumando en la sombra
> nos pasamos un viejo cigarro,
> solos, mientras del puente efímero
> oímos chirriar el maderamen. (*MM*, 28)

It is a scene replete with images of loss and ephemerality, from the final reference to the bridge, now described as 'efímero', to that of the dead smoking a cigar, that is, at a basic level, the turning of leaves (*hojas*) into smoke, air. The fleeting nature of life and its unavoidable end is reasserted, as all that remains is death and the dead.

Yet within this image there is a certain air of affirmation: the poet is now together with his dead relatives, relaxedly sharing a cigar in a quasi-communional manner whilst listening to the bridge creaking as the next person crosses into death to join them. And the positive note on which this

---

[12] Underlining the persistence of both this metaphor and the concern for the effects of time's passing, a variation on this image is also found in 'Pavana del hacha' (*FE*), where the tree assumes the identity as, itself, the individual life of a man, brought down by 'el hacha que nunca se da tregua' (*FE*, 49).

poem of cycles of loss ends is echoed in one of the most persistent cycles of
Montejo's poetry, what I shall term the 'generational cycle'. In the majority
of the poems in which this leitmotiv is developed, the cycle appears not as
one where, as in 'Otoño', all generations meet together in death, but, rather,
as a cycle which, whilst indicating the inevitability of death and loss as one
generation is succeeded by the next, is also perceived as a means of negating
death in the continuity of genetics. This emerges as early as *Élegos*, in particular in 'Había una vez un padre y yo era su hijo', which begins by declaring:
'Había una vez un padre y yo era su hijo, | el alud de su muerte y su primera
eternidad' (*É*, 26). The continuing nature of this cycle is then made clear in
the second stanza, where Montejo takes the cycle back a generation further,
altering the first line of the poem as he states that 'había una vez un hijo y
él era mi padre' (27), before expanding his initial reference to the 'eternidad'
implied by such a cycle:

> Ese roce con que la eternidad arma las piezas
> fugitivas nos ató hasta el final. [...]
> [...]
> Yo callo y recojo los fastos con que sonrío a la muerte
> por toda filiación. (27)

These lines, prefiguring the gathering and keeping of old leaves/lives in
'Otoño' and 'Setiembre', show the genetic bond between father and son to be
a way of allowing the father to live on (even as the son, as the next generation,
signifies his death), an idea which Montejo would go on to recast with reference to 'la antigua filosofía china [que] tiene el cuerpo por [...] la morada
donde perviven los antiguos, como a nuestra vez hemos de pervivir en
nuestros descendientes' ('Los números y el ángel', 2006b: 345–8, p. 348).[13]

In the later 'Nocturno al lado de mi hijo' from *Algunas palabras* (1976),
Montejo once more takes up this topos. Now a father himself, he takes the
cycle forward one generation rather than back. Looking at his son sleeping,
he writes:

> Allí en su sueño, tras las nieblas
> que nos separan, crece el árbol
> por donde torna hacia otro día
> mi sangre que aún en él es verde. (*AP*, 37)

The poet's blood is able to return to youth in the veins of his son, the greenness suggesting not just innocence, but a determined negation of the move
towards 'lo amarillo' ('Otoño', *MM*, 28), the autumnal yellow of the leaves

---

13 See also Cruz (2006: 368).

of life falling from the tree. Rather than a flowing towards death, then, the generational cycle, through the image of the same blood flowing in a new body, enables the poet to declare that 'Allí mi infancia se reencuentra' (*AP*, 37). And it is this identification of the eternity and the negation of death afforded by the generational cycle with infancy which is key.

Throughout Montejo's engagement with the themes of time, its passing, and the loss it effects, the period of childhood and youth, often depicted with the term *la infancia* by Montejo, is pivotal. As we have seen, the early poetry centres around the lost rural homestead of childhood and the loss of that time in general, and this focus continues into Montejo's later work, not least in a number of poems in Tomás Linden's *El hacha de seda*, where, removed from the specificity of Montejo's own childhood, poems such as 'El Ángel' and 'El planeta fugaz' are concerned above all with lost youth and/or the speed with which it passes. Similarly, in Montejo's essay 'Los números y el ángel', also dating from the mid-nineties, he argues that 'privilegia[mos] con razón el primer septenio de nuestra vida por encima de los otros', calling it 'nuestra edad perdida' (2006b: 348).

Clearly Montejo's presentation of childhood engages with the Romantic topos of the idyll of lost youth and resonates inevitably with Marcel Proust's *À la recherche du temps perdu* (1987–89 [1913–27]). But it is in Montejo's comments on the Spanish poet Luis Cernuda that the strongest indication of the particularities of his own approach can be glimpsed. Writing on Cernuda in 1974, Montejo, drawing on Philip Silver's work (1995), talks of how 'la sed de eternidad se manifiesta en su obra bajo una percepción estática del tiempo, que lleva al poeta a refugiarse en la infancia como en un presente eterno' (*VO*, 170), going on to describe this as an 'ansioso retorno a ese universo estático, atemporal, que se hubo forjado en la infancia' (171). Such statements reflect Montejo's own understanding of infancy in his poetry, in that he does not focus on it simply because it is a past period which is now lost. Rather, he does so because infancy itself is a time when, for Montejo, one is *not* aware of time, where one is immune from its effects: in control of it. This is repeatedly suggested in his poetry, and nowhere more explicitly than in 'Deshora' (*AP*), where Montejo describes his childhood as a time when 'poseía las horas' (*AP*, 87), echoing Cernuda's affirmation of childhood in the prose poem 'El patio' as when 'el niño [...] era dueño de lo que el hombre luego [...] tiene que recobrar con esfuerzo' (1974: 649).[14] In short, infancy appears not as a specific period but as an atemporal, ahistorical time,

---

[14] The motif of the patio of the past childhood home also emerges as a recurrent Montejian theme, being present in 'Lejano' (*MM*) and 'El girasol' (*MM*), for example, although it is unclear whether this latter poem concerns the childhood house. The thematic thread continues in poems such as 'Las nubes' (*AP*) and 'El otro' (*AP*); 'Los gallos' (*T*); 'Los almendrones' (*TA*); 'Ida y vuelta' (*AM*); 'La puerta' (*PC*); and 'La casa y el tiempo' (*FE*).

akin to a prelapsarian locale where death – the ultimate marker of time's course – is absent, as Montejo suggests with his reference to childhood as 'donde vivir no era pecado' (*MM*, 18) in 'Las ventanas'.[15] It is a time, then, in which loss is written out because time itself ceases to be a process of loss.

A clearer understanding of what is at stake here, as well as of the complex way in which the generational cycles fit into this concept of infancy, is hinted at in a later interview given by Montejo. Speaking to María Alejandra Gutiérrez in 2002, he stresses that an understanding of his poetry's concern for the past as one of a simple nostalgia largely misses the mark:

> No sé si la palabra correcta sea nostalgia. [...] [C]reo que ello tiene que ver, más que con la nostalgia del tiempo ido, con una percepción de la simultaneidad de las horas, digamos de un tratamiento no lineal, sino circular del tiempo; tal vez sea esto lo que nos lleva a evocar un instante y sentirlo en simultaneidad con otro que ya ha ocurrido o va a ocurrir más tarde. Se trata de una visión que debemos a la psicología de los amerindios y de los africanos, es decir, que no sólo nos valemos de los hábitos perceptivos que nos legaron los europeos, sino que con mayor asiduidad solemos percibir el tiempo como circular y simultáneo; en el fondo ello viene a representar cierto 'cubismo' del tiempo, donde todas las horas, las de ayer, las de mañana y las de hoy, conviven en nuestra imaginación simultáneamente. (2002)

Several important points emerge from this response. Not least, these lines signal a central difference between Cernuda's understanding of infancy as defined by 'una percepción estática del tiempo' (*VO*, 170), a 'universo estático' (171) and Montejo's, which, this citation implies, rather than being centred around infancy as a static, stagnated period, is caught up with a mode of thinking whereby the negation of the loss caused by linear time comes from a sense of a circularity of time which brings together past, present, and future in simultaneity. In other words, far from staticness, Montejo's understanding of childhood as a period freed from linear time is built around the idea of constant movement, but movement *not* in a linear direction. This contrast, as well as the points of similarity, between Montejo and Cernuda here are particularly clear from a reading of one of the latter's most notable prose poems on childhood, 'Escrito en el agua', where Cernuda affirms that:

---

[15]   The echoes of Cernuda are, once more, strongly felt here. In the prose poem 'El tiempo' Cernuda describes childhood as 'donde todo hombre una vez ha vivido libre del aguijón de la muerte. ¡Años de niñez en que el tiempo no existe!' (1942: 10), and his depiction of the move from childhood to adulthood is portrayed in similarly biblical terms in 'Escrito en el agua' as the moment when 'caí en el mundo' (43).

Desde niño [...] he buscado lo que no cambia, he deseado la eternidad. Todo contribuía alrededor mío, durante mis primeros años, a mantener en mí la ilusión y la creencia en lo permanente: la casa familiar inmutable, los accidentes idénticos de mi vida. Si algo cambiaba, era para volver más tarde a lo acostumbrado, sucediéndose así todo como las estaciones en el ciclo del año, y tras la diversidad aparente siempre se traslucía la unidad íntima. (1942: 43)

The family home, the annual cycle of nature, so central to Montejo's early verse, are present here, but the mention of these cycles – indeed of any movement – is largely pushed aside by Cernuda, whose focus remains on the notions of permanence and immutability. In effect, then, alongside his move away from the European understanding of the linear flow of time, what is implicitly revealed through Montejo's declarations in the interview cited is a move away from this identifiably European lyric model of infancy as a time beyond this linear flow into and of loss.

In contrast to these European models, Montejo here appeals to and affirms Amerindian and African temporal models, and it is these which help us understand how, as Montejo claims, a circular time could be construed as compatible with the notion of a conflational time of simultaneity. Scholars have frequently identified an understanding of time as circular within indigenous African and American communities: days, years, lives, and history are seen to operate as cycles, where what has been will be again and again in the future. In reference to Mayan and Aztec belief systems amongst others, Mircea Eliade, for example, with whom Montejo was familiar,[16] asserts that 'what predominates in all these cosmico-mythological lunar conceptions is the cyclical recurrence of what has been before, in a word, eternal return' (1971: 88–9).[17] In this understanding of time, then, there is, in a sense (and certainly as Montejo appears to read it), no beginning or end, no before or after, in that every moment can be conceived of as part of a whole existing 'permanently' and simultaneously with all equivalent moments in the cycle, rather than discretely as part of a linear progression. The obvious poetic model for Montejo's engagement with such an indigenous concept of time is Octavio Paz's 'Piedra de sol' (1988: 333–55),[18] and his concern for a prioritising of the Amerindian here certainly recalls elements of Paz's work.[19]

[16] See Montejo (2006b: 320).

[17] For a counter-argument regarding whether such an understanding of how time is and has been conceived of by indigenous peoples of America, Africa, and beyond is, in fact, accurate, see Read (1998: 105).

[18] The reference in 'Piedra de sol' to the 'tiempo total donde no pasa nada | sino su propio transcurrir dichoso' (1988: 349) offers a formulation of the vision which Montejo perceives in Amerindian understandings of time.

[19] See Wilson (1979: 78).

Yet it is important to add certain caveats to Montejo's presentation of his thought on time in this interview, not least because such a conception of circularity is found in many cultures and thinkers, both previous and subsequent to those alluded to by Montejo, from Ancient Greece and the notion of all of time as an *annus magnus*, found in Stoic thought and in figures such as Pythagoras,[20] to Nietzsche's eternal return and beyond.[21] Similarly, the idea of a conflated temporal simultaneity is found in Heidegger's *Being and Time*, with the notion of, as Pattison puts it, 'a "moment of vision" that enables Dasein to will the synthesis of past, present, and future and so (and only so) "to be" ' (2000: 14). And there is also evidence that Montejo's understanding of time here was influenced by his reading of Machado's heteronym Juan de Mairena's concept of a poetic 'tiempo vital' (*TB*, 103) and, consequently, to the thought of Henri Bergson (*TB*, 104), with which Montejo's rejection of linear time as separated into discrete moments resonates. Nevertheless, the indigenous influence claimed here by Montejo does, at the very least, point to the *affirmation* of a distinctly American understanding and development in his work. Indeed, it is notable that Montejo's recourse in this interview to the analogy with cubism, a movement to emerge from Europe, appears as far less appropriate to the line of thought he is pursuing, sitting uneasily with the image of this time, or instant, as *moving* in cyclical or circular fashion.

The understanding of time laid out by Montejo in this interview reflects and provides the basis for the persistent attempt in his work poetically to effect a conflation of temporal planes, which several commentators have noted.[22] It also helps us to see why this appears linked so often with the depiction of family generations, even in his late collections,[23] with the focus on the necessity of movement found in (t)his cyclical notion of time serving to set him apart from the conflationary schema of the early Heidegger, for example. However, what is most particular about Montejo's approach here is how he uses the thematic of the generational cycle to bring together his concept of infancy as a period beyond the effects of time's passing and his conflationary view of time, underscoring the special place that childhood has in Montejo's temporal schema. Initially, the presence of the movement of the generational cycle scarcely seems unproblematic, in that, as conveyed in parts of 'Había una vez un padre y yo era su hijo' (*É*), the generational cycle seems

---

[20] The *annus magnus* was the cycle of the heavenly bodies at the end of which they would return to their original position and all that had happened would happen again. There was no place in the thought of the period for the idea of a beginning to time (see Boas (1972)).

[21] For a general overview of the ways in which time has been viewed as non-linear, and frequently as circular or cyclical, see Pegrum (1996).

[22] See, for example, Cruz (2006: 367) and Chirinos (2005: 164–5).

[23] Beyond the poems discussed here, examples include 'Güigüe 1918' (*T*); 'Tiempo transfigurado' (*AS*); 'En casa' (*PC*); 'Caracas en el azul de enero' (*FE*); and 'Cerca del lago Tacarigua' (*FE*).

to fall into the same essential trap as the yearly and daily cycles of time, in that it is still bound by a linear flow. In this sense, it appears more as a spiral than a single, 'horizontal' cyclical movement, as portrayed in Fig. 1. But this is where the importance of infancy comes in, since in Montejo's verse it allows the generational cycle to operate in a way which – at one point in the cycle – escapes linear time, in that, with each new generation, the moment of infancy signals a re-joining of all infancies ('Allí mi infancia se reencuentra' (*AP*, 37)), a moment of simultaneity afforded by the cyclicity. Rather than a single circle repeated endlessly and timelessly, then, the generational cycle, with its focus on (the re-joining of) infancy, suggests a schema more like that described by Fig. 2, where the spiral conjoins at this point, escaping linearity and ('normal') temporality, in contrast to adulthood.[24] The generational cycle, that is, is a constant, circular, temporal movement centred around and endlessly re-joining the eternal present of infancy as a moment where time's effects are not felt, prefiguring precisely Montejo's description in 2002 of the 'instante [...] en simultaneidad con otro que ya ha ocurrido o va a ocurrir más tarde' (Gutiérrez 2002).[25]

Fig. 1.

Fig. 2.

[24] Towards the end of his life Montejo came to describe time explicitly as an 'inabarcable espiral' (2007b: 5).

[25] Again we see an alignment with Eliade's understanding of 'primitive' or indigenous concepts of time where 'all rituals imitate a divine archetype and [...] their continual reactualization takes place in one and the same atemporal mythical instant' (1971: 76). The 'moment' of infancy of each generation in Montejo's work would, then, constitute just such a sacred 'ritual' or rite.

Given the centrality of such an understanding of infancy, or childhood
more generally, it is not surprising that the contrast between the perception
of time as a child and as an adult should be underlined so forcefully in one of
the poems which engage most overtly with the topos of childhood, 'Deshora'
(*AP*), to which we can now return. The poem begins with the poet, now an
adult, referring to the inexorable passing of time which surrounds him:

> Los días se doblan en mi mesa,   1
> se esparcen, rotan, se suceden,
> pero ¿qué hace mi alma del tiempo?
> Iba a amanecer y ya es noche,
> vine a la ciudad y está desierta.   5
>   (*AP*, 87)[26]

In sharp contrast to this adult experience of time, Montejo, as I have noted,
then turns his attention to his experience as a child:

> Antes poseía las horas,
> me gustaba flotar en sus nieblas.
> En casa me decían: –¿dónde has estado?
> Me hablaban de los lobos,
> pero yo tenía tiempo. (87)

The difference could not be starker. And yet, towards the end of this poem,
the tone changes. Rather than moving towards an affirmation of the generational cycle as a way out of the move into loss through the re-joining in
infancy that it grants, as stated in 'Nocturno al lado de mi hijo' earlier on
in the same collection, we are given an insistence on the passing of time
which has important consequences for Montejo's poetics of infancy and the
generational cycle. The poem takes up the earlier image of the poet as a child
ignoring the adults' warnings regarding the wolves, shifting to the now-adult
poet's mind as he describes how, in the present:

> No queda en casa nadie que pregunte
> sino sus fotos en los muros.
> Busco las huellas de los lobos
> que me asustaban. Y los lobos son ellos. (88)

As a child, the stories of wolves waiting outside to attack or eat up the child
who dared stay out late after dark were tempered by the fact that 'yo tenía

---

[26] The speech-like rhythms recall those found in Cernuda's prose poems, not least 'Escritura
en el agua', whose lines 'Pero terminó la niñez y caí en el mundo. Las gentes morían en torno
mío y las casas se arruinaban' (1942: 43), for example, are echoed thematically and structurally
here in lines 4–5.

tiempo': the young boy possessed time, was immune to any concept of death, of loss. Now, as an adult, Montejo searches for a trace of his childhood, of the wolves which, though a threat, were part of this time when he possessed time, and he discovers that the wolves are not some external threat never seen but simply 'out there'. Rather, the wolves are the very relatives who used to warn him of them. The photographs of the now absent family members, then, become the 'huellas', pointing to the unseen, yet perceived, threat of the wolves, and this threat is that of death, the passing of time which will lead Montejo to the same place as his relatives. All along, then, their warnings were warnings of the absence into which time will take him. Like the wolves, and like his relatives, Montejo too will become an absence, leaving only a trace of himself, a photograph, perhaps, as both a warning and a marker of the result of time's passing. Not only, then, does the insistence upon death prove ineluctable in this poem, but previous generations serve as the way in which this insistence is marked. Far from acting to hold onto infancy and escape the linear flow through a re-joining of all infancies in a moment of simultaneity, the focus is placed firmly on the generational cycle as a symbol of the inevitability of time's effects, serving as a reminder of what is lost, as the coil in Fig. 2 springs back into place.[27]

Such an overrunning of the affirmatory presentation of the generational cycle by its linear reading is not just limited to the poem 'Deshora' either. It is also starkly apparent in the poem which engages most explicitly with the topos of the generational cycle, 'Nocturno al lado de mi hijo', even as it foregrounds the hope afforded by it. Immediately following the poet's decla-ration that, in his son, 'mi infancia se reencuentra' (*AP*, 37), the poem begins to acquire a plaintive edge. For a start, the poet is, in fact, not in the timeless innocence of infancy with his son, but in the adult world, watching him, and what he observes is far from calming:

> Y la inocencia en su reposo
> que en lentas ondas fluye
> mientras velo a su lado me atormenta. (37)

The serene affirmation of the innocence seen in the son is suspended along three lines of verse laden with long vowel sounds before the final word

---

[27] In the insistence on the linear progression of time Montejo's generational cycle appears to slide from the envisaged and hoped-for Eliadean oneness of the 'moment of infancy' of each generation towards an understanding more akin to that of Read, who argues that the cyclicity of time in, for instance, Aztec culture is to be seen as more of a spiral, where each subsequent replaying of a certain moment acts as an engagement, but not a oneness, with the previous enactments of that moment; that is, where the linear movement is not avoided (1998: 95–108). In this respect, it might be noted that Montejo's engagement with Amerindian thought, whilst declaring an Eliadean reading of the latter, serves to support Read's reanalysis of it.

reveals it is, in fact, a torture, precisely in acting as a reminder of what the poet has lost. And it is now that Montejo mentions for the first time in the poem the generations that preceded him, conveying, thus, the realisation that his parents experienced with him exactly what he is now experiencing with his son:

> A la mesa en que escribo
> llega la sombra de mis padres
> a zancos de otro tiempo.
> Ojerosos anillos me suspenden
> del velón que en sus ojos parpadea
> al verme dormido de pequeño. (37–8)

The scene is being repeated with the father now cast back as the son, as in 'Había una vez un padre y yo era su hijo' (*É*). Only this time the circles are signs of aging, of loss ('ojerosos anillos'), and, as Montejo echoes the first lines of each of the two stanzas of the *Élegos* poem, the result is not a laughing in the face of death, but quite the reverse: a shiver of fear:

> De padre a hijo la vida se acumula
> y la sangre que dimos se devuelve
> y nos recorre en estremecimiento. (*AP*, 38)

This shiver is the *mysterium tremendum* referred to by Rudolf Otto in *The Idea of the Holy* (1959 [1917]) and about which Derrida later writes in *Donner la mort* (1999): a shiver of dread in the face of the unknown, where 'Dieu est la cause du *mysterium tremendum*, et la mort donnée est toujours ce qui fait trembler' (81). For Montejo too, this shiver or shaking comes from the passing of time – synonymous with God in his poetry, as we have seen ('Fue Dios el que movió todos mis días' ('El inocente', *AS*, 16)) – and from the move into death it effects. And this is what the generational cycle comes to mean for Montejo, as the poem closes with a scene of a coming together of even more past generations in what should be a hymn to the fact that all generations live on in their offspring or to the notion of a suspension of time afforded by a collective return to childhood. But, instead, it is an 'amarga sobrevida | que da terror y quema' (*AP*, 38). Far from a re-joining of infancy in that of his son, it is this existential fear with which the adult Eugenio is left, just as, in his later collections, the continued appeal to past, present, and future generations in poems which aim at temporal conflation is countered by poems such as 'El tiempo ahora' (*AS*), 'Temblor de llama' (*PC*), and 'Pavana para una dama egipcia' (*FE*), to name but a few of many, which affirm the inevitable flow of linear time.

The privileged moment of infancy, then, as a timeless time, escaping loss and death, appears as a wish, a theoretical possibility denied a reality. Moreover, this feeds back into the presentation of the central infancy or child-hood in question in Montejo's poetry: that of the poet himself, with Montejo affirming in interview in 1982 that, with the sociopolitical reality of the time, '[la muerte] me había invadido toda la juventud, porque no he tenido juventud' (Szinetar 2005: 102). Further still, the death of his brother Ricardo shows plainly the possibility of the death of a child. In short, infancy, in being presented as a time beyond the effects of time and where an attainment of an end to the temporal flow of loss is possible, appears in Montejo's work as a mythic – and Pastoral – Golden Age, projected back onto the past by a poetics which undercuts such an affirmation. Infancy acts more, then, as a powerful and developed symbol and poetic image of what the poet desires, than an historical actuality which he seeks to regain, a fact underscored by the nature of the poetic composition in *Élegos*, whose almost total lack of punctuation (added in subsequent anthologies) and incursion into archaic encliticisation ('oréanse'; 'obsérvanme'; 'anúdase') speaks more of a highly literary imagi-nary than of the specificities of 1940s and 1950s semi-rural Venezuelan life.[28]

Having set out the problematic and lamented process of loss effected by time's passing which is constructed in Montejo's early poetry, I shall now turn my attention to how this loss is tackled poetically through his develop-ment of two central and recurrent motifs: *caballos* and *café*, taking each in turn. The primary distinction brought about by time's passing in Montejo's poetics of loss is, as I have hinted, the separation of the dead and the alive, the absent and the present. This is the fundamental result of time's flow and it is on this distinction that Montejo focuses in his engagement with these two motifs. Through each, he both addresses this lamented binary and attempts to bring about a poetic annulment of it.

Poetic responses to time and death: *Caballos* and *café*[29]

One of the most consistent characteristics of Montejo's earlier verse is his presentation of both life and death either as a journey on a horse or, more abstractly, as both themselves being a horse. In the case of life, this align-ment emerges particularly explicitly in *Muerte y memoria*'s 'Caballo real'. Here, Montejo talks of his father as, 'Aquel caballo que mi padre era | y que después no fue' (*MM*, 40), and it is in these equine terms that the poem depicts the arrival of Montejo, the son, as he joins his father:

---

28 Miguel Gomes highlights these and other alterations made to subsequent publications of poems from *Élegos*, considering certain lexical changes to be due to the attenuating of 'ciertas estridencias juveniles' (1990: 100).

29 An earlier version of this section is found in Roberts (2007).

> Sé que vine en el trecho de su vida
> al espoleado trote de la suerte
> con sus alas de noche ya caída. (40)

From this birth moment on, the son is portrayed as riding with his father, until the time comes for the now-older Montejo to strike out on his own, signalled by the father's setting down of his son ('y aquí me desmontó de un salto fuerte, | hízose sombras' (40)). But this culmination of the period of fatherly guidance does not lead to the end of the image of the horse of and as life, in that, we are told, his father 'me dio la brida | para que llegue solo hasta la muerte' (40). The son, then, now takes up the reins of his own horse of life, in what is, once more, a cyclical movement, a repeated journey from birth to death recalling that of the horses of Helios pulling the sun across the sky from dawn (birth) to dusk (death), as the final image of the son now alone on his own journey of life makes plain that it is a journey which, like the father's, can lead only to death.

It is notable, however, that this final image is one of the son's riding the horse rather than being the horse, in contrast to the father. This may appear as a contradiction in the poem's internal logic, but it is precisely the play between these two descriptions of the same journey that is central. On the one hand, the use of both metaphors points to the indivisibility of the person embarked on the physical journey of life from the abstract 'life': in journeying through life one *is* 'life'. This is also the case in Montejo's identification of an individual life with both a tree and an individual leaf on a tree, to which I referred earlier. But, more importantly, the description of the father as inseparable from the horse and, hence, unable to halt or deviate its progress towards (his own) death also serves to highlight the latent irony in the notion of the son's – or father's – agency in the journey of life found in the reference to the bridle passed from father to son. Similarly, it is significant that Montejo should choose to revert here to the strict sonnet form for the first time since *Humano paraíso*, the strictness and predictability of the metre, number of lines, and organisation of the four stanzas mirroring the ineluctability of the journey and destiny of the horse.[30]

Within Montejo's *œuvre*, 'Caballo real' by no means stands alone in its depiction of life as such a journey. On the contrary, the piece echoes and develops the earlier 'Piafa y me ausculta a cada hora' (*É*). The opening lines of this poem suggest a similar alignment of life with riding on a horse, which is then passed on to the son, as the horse comes to represent the generational cycle of life we have seen to pervade much of Montejo's earlier work in particular:

---

[30] Following this poem, the sonnet will only reemerge in the heteronymic *El hacha de seda*, and never again under Montejo's own name.

Piafa y me ausculta a cada hora
aquel caballo en que mi padre
llegó hasta mí. (*É*, 7)

And, like 'Caballo real', this identification of the horse contains within it the inevitable move towards death. In the later poem the horse is described as being where 'calla | su filiación fatal [del padre] en la quimera' (*MM*, 40), indicating how the father's death is inscribed in his son's life, even as his son's life is his chimeric hope of eternalisation. Likewise, in 'Piafa y me ausculta a cada hora' the horse is depicted both as an eternal cycle of life ('La herradura combada a un límite de obsesiva eternidad | donde todo venir es volver' (*É*, 7)) and yet, concomitantly, as Juan Medina Figueredo (1997: 79) has noted, as an augur of death:

Piafa y orejea su capa de murciélago
modula un relincho de dádivas oscuras
y aletea magro de toda fatalidad
siempre con esa víspera en los ojos
listo para llevarme en su trote sin fin. (*É*, 7)

As is suggested by this poem, alongside the schema of life as a (journeying on a) horse, Montejo also frequently refers to death itself in the same way, echoing the mirroring counterpoints in Greek myth of Helios's horses and the black horses of Pluto. This is most explicit in 'En los bosques de mi antigua casa', which ends with the line 'los muertos andan bajo tierra a caballo' (*É*, 5). It is a line that resonates throughout much of Montejo's poetry, informing, as many critics have noted,[31] the opening poem of *Muerte y memoria*, 'Cementerio de Vaugirard', which describes the 'muertos' which dominate the poem as also 'bajo tierra a caballo' (*MM*, 7).[32]

This ambiguous presentation of the horse as a cipher for both death and life is not, of course, unique to Montejo; he is following a well-established literary and, particularly, poetic tradition, dating back at least as far as Greek mythology. This *doble naturaleza* of the horse in human culture and history is described in some detail in Luis Alberto Crespo's preface to the book *El caballo en la poesía venezolana* (Crespo, *et al.* 1981), co-edited by Montejo himself:

---

[31] See, for example, Medina Figueredo (1997: 104); Ferrari (1988: 16–18); and Lastra (1984: 213).
[32] For further examples of the alignment of the horse and death in *Muerte y memoria* see Roberts (2007: 1046).

Dador de vida y dador de muerte, el caballo ha sido identificado por el hombre con las fuerzas del bien y del mal. Los caballos del Apocalipsis galopan para asolar al mundo como los corceles de Atila, al tiempo que tiran del carro del sol y celebran con su desenfreno la vida, abren los ojos del visionario y el profeta. Ambiguo, mitad ángel, mitad demonio, cercano e inalcansable [*sic*], el caballo es el enigma, la más pura claridad y la más cerrada tiniebla. [...] La muerte fue siempre ese potro rápido y negro que nos cruza la mirada o el sueño, en cualquier llanura de la tierra, en cualquier extensión o comarca donde solemos perdernos mientras dura la zozobra o la pesadilla. La vida fue ese otro, como un ciervo en el salto, un galgo en la pista del hipódromo o el que se convierte en centauro en la fiesta del coleo. (Crespo, *et al.* 1981: 8)

Moreover, as the title of this book implies, Venezuelan poetry itself is notable for the prominence of the horse as a poetic symbol, thus revealing Montejo's own concern for the horse as being part not just of a general poetic and cultural tradition, crossing boundaries of time and place, but of an ongoing national poetic – as well as more generally artistic – tradition.[33] The same ambiguities are still found in this tradition, but with the added meaning acquired by the horse, as a symbol, as a result of its place in Venezuelan history, specifically as the instrument of both conquest and liberation:

También entre nosotros subsiste aquella doble naturaleza que los antiguos acordaron al caballo. La hazaña de la conquista tinta en sangre, cruel, espantable, convirtió al caballo en criatura de la muerte y el horror. El indio identificó al español con el centauro. La guerra de Independencia, la campaña libertadora, devolvieron al caballo su otra imagen, la de la libertad y el coraje. Bolívar y su cabalgadura conforman una unidad en el mito y en la historia de nuestro destino donde vemos encarnada la simbología del caballo y el hombre como cuerpo único de lo sublime.

(Crespo, *et al.* 1981: 10)

In general cultural terms, in specifically Venezuelan cultural terms, and in Montejo's poetry, that is, the horse cannot be just life *or* death, positivity *or* negativity. Furthermore, this factor underlines to what extent Montejo's use of the horse as a symbol of both (the journey of) life and death goes hand in

---

[33] *El caballo en la poesía venezolana* includes poems by, for example, Ramos Sucre, Sánchez Peláez, Paz Castillo, Gerbasi, and Montejo himself. Beyond the poetic field, the horse is a central figure in Venezuelan culture generally: a number of popular legends are centred around horses, including those of 'el Caballo Encaramao, el Jinete Sin Cabeza y la Mula Manéa' (Medina Figueredo 1997: 196), and arguably the most well-known Venezuelan popular song is Simon Díaz's 'Caballo viejo'. Montejo himself also underlines the prominent presence of horses in the work of the Venezuelan engraver and painter Alirio Palacios (Montejo 2006b: 320).

hand with his interest in Eastern thought, effectively representing a particular
formulation of the yin/yang symbol of Taoism. Just as in this symbol neither
the black nor the white is wholly black or white respectively, each containing
a spot of the other, so too is the symbol of the horse here never purely life or
death: the other meaning cannot be escaped, but is always there, implied, felt.

There is, however, one vital difference between Montejo's poetics of the
horse and the yin/yang. As Montejo points out in his essay '*I Ching*, el libro
de las mutaciones' (*VO*, 101–9), the symbol of the yin and the yang, as
with the thought behind the *I Ching*, is based on the consideration of 'estos
opuestos alternos no como cifras separadas [...], sino como parcialidades de
una totalidad cíclica' (108), where each leads into the other. Along similar
lines, in *El caballo en la poesía venezolana* the horse is described as 'la
representación de lo absoluto [...] lo eterno' (Crespo, *et al.* 1981: 9), and
as a symbol of 'el principio de la *unidad*, la montura iniciática' for both 'el
santo y el chamán' (10), highlighting both the dual tradition, European and
Indigenous American, which feeds into Montejo's poetics here, alongside
the Taoist elements, and hinting at the religious transcendence which the
attaining of such a cyclical totality would represent.[34] The journeys on horse-
back described in Montejo's poetics, however, do not both lead into each
other, forming a unified cycle: that of life leads to death, as we have seen, but
there is no return to life for the dead horsemen. In 'Llueve en el fondo del
caballo' (*É*), for example, the dead attempt to return but cannot then remount
the horse of life: 'allí donde regresan a galope los muertos | donde no queda
nada de caballo' (*É*, 19).

Nevertheless, as is made clear in *El caballo en la poesía venezolana*, in
engaging with the symbol of the horse, Montejo's poetry does affirm the
potential for 'el principio de la *unidad*', even as it bemoans the inevitable
and one-way movement of life into death, the separation of the past from
the present. And, as the failed attempt at return in 'Llueve en el fondo del
caballo' (*É*) indicates, it is by following the Taoist schema and leading the
horse of death back into life that this potential can, it is hoped, be realised,
bringing together (the horse of) death and (the horse of) life into one whole,
a cyclical whole, rather than two distinct entities. Such a reading of the two
horses in question is explicitly pointed to by the later poem 'Visiones II'
(*AS*), where the two horses of the earlier poetry find themselves now as a
single horse, with half above ground and half below: 'Sólo medio caballo
para tanto horizonte | y lo demás dormido, bajo tierra' (*AS*, 64).

---

[34] Underlining this, Montejo himself refers to Eliade's argument that 'el caballo [es] en
la mitología del chamanismo [...] un animal funerario por excelencia, que es utilizado por el
chamán como medio de obtener el éxtasis, esto es, la salida de uno mismo que hace posible el
viaje místico' (2006b: 320).

Returning to *Élegos*, this notion of and desire for a leading of the horse
of death back into life can inform our reading of its opening poem 'En los
bosques de mi antigua casa'. Here, as he stares out onto the house of his past,
the poet writes:

> Atisbo a la mudez del establo
> la brida que me salve de un decurso falible
> palpo la montura de ser y prosigo
> cuando recorra todo llamaré ya sin nadie
> los muertos andan bajo tierra a caballo. (*É*, 5)

From within the stables of the house of the past Montejo glimpses a bridle.
This is not the bridle of the horse of life of 'Caballo real', but that of death,
the 'brida muerta' (*É*, 12) of 'De quién es esta casa que está caída'. And it is
this bridle that Montejo here envisages taking up and taking out of the house
of the past. The result of such a move would be the avoidance of a 'decurso
falible', life as a fallible journey which leads inevitably to death, and, by
implication, the attainment of an infallible path (which can be understood
as the Tao or in biblical terms). In short, in the reading I am proposing, the
retrieval by the living poet of the horse of this place of the dead can be seen
as an act of restitution of wholeness, wiping out the difference between (the
horse of) life and (the horse of) death and, hence, the one-way movement
from the former to the latter. The 'montura de ser' that the poet envisages
touching (and, one infers, mounting) at such a moment is not, then, a reference to life in contrast to death, but one that corresponds to a wholeness or
unity of being ('ser'). Read thus, the 'dádivas oscuras' (*É*, 7) offered up by the
somewhat ambiguous horse in 'Piafa y me ausculta a cada hora' now come
to be seen as the potential gifts of both life and death together ('Dador de
vida y dador de muerte' (Crespo, *et al.* 1981: 8)), the gift of the eternal, of
complete being without loss, which it is the poet's task to attain.

Bearing in mind the Orphic undertones to Montejo's work as a whole, the
poetic quest revealed in this opening poem of Montejo's first major collection
to touch, bring out, and mount the bridle of the horse of death can be seen
to insert itself into the poetic tradition described in *El caballo en la poesía
venezolana* as the search for 'la proyección totalizadora de aquella posesión
órfica que permitió al hombre acercarse al caballo, *tocarlo* con su voz, con el
lenguaje y encantarlo, poetizarlo para apoderarse de su esplendor' (Crespo, *et
al.* 1981: 8). The poeticising of the horse is this act of touching and appropri-
ating the bridle, incorporating the horse into the poem which thus embraces
both death and life, and it is significant that the poet should go on to imagine
himself in just such a totalising position, with there being no outside of his
sphere ('cuando recorra todo' (*É*, 5)), and hence no one to whom he may call
('llamaré ya sin nadie' (5)). The implication of Montejo's totalising poetic

quest is that, with no longer any dead, there would be only subject, with no 'other' outside the totality of the unified horse-self, and such an idea is found in the grammatical ambiguity of this 'ya sin nadie', implying there would be no more 'no one', no 'nothingness', as the music of the dead ('el jazz de los muertos' (5)) and the silence of their locale ('la mudez del establo' (5)) are incorporated into the language of the poem in front of us. In short, what is being imagined in this envisaged recuperation of what is past is the ending of absence, an achievement whose realisation is immediately postponed by the final line's insistence on the dead who, despite the poet's efforts, 'andan bajo tierra a caballo' (5).

For all its philosophical and ontological implications and resonances, it is, nevertheless, crucial to note that the recuperation described in Montejo's poetry here and elsewhere is firmly rooted in and concerned with the familial and the Venezuelan. As we have seen, the poems in *Élegos* and *Muerte y memoria* are largely centred around the move into loss and death of places and people from Montejo's life, and the potential recovery of the horse of death, bringing life and death together into one totality, is played out specifically in this familial context, not least in 'En los bosques de mi antigua casa' itself, where the poet's childhood homestead (and the family and wider community associated with it) takes centre stage. And yet, as the importance of the horse as a national cultural and literary symbol suggests, over and beyond the recovery of this personal past, Montejo's poetry is also concerned with a national recovery, that is, one where the wider setting of Venezuela assumes an important role. Following the particularly personal characteristics of *Élegos* and *Muerte y Memoria*, this underlying preoccupation for the national begins to emerge more explicitly in *Algunas palabras* (1976), specifically in 'Un caballo blanco', which concerns a horse that the poet seeks to capture and describe in his writing. Whilst not explicitly associating itself with Montejo's personal quest for the bridle of the horse of death, and thus complete being, of 'En los bosques de mi antigua casa', the poetic nature of the search described in 'Un caballo blanco' clearly aligns it both with the poetic traditions to which I have referred and with the existing equine discourse of Montejo's poetics. In short, the 'caballo blanco' represents a possible identification of the horse of Montejo's earlier poetry, the horse that he wishes to incorporate into his poetry or *poetizar*:

> Sentí el deseo urgente de anotarlo
> en mi cuaderno,
> no sé con qué palabras (es lo que indago),
> no estoy seguro de que lo haya visto,
> hablaba, perseguía unas imágenes
> con sonidos de cascos en la hierba
> pero errantes, de paso.

El bulto aéreo de su cuello
y las sombras detrás de los celajes
me desviaron tal vez, iba a alcanzarlo,
iba a palpar el aleteo
de su visión o casi,
el fuego en un caballo blanco! (*AP*, 73)

But the 'caballo blanco' in question here, read within a Venezuelan context, cannot but recall Simón Bolívar's horse Palomo. The personal and the national meet in these verses as the recuperation of a national past is tied up inextricably with the poetics of the personal horse of the dead from Montejo's earlier verse, the connection between the two being emphasised by the recurrence of the verb 'palpar' in the description of the poet's attempt to attain the horse both here and in the distinctly personal 'En los bosques de mi antigua casa'. The loss that Montejo describes himself as feeling in *Élegos*, *Muerte y memoria*, and beyond is thus seen as symbolic of a wider national loss felt by Venezuela and Venezuelans as a whole. Moreover, there is an interesting juncture here between Montejo's poetry of the family 'muertos [que] andan bajo tierra a caballo' (*É*, 5) and the Venezuelan national coat of arms (opposite),[35] where Bolívar's white horse is depicted in the lower portion, below both the ears of corn, which stand as symbols of the earth, and the standards, which are suggestive of battles fought on land by man and horse during the fight for independence. The national horse of the past, then, is similarly 'bajo tierra'. Further still, the loss or lack synonymous with death and the passing of time is shown to be inescapable in any definition of the life or being both of the individual and of the nation here. On the personal level, for example, the poet is seen to carry around his 'muertos que andan bajo tierra a caballo' as a constitutive part of himself on his journeys to Paris in 'Cementerio de Vaugirard' (*MM*), whilst on the national level the loss is inscribed into the country's very being in its inclusion in the national coat of arms. We thus see how far the attempted recovery of (the horse of) death and loss is, as I have argued in my reading of 'En los bosques de mi antigua casa' (*É*), tied to a consequent move into an ontological wholeness not just on the personal level, but on the national level too.

What is made clear in 'Un caballo blanco', however, is that the task of the poet is impossible to effect. Despite the affirmations of the poet in 'En los

---

[35] The Venezuelan coat of arms, along with the flag, was changed on 12 March 2006 by the government of Hugo Chávez. The new coat of arms has the white horse of Bolívar galloping towards the left rather than the right and with his head facing forwards. An African-American machete, an indigenous bow and arrow, and typical fruits and flowers have also been added. The new coat of arms maintains the location of Bolívar's horse 'bajo tierra', but it is the old coat of arms which I use here, given the dates of the poems discussed.

The Venezuelan coat of arms

bosques de mi antigua casa' to be touching 'la montura de ser' (*É*, 5), it is always only a potential, as indicated by the use of the subjunctive ('la brida que me salve' (5)). Similarly, in 'Un caballo blanco' the use of the imperfect tense ('iba a palpar el aleteo' (*AP*, 73)) underlines the failure ever actually to achieve the goal of a whole being, to 'alcanzarlo' (73).

Underlying this preordained failure is the basic fact that the horse which needs to be brought back to life is that of death: the first step of the poet – that of reaching and attaining the horse – is thus also his last in being synonymous with the end of his life. Yet there is a further reason behind this failure, which emerges in the poem 'Uccello, hoy 6 de agosto', also from *Algunas palabras*. The poem concerns a reading of the events of Hiroshima on 6 August 1945 and a painting by the fifteenth-century Italian painter Paolo Uccello. Although which painting is being referred to is never made clear, it would seem to be the three-panel piece *Battle of San Romano*,[36] since the poem centres around a comparison between the shocking annihilation of Hiroshima and the 'mapa de la guerra | arcaico' (*AP*, 21) depicted in this work. Underlining its place amongst what we might term Montejo's horse poems, and inserting itself, more narrowly, into the existing Montejian discourse of the horse and death (and the horse as death), the poem begins: 'En el cuadro de Uccello hay un caballo | que estuvo en Hiroshima' (21). The painting *Battle of San Romano* is in fact replete with cavalry horses, horses that are linked with death and destruction, and the reference suggests that a similar horse of death was present at Hiroshima in a symbolic sense. But the poem ends by disclosing that the horse of Hiroshima to which Montejo refers in the opening

---

[36] Uccello's *Battle of San Romano* is made up of three separate panels, created c. 1454–57. All three panels can be found at http://www.abcgallery.com/U/uccello/uccello.html [accessed 1 January 2009].

lines is not any of the visible horses of the painting. Rather, it is 'present' as
a hidden entity:

> Es un caballo torvo, atado a un árbol,
> siempre listo en su silla.
> Uccello lo cubrió con capas de pintura,
> lo borró de su siglo,
> y hoy aguarda en el fondo de la cuadra
> con los jinetes del Apocalipsis. (21)

The horse in question, then, is not represented by the images on the canvas.
Quite the contrary, they act merely to cover it up, and it is here that Uccello's painting serves as an indicator of how we are to understand Montejo's
attempt to describe, touch, and attain the horse of death in the poems 'Un
caballo blanco' and 'En los bosques de mi antigua casa'. (Indeed, the reference to the horse waiting 'al fondo de la cuadra' echoes the latter poem's
depiction of the poet glimpsing the bridle of the death-horse in the 'mudez
del establo' (*É*, 5).) Desiring to bring the horse of death, and thus all that is
dead or lost (back) into life, both poetry and art in fact fail to do so, writing
the elision of the horse even as they seek to present it. And what 'Uccello, hoy
6 de agosto' indicates is that this is not linked simply to the death of the poet
(or artist) implied in such a move, but to a resultant widespread annihilation,
as, we are told of the horse of death present in Hiroshima, 'sus patas llevan
en la noche | a la desolación del exterminio' (*AP*, 21).

But what is at stake in this annihilation is also more complex. Significantly, in depicting the horse in this way Montejo's poem recalls and echoes
Jacques Lacan's (1973: 75–86) famous reading of Hans Holbein's painting
The Ambassadors.[37] Lacan's account focuses on the stretched, distorted,
and unsettling form which appears at the bottom of Holbein's work. When
viewed from a very oblique angle, this form is revealed to be a skull, an
image 'hidden' from the onlooker when not viewed in this unorthodox way,
what Lacan describes as an anamorphotic object, always 'there', but usually
hidden from view. The skull symbolises the inescapable 'presence' of death
which pervades all life and awaits us all, and its revelation acts as a moment
of *frisson*, as we are brought face to face with an object which 'nous reflète
notre propre néant' (86), that is, 'quelque chose qui n'est rien d'autre que le
sujet comme néantisé' (83). The hidden horse in Uccello's painting, like the
elusive horse of death in Montejo's poetry, is just such an object.

The key to understanding the horse's necessary elision in both the
painting and poetry is found more precisely in the particular way in which

---

[37] Holbein's *The Ambassadors*, located in the National Gallery, London, can be seen at
http://www.nationalgallery.org.uk/cgi-bin/WebObjects.dll/CollectionPublisher.woa/wa/largeIm
age?workNumber=NG1314&collectionPublisherSection=work [accessed 1 January 2009].

this anamorphotic object is understood by Lacan. In Lacanian terms, the skull – or, in Montejo's case, the horse – is associated with the real, lying beyond both the imaginary and the symbolic, that is, outside of signification and the signifier. In short, the skull/horse threatens to dissolve the subject, should he or she ever attain it, in that this object is concomitant with a move outside of language and symbolisation. This is why any attempt to name or represent such an object in poetry or art, that is, in language, in the widest sense of the term, works as an ineluctable avoidance or covering of it: it is an avoidance which serves the interests of the work of art itself in that, with the revelation of the object, would come the loss or dissolution of the poetic or artistic representation. Thus, in Holbein's painting, the skull is elided, and, significantly, can only be seen at the moment when the rest of the painting is blurred or lost to the sight of the person gazing at it; in Montejo's reading of Uccello's painting the horse of death is hidden from sight and would only be glimpsed by wiping out the layers of paint, of representation; and in Montejo's own poems the horse of death is likewise always elided, alluded to but never attained within the language of the poetry on the page. Moreover, even the appearance of the object, as in Holbein's painting, is finally a *representation* which can only afford a glimpse of 'notre propre néant' (Lacan 1973: 86), to use Lacan's terms once more, without constituting an arrival at such a beyond of representation.

Read in this way, in 'Uccello, hoy 6 de agosto' Hiroshima on 6 August 1945 represents the consequence of the irruption of the real into the world in the form of the horse of death. It is a moment in human history where the horse of death was present ('un caballo | que estuvo en Hiroshima' (*AP*, 21)), dissolving being and the layers of representation which had covered it, layers which had acted not as a way of bringing the horse into presence but of shielding us from it and the nothingness, the 'desolación del exterminio' (21) that its presence would bring. And this is the central paradox that Montejo's poetry comes up against here. In bringing out the horse of death Montejo sees a potential for an end to the difference between life and death, an end to the irrecuperable fall into absence. And, certainly, Lacan's presentation of the real suggests such a collapsing of the absent/present binary would indeed be the result: as Dylan Evans, citing Lacan, states, 'unlike the symbolic, which is constituted in terms of oppositions such as that between presence and absence, "there is no absence in the real"' (1996: 159). But any ending of the difference between death and life, thus ending the fall into loss and death brought about by time, would itself signal an end to life as much as it would an end to death, an end to presence as well as an end to absence, to extend Lacan's assertion. In Montejo's 'horse poems', poetry, like art, may be seen ineluctably to hide and/or elide the horse of death, thus ensuring the separation between the absent and the present, the dead and the living. But in so doing, in bolstering the symbolic and the imaginary, poetry acts to bolster what we know and perceive as life as well as its own existence. In just such a way, and despite its pretensions to the contrary, Montejo's attempt to incorporate the horse of death into his verse likewise serves merely to buttress and assert the side of the living, that is, language and the self: that which is deemed to be present. In short, Montejo's poetry most desires what it most fears and works to avoid, and that which, as poetry and as representation, it can finally only elide.

Despite the apparent impossibility of the quest constructed around the symbol of the horse, Montejo's poetics nevertheless continues to attempt to present a potential way in which the dead might be brought back together with the living in a process which would once and for all do away with the move into loss and death that the passing of time effects. Central in this regard is the motif of coffee, recurrent, like the horse, in Montejo's early poetry, as we have seen, but which is only developed fully by Montejo in later works.

   An early indication of the direction in which Montejo takes his quest is found in the trance-like ambience of 'Sobremesa' (*MM*). Here Montejo describes a scene where the dead and the living come together around a table to converse. It is a nebulous scene, lacking a firm sense of time or place, and where no one – dead or alive – can see anyone else:

> A tientas, a nivel de la niebla
> que cae de los remotos días,
> volvemos a sentarnos
> y hablamos ya sin vernos.
> A tientas, a nivel de la niebla. (*MM*, 27)

As the poem progresses, the quasi-religious atmosphere is built up: adding to the fog, there is now reference to 'el aire', 'el sueño', and, crucially, 'vapores de café', which act both as incense, adding reverence and mystery to the scene, and also as an invocation of the dead ('los ausentes') to make their presence felt:

> Sobre la mesa vuelve el aire
> y el sueño atrae a los ausentes.
> Panes donde invernaron musgos fríos
> en el mantel ahora se despiertan.
>
> Yerran vapores de café
> y en el aroma, reavivados,
> vemos flotar antiguos rostros
> que empañan los espejos. (27)

The dead are raised, made living again, as are even the 'panes' which harboured 'musgos fríos' on the table cloth, a further hint at the religiosity of the scene, and, specifically, the Christian symbolism present in the poem's overall resonances with the Last Supper.[38] Now gathered, 'comenzamos a hablar | sin vernos y sin tiempo' (27). Time is no longer, as the loss effected by the passing of time is reversed and the poem ends with an affirmation of the end of the differentiation between life and death:

> A tientas, en la vaharada
> que crece y nos envuelve
> charlamos horas sin saber
> quién vive todavía, quién está muerto. (27)

'Sobremesa' pervades and supports much of Montejo's later poetry in which he tackles this notion of the bringing together of the dead and the living, and the aroma of the coffee is a particularly significant element in its claims to have made the two indistinguishable. The meaning and power of coffee as a motif, and the underlying reason for Montejo's recourse to it here, are suggested in numerous poems from this early period which deal with or make reference to coffee. As I set out earlier, in these poems coffee is associated with the past and, specifically, the poet's familial past; it is a part of childhood memory which comes to stand as a symbol of a lost 'homeliness' and of the now absent family and wider community members, as we have seen in 'En los bosques de mi antigua casa' and 'Mi ayer es una bizca tía' from *Élegos*, and in 'Otra lluvia' from *Muerte y memoria*. In each of these poems the people from the childhood past connected with coffee are now gone, but the memory of the making and drinking of coffee remains, appearing as a past and familial ritual.

Much like the horse, however, coffee as a personal and poetic symbol is also, in a Venezuelan poetics, inseparable from its wider meaning as a national symbol. Just as the white horse of Bolívar represents the birth of the nation, so too is coffee, which was first cultivated in Venezuela in c.1779, linked with this moment of national incipience. Writing in 1952 – when Montejo was a child – on the place of coffee in the national mindset, the Venezuelan essayist Mario Briceño-Iragorry describes how 'el café aparece en nuestro país coincidiendo con la revolución comunera y con el propio nacimiento de la venezolanidad integral' (1983 [1952]: 38).[39] Moreover, he goes on to describe coffee in terms which underlie and are echoed by Montejo's own

---

[38] In its focus on the breads which 'se despiertan', 'Sobremesa' also appeals to pagan symbolism. The Christian form of the Eucharist is very similar to the ritual practised as part of the Greek Eleusinian Mysteries, in honour of both Ceres, goddess of wheat, and Bacchus/Dionysus, god of the vine (see Taylor (1829) for a thorough discussion).

[39] The title of this essay is 'Una taza de café' (1983 [1952]: 35–41), complementing the preceding essay in the collection 'Café' (31–4).

understanding of coffee as a personal custom, when he instructs Venezuelans: 'tomemos como símbolo de nuestros valores vernáculos, el aromoso
café; tomémoslo hasta con un valor de rito sagrado' (41). On both levels,
coffee is understood by these writers as a sacred, communional rite, signalling familial and national 'wholeness', an identification which lies at the heart
of Montejo's use of it in the trance-like religiosity of 'Sobremesa' (*MM*) and
which enables the poem's final affirmation of success in bringing together
and conflating the living and the dead.

In this respect, it is significant that both in Montejo's personal poetics and
in Briceño-Iragorry's depiction of it as a national symbol, coffee does not just
appear as an element of and from the past. Rather, the emphasis is placed on
the coffee ritual as a more general act of welcoming or communion, which
does not just take place *in* the (now) past but *between* the past/dead and the
present/living. This is the case in 'La silla' (*MM*) ('A veces un hombre de
otro siglo | baja de su carreta, | llega por una taza de café' (*MM*, 21)), 'Casa
agreste' (*AP*) ('Morada detenida en ausencia | donde la noche nace del café |
que me sirven sus dueños' (*AP*, 39)), and, most powerfully, in 'Sobremesa'.
Similarly, Briceño-Iragorry talks of how 'al regustar el licor de nuestro criol-
lísimo fruto, estamos comulgando con la tierra de nuestros padres, estamos
respirando el aire que en nuestros campos acarició las rojas bellotas' (1983
[1952]: 41). On both the personal and the national level, then, coffee effects a
bridging between past and present, dead and alive. Thus, when Montejo talks
in 'En los bosques de mi antigua casa' (*É*) of hearing the jazz of the dead and
how 'Arde en las pailas ese momento de café | donde todo se muda' (*É*, 5),
it is uncertain whether this moment is one remembered from the past or the
moment in which the poet is now looking out onto the absent scene, or both.
It also underscores that the poem itself is – as in 'Sobremesa' – a potential
momento de café: through the poem there can be a glimpse in the present of
this moment from the past, uniting for one brief instant the dead remembered
and the living poet and reader.

The striking poem 'Café' from the later collection *Alfabeto del mundo*
finally brings together these strands and lays out explicitly the reading I have
been suggesting, as well as deepening and developing the significance of
coffee as a symbol in Montejo's poetics. From the very beginning of the
poem it is clear that the aroma, taste, and rituals involved in the preparation
and drinking of coffee are intimately bound up with the aims of Montejo's
verse:

> Al dibujar cada palabra,
> detrás de su color, ritmo, latido,
> siempre soñé dejar llena, secreta,
> alguna taza de café
> que se beba entre líneas. (*AM*, 162)

The poem then goes on to describe in more detail the signification of this coffee and in so doing reminds us explicitly of 'Sobremesa' and the end of the life/death separation. It is:

> Café con el aroma de las horas
> y la mesa en el aire
> donde al primer hervor los vivos y los muertos
> levitemos. (162)

In addition, Montejo reiterates its link with both homely scenes of rural family life and the dead, as he describes the coffee as:

> café del alba, amargo, recién hecho,
> que nos trae a la cama
> algún canto remoto de gallo.
> [...]
> el café sin café de los ausentes
> dormidos en nuestra sangre. (162)

And, as this last line suggests, the poem also taps into the place of coffee within the national sense of identity and belonging, referring to it specifically as 'café natal, sentimental', the 'café de las ciudades fugaces, imprevistas, | que sabe a las voces de su gente, | al rumor de sus ríos imaginarios' and 'el café azul del pájaro, | el verde inmenso de los soleados platanales' (162).

For Montejo, this communal, quasi-religious, and salvational coffee, working on both the personal and the national level, is always there, offering itself up to be smelt and consumed, an 'amable duende que nos sigue por el mundo | con densas vaharadas' (162). The question is whether the poem can successfully evoke its aroma, and here the poem moves towards greater affirmation. Whereas at the beginning of the piece there is a questioning uncertainty as to whether the poem can produce this coffee 'entre líneas', indicated by the use of the subjunctive ('que se beba'; 'donde [...] | levitemos'), by the end this has shifted to a reassured sense of repeated success:

> Sólo para avivar su aroma escribo a tientas
> al dictado del fuego.
> Sólo para servirlo siempre dejé oculta
> alguna taza que se beba entre líneas,
> detrás de mis palabras. (162)

Montejo paints himself as always having left coffee hidden between his words, with the uncertainty now placed onto whether the reader will be capable of sharing in this communal cup, as the coffee assumes its religious charge once more, both Christian, as a cup of divine coffee served up to other mortals to partake of, and pagan, as an offering served up to the gods, for them then to accord the poet in return the divine gift of a bringing together of dead and alive. (Such an image is conjured up explicitly in the poem 'Ulises' in the same collection, as Montejo writes in the first person of how 'llevo un poco de café para los dioses | que nos prometen un viaje propicio' (*AM*, 182).) In short, 'Café' underscores that it is the poet's task to serve up the potential for the scene and the opportunity for the coming together described earlier in 'Sobremesa' (*MM*), the connection between these two poems being signalled by their both using the phrase 'a tientas': the blind act of writing such poetry in 'Café', relying on touch, on feeling, intuition ('escribo a tientas' (*AM*, 163)), is thus inseparable from the creation of the potential realisation of the scene in 'Sobremesa' ('A tientas [...] volvemos a sentarnos | y hablamos ya sin vernos' (*MM*, 27)).

Most significantly, however, 'Café' also reveals a crucial problematic of the quest and schema proposed by these 'coffee poems', as well as a potential way forward. For whilst it may appear as an element that enables a communion between the past and the present, the coffee which the poem seeks to serve up – and of which Montejo's early poems speak – is essentially that of the dead, of the past, and of the poet's childhood ('el café sin café de los ausentes' (*AM*, 162)). The poem's evocation of the coffee and/or its aroma effectively repeats the idea of the horse of the dead being made present, with both figured as ending the separation between life and death. The implication of the similarity between the two, however, is that, as with the horse, so too would the recovery or presentation of the coffee of the dead work to annihilate both the present and the poem itself. And this is precisely what emerges in 'Café', where the coffee cannot be expressed in the symbolic: the description 'el café sin café de los ausentes' elides and eludes 'café' as both signifier and signified. It is, in its essence, absence and silence, and it is the poet's task to attempt to make this absence and silence of the dead present, but without falling into the trap of annihilation, without actually writing it, since such writing would be the end or death (the absenting or silencing) of writing. In its focus on the need to make the coffee present 'entre líneas', 'Café' thus represents a move beyond 'Sobremesa' in showing the naivety of the earlier poem's attempt to do – and claim to have achieved – *in* words ('charlamos horas sin saber | quién vive todavía, quién está muerto' (*MM*, 27)) what can only be done *behind* them and *between* them.

It is this naivety which, in the light of 'Café', is then explored in 'De sobremesa', also in *Alfabeto del mundo*. As a secondary meaning of its title suggests, it is effectively a reading of and commentary on the *Muerte y memoria* poem 'Sobremesa'. The poem describes a similar scene to that of the earlier poem, although on this occasion the poet is looking on rather than actively participating in the conversation at the table. As before, the poem begins by suggesting that we are in a timeless scene, in that it takes place 'cuando relojes zurdos | vuelcan intacto el cofre de sus horas' (*AM*, 202). But the tone of the poem is soon very different. Far from the nebulous, aethereal ambience of 'Sobremesa', here the conversation is portrayed first and foremost as 'billaresca', as the voices or words ('voces') of those sitting at the table reverberate around, with time being imagined as the cushions of a billiard table:

> siento rodearme la billaresca charla
> de voces que rebotan contra el tiempo
> y se repliegan en un rumor de sombras. (202)

The scene also marks a change from that of the earlier poem in the lack of people. For all its focus on the fact that those who were there were speaking 'ya sin vernos' (*MM*, 27), 'Sobremesa' at least talks of 'antiguos rostros' brought back to life. 'De sobremesa', however, is bereft of such mention. When the poem finally does refer to 'alguien' it is the start of a series of four lines which signally negate the very idea of any people or faces being present:

> Alguien habla por sombras o por ecos,
> alguien desde ninguna silla dice un nombre
> que al instante ya es otro o tal vez nadie,
> un nadie más, sin rostro, sin persona. (*AM*, 202)

The unknown 'alguien' in question is a total non-existence: it speaks in shadows and echoes, sits in no chair, and says a name which immediately changes, slips into something else, cannot be fixed, so much so that it is essentially meaningless: it refers to no one at all, 'un nadie más', suggesting that all there is is '*nadies*'. That this is set up in direct opposition to 'Sobremesa' is implied by the specific reference to the 'nadie más' being 'sin rostro' (cf. 'vemos flotar antiguos rostros' ('Sobremesa', *MM*, 27)), and made particularly evident in the way in which the two earlier lines:

> Sobre el mantel ruedan insomnes las palabras,
> desenterradas pero anónimas. (*AM*, 202)

offer themselves up as a counterpoint to the parallel lines in 'Sobremesa':

> Panes donde invernaron musgos fríos
> en el mantel ahora se despiertan. (*MM*, 27)

In so doing, they deny the earlier poem's idea of actual physical and individual resurrection: the focus in 'Sobremesa' on the biological ('musgos fríos') and on the bread waking up (an image which, especially in the context of the rest of the poem, has connotations of the Eucharistic bread becoming the living body of Christ at the sacramental moment) is now rejected, as the later poem insists that the only thing brought back from the underworld, the 'bajo tierra' of Montejo's 'muertos', is words, and words devoid of a speaking subject ('anónimas'), a long way indeed from the individual 'antiguos rostros' present in 'Sobremesa'.

Rejecting thus the physical and individual in 'De sobremesa' Montejo effectively rewrites the *Muerte y memoria* poem, revealing the *actual* result of its attempt at bringing together the dead and the living both in the language *of* the poem and in the language of the scene referred to *by* the poem ('hablamos'; 'charlamos' (*MM*, 27)). Rather than bringing the two into communion with each other in a timeless place which is neither life nor death, 'De sobremesa' discloses that the earlier poem merely revives and repeats words. The fact is that we are not in a timeless realm without a difference between dead and alive, absence and presence; we are in a realm constituted by nothing but language, with the dead left in absence as they are reduced to anonymous, bodiless signifiers, firmly locked in the symbolic, that is, within a logic and structure of oppositions. Indeed, this is implied by the final lines of 'Sobremesa', in that, even as they claim to affirm the contrary, in describing how 'charlamos horas sin saber | quién vive todavía, quién está muerto' (*MM*, 27), they effectively underscore that the poem is an act of inscription within precisely these oppositions of dead/ alive, absent/present.

To understand what is at stake in this rewriting of 'Sobremesa' and the particular importance of coffee in these poems we need to consider that, as the resonance with the Christian Eucharist in 'Sobremesa' suggests, Montejo's 'coffee poems' are also a commentary on the value of ritual itself. And it is this commentary that helps us see why the ritual of 'Sobremesa' fails, falling into language, as well as disclosing why the coffee Montejo seeks is repeat-edly portrayed as that of (a mythic) infancy – with all that that implies in Montejo's poetics – and one which is elided by language, rather than simply coffee *per se* or the coffee of the present. The communional ritual of coffee, like that of the Eucharistic wine with which it is identified in 'Sobremesa', both in being coupled with bread and in the reverential and quasi-religious atmosphere found in the poem, serves as a symbolic repetition of an origi-nary, transcendental communion. But, as a symbol and ritual, the preparation and drinking of coffee points only to the absence of that which it pretends to repeat and make present, as Montejo's portrayal here of ritual and language, and of ritual as language, resonates with Derrida's disclosure of the iterability of every ritual – and speech – act (1972a: 365–93). In seeking a past, mythic coffee, as in 'Café' – a coffee both tied to the timeless period of childhood and outside of language – Montejo's poetry underscores the insufficiency both of the (current) rite of coffee and of the poem which attempts to convey and be such a rite in its language, and affirms the need for an originary coffee, an originary communional moment before its repetition as ritual and as language if the timeless, communional state to which he aspires *through* his poetry is to be attained.

It is thus significant that, just as 'Sobremesa' discloses the ineluctable inscription of the communional scene it portrays in language and its dialectical terms, so too does it reveal the poet engaged in the representation of such a scene to be incapable of escaping temporal references. As Montejo's heteronym Blas Coll later states, language is inherently tied up with 'la estructura lineal presente-pasado-futuro' (*BC*, 42), and the move into it implies a concomitant move into this linear temporal structure. Accordingly, and as 'De sobremesa' suggests when it refers to the 'voces que rebotan contra el tiempo' (*AM*, 202), far from creating and describing a timeless realm, beyond the effect of loss, the language of 'Sobremesa' abounds with references to repetition ('volvemos a sentarnos'; 'vuelve el aire' (*MM*, 27)) and sequential time ('ya sin vernos'; 'retornarán más tarde'; 'comenzamos a hablar'; 'quién vive todavía' (27)), underscoring once more the unavoidable inscription within the linear progression of time that dominates Montejo's poetic leitmotivs.

It is, though, in the last two lines of 'De sobremesa' that we find the most succinct précis of this attempt to bring the dead and the living into communion in and through the words of the poem. Here the poet affirms that the scene described – which is that originally evoked in 'Sobremesa' – is 'como si tanta ausencia viniera a decir algo | que la vida convierte en otra cosa' (*AM*, 202). The dead, the absent, that which is past, are figured like the Lacanian real as exerting pressure on the symbolic and the imaginary: in Montejo's terms, on the world as we know it, temporal and linguistic. Yet any attempt to allow the absent to burst forth in the world, to express itself, hence annulling the loss effected by time, and despite its assurances to be evincing a timeless, opposition-less realm, is inevitably a drawing of the dead and the absent *into* time and language, the imaginary and the symbolic, which thus fails to grasp the essence of what they are: an extra-linguistic absence. Their essence is not maintained together with that of life, that which is present, in a quasi-religious limbo. Rather, it is converted into language and made temporal, with the insistence on cyclical repetition in 'Sobremesa' falling into the same problematic as the repetition of infancy in the generational cycle in coming to stand not as a moment of atemporal oneness, but as a reenactment and a reminder of what has already been and is now lost. In short, it shows merely how the poem which seeks to make present in language the apparent moment of communion offered by the sacred personal and national rite of coffee is – like rite and ritual itself – a cycle of a repeated loss, a repeated failure to recover the dead without converting them 'en otra cosa', just as, working with the symbol of the horse, the poet's attempt to incorporate the jazz and silence of the dead into the language of 'En los bosques de mi antigua casa' led, likewise, to the continued elision of these figures.

Reflecting on this attempted recovery of the dead and the past in Montejo's poetry, as ciphered in the motifs of both coffee and the horse, a final word needs to be said of the latent and persistent presence of Orpheus here, not least because 'Orfeo' (*MM*) and 'Orfeo revisitado' (*AM*) are central poems in the period in which both these motifs are developed. Like Orpheus, Montejo, as poet, is involved in a quest to end loss and recover what is dead. But the fruit of his quest is the inevitable, continued loss of 'los muertos': his Eury-dice. Maurice Blanchot, writing on Orpheus and the reason for his turning back to look at Eurydice, comments on the fact that he wants 'non pas la faire vivre, mais avoir vivante en elle la plénitude de sa mort' (1968: 228). Such, too, is the goal of Montejo, whose poetry speaks of the desire not to convert *muertos* into *vivos*, but to bring together and *confuse* them. Yet, as 'De sobremesa' shows, the only way the poem, *in* its language, can bring out the dead from their place 'bajo tierra' – the Montejian Underworld – is by changing them into words and the temporal, that is, by once more effacing them 'sous un nom qui la dissimule et sous un voile qui la couvre' (Blanchot 1968: 227), just as the horse of the dead is hidden in Uccello's painting.

2

Language, Memory, and Poetic Recuperation

Language and loss

At the end of the previous chapter I alluded to the connection between (linear) time and language in Montejo's work. However, such a connection is not just a matter of the language of Montejo's poetry reflecting the inevitable succession of moments in 'la estructura lineal presente-pasado-futuro' (*BC*, 42). Neither is it simply a case of language being 'on the side of the living' and hence failing to bring the dead back without converting them 'en otra cosa' (*AM*, 202), although both these elements are present in Montejo's poetics, as I have shown. The connection is more fundamental. Earlier we saw how Montejo's essay 'Tornillos viejos en la máquina del poema' (*VO*) can be read as disclosing the presence of death within language *per se*, a reading suggested, moreover, by the terms and argument of the essay as a whole. And this reading is central in revealing to what extent Montejo's quest to bring back the dead and all that is past is tied in with a parallel quest to evade the deathly nature of language. It is on the ramifications of this essential linguistic problematic within the presentation of loss over time in Montejo's work that the present chapter will focus.

Looking more closely at the terms Montejo uses in his engagement with the symbol of the horse, we begin to see just how far language is implicated in his portrayal of (the effects of) temporal loss. In my analysis of how Montejo's poetics envisages the notion of a uniting of the horse of life and that of death into one (cyclical) whole, I alluded to the importance of the reference to 'la brida que me salve de un decurso falible' ('En los bosques de mi antigua casa', *É*, 5). However, beyond what is explicit in this line, a crucial aspect of the envisaged quasi-religious salvation is found in the implicit morphological link between *decurso* and *discurso*.[1] The fallible *course* of the journey of life leading inevitably to death, which Montejo seeks to avoid is also to be seen as the fallible *discourse*: language as inherently pervaded by death and loss. In effect, it is not just that language elides

---

[1] The word *decurso* found in the original version of this poem was changed in subsequent anthologies to *senda* (see, for example, *AM*, 36). It appears as if, on some level, Montejo were fighting against the slippage of signifiers which I identify here.

the dead. Rather, it is in being named in language that the dead are made dead, are made past. Thus, when Montejo asks 'De quién es esta casa que está caída | de quién eran sus alas atormentadas' (É, 12), the juxtaposition of 'es' and 'eran' does, as Américo Ferrari notes, '[abre] toda la perspectiva de la incesante confrontación de la presencia y la ausencia, del presente y el pasado, de la vida y la muerte' (1988: 15). But, more importantly, it shows the inevitable slippage into death which language itself effects: no sooner is the house named than it is made past.

The relationship between language and absence in Montejo's work here has echoes of Mallarmé, a poet with whose work Montejo was familiar. One thinks, for example, of the former's aim of 'peindre non la chose, mais l'effet qu'elle produit' (1959: 137). Yet rather than accepting (and aiming for) this excision of the referent by language, Montejo's work, here at least, speaks of the frustrating impossibility of avoiding such an outcome. To this extent, working within a Mallarméan heritage, Montejo's poetics reflects more particularly the overlaying on that heritage of a distinctly Derridean understanding of the nature of language, not forgetting that Derrida was himself an attentive commentator on Mallarmé.[2] For Derrida, language is permeated by division and deferral, as captured in his term *différance*. Every signifier has meaning only in its relation to other signifiers; meaning is a matter of constant referral and deferral on from term to term (1972a: 1–29). Similarly, Montejo's use of language to evoke and invoke the dead immediately defers the arrival at any fixed meaning, at any beyond of language, that is, at that which he seeks to name in the text, recalling the absent referent which Derrida and others have noted in Mallarmé's poetry.[3] This is what is described, for example, in 'De sobremesa' (*AM*), where, as soon as they are spoken, the words and the name called out cannot be fixed, referring ultimately to no one ('sin persona' (*AM*, 202)), as we saw in chapter 1. Furthermore, this example also underscores that one of the most pertinent resonances with Montejo in Derrida's work is his specific focus on the production of language as an *immediate* move into an absenting of what it names or in whose name it is produced. In *Limited Inc.* (1988), Derrida refers to the idea that 'the break intervenes from the moment there is a mark, at once' (53), and this serves as an accurate indicator of how Montejo's poetic texts immediately write out the presencing of that which is named (the 'muertos', the past, infancy).

The extent to which Montejo's poetics opens itself up to a Derridean reading becomes particularly evident in 'Tan ululante vuelve y no verídica' (É). The poem begins:

---

2   See, for example, Derrida (1972b: 199–318) and (1974).
3   For instance, Derrida (1972b: 289) and McCann (1996).

Tan ululante vuelve y no verídica
la fabla de mis loros nonagenarios
reyes en la ceniza de un vano parloteo. (*É*, 13)

As in 'Sobremesa' (*MM*), already here the cyclical repetition of a repetitious language is underlined, the age-old parrots repeating once more ('vuelve') the same 'vano parloteo', vain precisely in its inability to effect the end to loss desired by Montejo. It is a language which, in this sense, is 'no verídica' (note the alliterative *v*s connecting the three terms 'vuelve', 'verídica', and 'vano'), and it is significant here that Montejo should use the archaic term 'fabla' to describe it. This word, seemingly indicating an old language, more connected with the past and thus, potentially, more capable of presenting that past, is shown to be quite the opposite, disclosing that this failure stretches back into time and is a characteristic of language *per se*. Its etymological connection to the term *fábula* further adds to the connotations of myth, tale, and lie contained in its being 'no verídica', connotations which are directly relevant to Montejo's own language and poetic production, in that later in *Élegos* he refers to the endless cycle of the writing of poetry in which he is engaged as 'fabla de esquivez' ('Mi vivir es araña en la tela del poema', *É*, 37).

The most significant element of these lines, however, is the reference to the 'vano parloteo' as 'ceniza'. Not least given Montejo's stated attraction to Quevedo's work, it is impossible not to be alert to the echoes of the latter's famous 'Amor constante más allá de la muerte', with its final lines 'serán ceniza, mas tendrán sentido; | polvo serán, mas polvo enamorado' (1995: 507), although here at least there is nothing of the affirmation found in the Quevedean sonnet, with the tone and focus on degradation and finitude here and in *Élegos* generally being more reminiscent of Eliot's *The Waste Land* (1922). Yet in talking specifically of ashes of language, it is once more Derrida who provides the most telling resonance. Derrida talks of cinders as a cipher for the workings of language in that they are the irreducible presence of what is absent, a sign of what once was, standing for its absence even as it stands for it: 'C'est là la cendre: ce qui garde pour ne plus même garder' (1991: 35), and such is the nature of language for Montejo, for whom all that is left is 'tan ululante grito de mis nombres perdidos | ecos en la memoria sin edad' (*É*, 13): what we might term the 'originary names' are replaced by echoes circling in the realm of *différance*, as the idea of timelessness ('sin edad') takes on the negative sense of endlessness: endless language, endless loss.

Memory

Amidst these poems of temporal and linguistic loss, Montejo neverthe-less identifies a potential way of overcoming the effects of both time and

language. Effectively seeking to rescue it from its negative depiction in 'Tan
ululante vuelve y no verídica', memory comes to represent, for Montejo, the
potential for an elision of death and loss, thus providing one way of understanding the title of *Muerte y memoria*. The importance of memory here for
Montejo is highlighted by his depiction of loss as synonymous with 'olvido':
what is forgotten is what is lost or dead. In *El cuaderno de Blas Coll*, for
example, Montejo sets up his role as editor of Coll's notes as being primarily to 'defenderlo del olvido' (*BC*, 33), and as early as *Élegos* he is found
suggesting the same alignment:

> Mi ayer es una bizca tía
> y una casa emplumada donde los muertos
> hacen café. Olvido es lo demás. ('Mi ayer es una bizca tía', *É*, 17)

Memory, then, acts as a potential counter to this loss, and this is what is seen
in *Muerte y memoria*, in particular in 'Metamorfosis', which, with specific
reference to the terms of the childhood homestead of *Élegos*, conveys memory's ability to make what is past reappear or revive in that it:

> Abre un tiempo remoto
> donde otras voces reaparecen,
> escucha el río de la casa caída
> tatuado entre las piedras. (*MM*, 25)

In fact this poem initiates a persistent thematic thread of the *casa* and its
restitution in memory. In 'Setiembre' (*T*), we recall, the loss of youth, the
death of Ricardo, and the destruction of the old family house are countered
not just with the reference to autumn gathering up the leaves, but with the
declaration that 'la casa fue derrumbada, no su recuerdo' (*T*, 19), an image
taken up at several points in Montejo's subsequent *œuvre*, including his last
collection *Fábula del escriba*, where both 'Un parpadeo' and 'La casa y el
tiempo' speak in similar terms of how 'En pie sigue la casa ya sin casa' (*FE*,
60) and how 'La casa sigue intacta en esta calle | aunque el tiempo deshizo ya
los muros' (*FE*, 65), respectively. Likewise, Montejo's heteronymic work also
engages explicitly with this topos. In the gloss to copla XXXI from *Guitarra
del horizonte*, for example, Sergio Sandoval specifically affirms the power of
memory in rebuilding and re-presenting the house of childhood:

> Pero la copla no es fiel del todo cuando asegura que ahora, en la intemperie,
> nada permanece de mi antigua casa. Si la dibujo es porque mi memoria
> sabe restituirla piedra a piedra, con sus ecos que están y no están dentro
> de los largos corredores. (*GH*, 59)

Throughout his discussion of the restitutive powers of memory, Montejo places great importance on the role of household objects. This is especially noticeable in *Muerte y memoria*, where objects, invariably associated with everyday life, are envisaged as accumulating the memories of the events they have witnessed over the years. The objects, ranging from a chair ('Regreso'; 'La silla'), to shoes ('Viejos zapatos'), and a bed ('Antigua sangre') come, thus, to represent what I shall term 'memory-stores', inscribed somehow with the events and people of the past. These events and people are then offered up to the poet as he contemplates and writes the objects. In 'Antigua sangre', for instance, we read:

> La antigua sangre corre intacta
> entre las venas de la cama
> mientras se oye que guarda en su pasar
> tantas memorias de otros años.
> [...]
> Y al restallar ahora la madera
> creemos ver que flotan
> almas o voces en el aire
> con que la noche decora los sueños
> cada vez que regresan y nos hablan. (*MM*, 17)

The moment of release of the memories stored up by the bed, as its wooden frame cracks, produces a moment akin to those described in 'Sobremesa' (*MM*) and 'De sobremesa' (*AM*): the dead's 'almas o voces' come back and enter into a conversation with the living. The objects, as memory-stores – as *memoria* – represent a potential for bringing back the dead.

Montejo's treatment of everyday objects here reverberates with two distinct strands of thought. In the first instance, the focus on the world in which these objects are found and the role they have played in the lives of people down the years once again recalls a Heideggerean mode of thought. The presence of the latter is made particularly evident in the light of Montejo's comments in a later interview, where he states that:

> Hay un diálogo de intimidad con las cosas, que me permite ver una mesa, y estar con ella. [...] Por ejemplo, una mesa largo tiempo tallada quién sabe por quién, manchada por miles de tazas de café, es irremplazable, aunque sea por una mesa muy nueva y costosa, porque eso no tiene nada que ver ante aquella otra mesita. Esa cotidianidad que celebro viene de allí, del diálogo secreto, íntimo, con las cosas. (Posadas 2002: 306–7)

It is difficult not to hear echoes here of Heidegger's discussion of Van Gogh's 'A Pair of Boots' in 'The Origin of the Work of Art' (2001: 15–86), where the boots, imagined as belonging to a peasant woman, are revealed by the

painting in terms of lived experiences and of use: 'in the stiffly rugged heavi-
ness of the shoes there is the accumulated tenacity of her slow trudge through
the far-spreading and ever-uniform furrows of the field swept by a raw wind'
(33). It is this sense of the history and 'equipmental being of equipment'
(34) of the shoes which is 'what the shoes are in truth' (35), as disclosed by
the work of art. Likewise, Montejo's poetry presents itself as revealing the
'truth' of these everyday objects, at the same time as the above interview
citation shows how such a presentation carries with it an implicit rejection
of the postmodern world of consumerism, again a stance found in Heidegger
(1973a: 107).

The second strand of thought invoked by Montejo's poetics here relates
more particularly to the nature of the memory-stores which these objects
are conceived of as being, and reveals profound problematics in Montejo's
presentation of their potential in 'Antigua sangre'. The way the bed works in
this poem as a registry of memories (in the sense of *recuerdos*) has strong
resonances with Freud's famous model of memory (in the sense of *memoria*):
the Mystic Writing-Pad (1961 [1925]). The bed, as with the pad, retains the
imprint (inscription) of the events and people it has been in contact with, with
the blood acting as a constantly renewed and renewable writing surface, able
to take in each inscription, retain its imprint, and be ready, in its flowing, to
receive the next. But where Montejo's schema differs from Freud's is that
the objects used by Montejo as metaphors for how memory works are, first
and foremost, *not* metaphors in themselves: they are objects in and of their
own right, lying in front of the poet, which are seen as, in some way, actually
containing memories. What is being described, then, is not just the process
by which memories are formed and retained, but that by which every object,
every thing, accrues meaning. To put it another way, 'Antigua sangre' is a
description of the bed as a signifier which has accrued meaning in its relationships with other signifiers: the events and people with and through which it
situates itself, themselves only understandable as signifiers ('almas o *voces*'
(italics mine)).[4] Montejo's presentation of memory, that is, chimes with Derrida's interpretation of Freud's Mystic Writing-Pad (Derrida 1967b: 293–340).
For Derrida, such an image of memory as based on inscription or writing is
not simply a metaphor, but reflects how perception and memory actually
work: each memory/perception only gains meaning in its relationships with
previous memories or writing. What emerges from Montejo's poetics, then,

---

[4]   This reference to 'almas o voces' does not imply that there are *either* souls *or* voices/
words. Rather, it is a declaration of synonymity, the poet hesitating between two terms representing the same thing. This anticipates the revelation in 'De sobremesa' (*AM*) that the dead
can only be revived as language.

is that there is no place nor function of memory which itself is not a function of language, that is, which is not *écriture* in its widest (Derridean) sense.[5]

Given our discussion regarding the nature of language, the revelation that memory is itself language, or linguistic in structure, suggests that, like language, memory too is incapable of fixity, incapable of ever halting or univocally defining its meaning, and, concomitantly, of making present what is remembered. And this is what we see in 'La silla' (*MM*), where the process and result of a (past) life being conceived of as part of history and memory is described. The poem, in full, reads:

> Qué está claveteado en esta silla,
> sobre su rugoso cuero, bajo sus patas,
> para que aceche aquí un peligro tan fuerte?
>
> Al tacto es una araña de madera   4
> cuya astucia la salva del polvo
> mientras vela en su antiguo reposo.
>
> A veces un hombre de otro siglo
> baja de su carreta,   8
> llega por una taza de café
> y sin saber toca sus hilos,
> se anuda en la invisible red.
> Entonces la silla lo captura,   12
> lo arrastra hacia la historia
> más cerca del estar que del ser.
>
> Y el huésped deberá ya vencido
> colgar su abrigo desdichado   16
> en los clavos del viejo perchero,
> despedir su caballo,
> recomenzar con otros argumentos
> el monólogo estéril de la vida.   20
>
> (*MM*, 21)

Like the bed in 'Antigua sangre', the chair is a memory-store object, with the poem setting out the process by which events and people become part of historical memory. Far from affirmatory, the poem lends an explicit air of entrapment and threat to how this occurs, emphasised by the alliterative *ss* in the third stanza: the object appears as a spider which captures the victim, dragging him off into history, as he becomes, in some way, connected with it. Such is the result of entering into a relationship with an object or signifier: one is forever connected to it and the production of its meaning, no matter

---

[5] For a detailed exposition of the (use of the) term, see Derrida (1967c: 145–202).

how passing or insignificant the contact is ('llega por una taza de café' (line 9), a line which foregrounds the specificities of Montejo's poetic world). Despite its apparent negativity for the unfortunate man, however, it would seem as if the poem were depicting memory as grasping the past highly successfully. But the significant line here is that which refers to the result of this dragging off into history as leaving the man 'más cerca del estar que del ser' (line 14). The man no longer 'is', in the sense of no longer being ontologically definable. Rather, he now has only positionality, positionality, that is, within a system of signifiers, locked within the chair and the play of *différance* (lines 19–20).

In depicting memory as *écriture*, Montejo is, once more, figuring language as the only way in which the past can be brought back, as in 'Sobremesa' (*MM*) and 'De sobremesa' (*AM*), where, likewise, the dead are made present only as language. What is retained in Montejo's model of memory is disassociated from any identification as materiality or specificity. Indeed, as language, the disassociation of memory from what is apparently being remembered is total. After all, as memory-stores, the bed in 'Antigua sangre' and the chair in 'La silla' contain not the actual voices, but, as Freud's Mystic Writing-Pad image informs us, an inscription of them. In functioning as language, then, the memory-store itself constitutes the inscribing of a thing as a mark (and thus a *recuerdo*), as we recall Derrida's affirmation of 'the break [which] intervenes from the moment there is a mark, at once' (1988: 53). In this respect, it is significant that the poem 'Antigua sangre' should go on to describe the 'antigua sangre' as being:

> esta ausencia,
> este reposo desdichado
> de quienes antaño se durmieron
> para siempre en sus sábanas. (*MM*, 17)

Like language, like any signifier, memory is cinders: a marker of the absence of that which it apparently brings back to presence.

The implications of this break for Montejo's writing and the way in which he develops his presentation of and claims for memory are far-reaching. But, before examining them further, it is necessary to add a caveat to the Derridean reading I have been invoking. For, alongside the loss effected by the move into language, Montejo's work remains pervaded by a concern for the problem of continuing, and continual, temporal loss, a problem which, moreover, is intricately caught up in his portrayal of the problematics of memory. Nowhere is this clearer than in the development of the metaphor of rain which Montejo employs when discussing the separation from the past. In several poems, rain appears as a sort of curtain, continually descending between present and past and aligned with the incessant passing of time. In

'Las ventanas' (*MM*), as we have seen, Montejo talks of the 'persistencia de la lluvia | que cae con los años' (*MM*, 18), an image reiterated some twenty years later in 'Visiones II' (*AS*), where he writes of how 'Sonaba el tiempo | [...] | sonaba la lluvia en la ventana ...' (*AS*, 64). It is a barrier of rain which appears gradually to cut off the past in a detachment which not even memory can overcome, as suggested in 'Rue du Moulin des Près' (*MM*):

> Cruzo la calle fría de esta memoria
> y en la erizada alcoba me detengo
> hasta que el agua me cubre la mirada. (*MM*, 20)

The poet's view of the past in his memory is increasingly obfuscated by the water falling in front of his eyes, until it disappears from view completely. These 'rain-poems' thus allow us to extend and adapt Derrida's model, not least because of the identification made between rain and language in Montejo's poetry, most explicitly in 'La lluvia afuera' in *Fábula del escriba* (itself an indication of how rain continued to play a role in Montejo's poetic discourse until the end of his life), where the rain is described as a writer working away at night:

> Oigo la lluvia afuera, trabajando,
> toda la noche en vela, sin reposo,
> la alfabética lluvia que siempre escribe a máquina. (*FE*, 24)

Whereas the play of *différance*, in writing out a univocal and wholly present-ing connection with what it seeks to make present, is very much not a temporal process, being based, rather, on a break which is 'always already' in place, at least in this repeated metaphor in Montejo's work there is still very definitely an important temporal aspect working alongside the loss inscribed within the move into memory/language. Indeed, it is here that Montejo's approach to memory diverges most strongly from that of Freud and Derrida. In main-taining the temporal cause of loss alongside a poststructuralist depiction of language, Montejo's work effectively offers a critique of both figures. Rather than focus on the effect of the continual wiping and overwriting of memory with new memories, as Freud does, with the invisible trace of previous memories in some phantasmal sense still 'there', or on the loss involved in the very emergence and production of memory *tout court*, in a Derridean fashion, Montejo's discussion of memory, whilst engaging with the effect of the move into memory of past events and people, also concentrates on the way in which one memory is changed *over* time. Indeed, the continual thematic focus on the return to and of the past in poems such as 'Sobremesa' (*MM*) and Montejo's overarching concern with cycles and circles both point to the question of the persistent return of the same memories over time.

Certainly, this can be seen in Derridean and, to an extent, Freudian terms as simply the change in meaning of a memory as it accrues new relationships and connections with more signifiers (memories). But Montejo's work places the focus very much on the passing of time itself. This is made most apparent in 'Cementerio de Vaugirard' (*MM*), which demonstrates aptly the gradual *loss* of a memory (*recuerdo*) over time, despite – or might one say because of – the accrual of more time, language (memories), and, hence, meaning in the memory (*memoria*):

Los muertos que conmigo se fueron a París
vivían en el cementerio Vaugirard.
En el recodo de los fríos castaños
donde la nieve recoge las cartas   4
que el invierno ha lacrado,
recto lugar, gélidas tumbas, nadie, nadie
sabrá nunca leer sus epitafios.

Un alba en escarchas de mármol   8
y el helado aguaviento
soplando sobre amargas ráfagas.
Alba de Vaugirard, rincón donde la muerte
es una explosión interminable. Piedras, huesos, retama.   12
¿Quién oía el tintinear de sus pailas
a la sagrada hora del café
cuando son interminables sus cháchéras?
¿Qué silencio tan hondo allí suplía   16
el canto de uno solo de sus gallos?

Muertos de sol, de espacios, de sábanas,
muertos de estrellas, de pastos, de vacadas,
muertos bajo tierra a caballo.   20
Los muertos que conmigo se fueron a París
vivían en el cementerio Vaugirard,
estéril pabellón de graníticas tapias.
¿Qué queda allí de esa memoria   24
ahora que la última luz se ha embalsamado?
¿Qué recordarán sus camaradas
de sus voces, de sus humildes hábitos?

Alba de Vaugirard, niebla compacta,   28
amistad con que la luna clavetea las lápidas,
¿qué quedó allí de aquellos huéspedes
agradecidos de tanta posada?
¿Qué noticias envían ahora lejanos   32
a los caídos, a los vencidos, a los suicidas olvidados?

Un alba en escarchas de mármol
y el helado aguaviento

soplando sobre amargas ráfagas.   36
Oscuro lugar donde la muerte
es una explosión interminable
sobre recuerdos, átomos, retama.
¿Qué permanece de tanta memoria?   40
¿Quién llega ahora a oír sus chácharas
cuando la nieve recoge las cartas
que el invierno ha lacrado? Nadie, nadie
sabrá nunca leer sus epitafios.   44
                    (*MM*, 7–8)

On the one hand, the poem recalls Borges's 'El testigo' (1997a: 39–40) in asking whether the death of a person is also the irrecuperable death of that person's memory, in particular in lines 24–5 and line 40. But, significantly, the poem also raises the further question of how something is remembered, that is, of how the memory of someone (or something) past is retained by someone else throughout their life. Although seemingly limited to a few lines, in particular lines 26–7, it is a question which the poem as a whole itself addresses in its very form, with the last stanza reading as a summary – in effect, a *recalling* – of the rest of the poem. Only, now, details are missed, alignments slightly altered, the meaning not quite the same: the 'Alba de Vaugirard, rincón donde la muerte' (line 11) becomes simply 'Oscuro lugar donde la muerte' (line 37); the asyndeton of 'Piedras, huesos, retama' (line 12) becomes 'recuerdos, átomos, retama' (line 39), the reduction of bones to atoms reflecting within the line the loss symbolised by the line; and lines 3–7 and lines 24–7 are reduced considerably in their reformulation in lines 40–4. The poem, remembering itself, remembering the lines from its own past, loses what it attempts to recall, thus exemplifying the gradual loss it effects as both language and memory (which are synonymous) over time. Indeed, such loss and disintegration is also played out in the metre of these lines, as the twelve syllables of line 11 – a nod towards the French Alexandrine perhaps, given the French setting – become nine in line 37, and the two hemistiches of the long line 12 are fragmented into two lines in their recasting in lines 38–9.

Returning to Derrida's comments in *Résistances de la psychanalyse* on which I commented in the Introduction, we thus see how Montejo's work both anticipates and supplements Derrida's reference to the tape recorder as indicative of how language works on the basis of inscription and iterability. If memory is an inscription, a recording, which, thus, alienates or cuts off that which it seeks to re-present, it is nonetheless a recording to which one returns again and again, replaying, and, in a sense, thus rewriting, reinscribing each time. As anyone who has lived in the pre-digital age will know, this process, in its analogue cassette form, is one where, with each successive playing and/or rerecording, more background hiss is added, more rain falling on the inscription. This does not annul Derrida's poststructuralist comments on the alienation of *écriture*, but it does add a temporal dimension which continues to play an important role in Montejo's poetics.

The image of increasing loss in the continual return to a memory over time is also found in 'Otra lluvia' (*MM*). Here, the retrieval of memories is portrayed as a crossing of puddles – fallen rain – which lie on the mind:

> Siempre sobre la mente quedan charcas
> y nunca es fácil atravesarlas
> sin regresar con los zapatos anegados. (*MM*, 30)

These lines tell us that with each and every expression of the (linguistic) memory in question, there is further alteration, confusion, and inaccuracy, the puddles, we imagine, getting bigger as the persistent rain keeps falling 'con los años' (*MM*, 18). Each crossing, then, is through another 'layer' of water, of yet more time, of yet more language, and accrual of *différantial* relationships, as the memory retrieved is ever more 'anegado'.

And yet this very poem also points us back towards the centrality of the initial (Derridean) break, that is, the initial move into *écriture* of the thing perceived and stored as memory, before its subsequent alteration *as* a memory over the years. Moreover, it does so by hinting at the radical implications of the break for the nature of the relationship between a memory and the event, time, or person to which it corresponds, even before the effects of gradual loss over time come into play. The poem suggests that, rather than memory being a marker of the absence of the thing, and an imperfect or skewed version of it, it in fact gives an image of the past which one cannot be sure has any relation to the actual past:

> Por los tejados baja a los canales
> un tiempo muerto en verdes goterones
> pero no rueda lo que imaginamos. (*MM*, 30)

Memory talks of and claims to re-present the past, but the events which happen in the passage of time are not what we imagine them to be; memory can have no claim unerringly to know or to present the 'actual' past, and there can thus be no claim for memory as being in any way authentic or true to the past it 'remembers', as Montejo reiterates in 'Gramática de la ausencia' in *Fábula del escriba*, a poem which also engages with the topos of rain:

> La gramática de la ausencia
> declina voces tan amargas
> que siempre significan otra cosa
> sin que nos demos cuenta. (*FE*, 27)

The past as we see it, then, is merely an *effect* of memory (*memoria*), an effect of the play of language, explaining why the poet declares in this late poem that 'Ya no quiero volver a aquella calle | donde las casas demolidas | siguen en pie' (27). In short, the curtain of rain also implies an absolute curtain, and the effect of the continuing fall of rain, the continuing temporal loss, is not to lose yet more details of an 'actual' past. It is, rather, the gradual loss of details of the memory, which itself is utterly separate(d) from that past.

Far from the affirmations of memory in Montejo's work with which we began, then, a close analysis of his poetics shows it to be increasingly undermined as a potential way of making the past present.[6] And such an undercutting of memory also emerges from several of his essays, both early and late. In 'Un recuerdo de Jean Cassou' (*VO*, 179–84), for instance, Montejo draws attention early on to the untrustworthy nature of memory, even as he begins an essay which is concerned precisely with recounting a memory:[7]

> Es Jean Cassou, tal me lo devela el escorzo anieblado de mi remembranza; pero podría no serlo. Las mudanzas del tiempo enseñan a desconfiar de la memoria, y lo que vimos una vez, si de verdad lo vimos, pudo ser de otra ciudad, en una estampa imprecisable o en el espacio de algún cuadro, digamos de Vermeer. Los recuerdos no advienen nunca libres de las trasmutaciones de los sueños. (*VO*, 181)

The complete break between a memory and what that memory is supposedly of is foregrounded here ('si de verdad lo vimos'), as Montejo also alludes to how diverse memories mix and blend together, as well as to how they are inevitably altered by dreams. Indeed, this latter description represents a further indication of memories' being open to the slippage of the signifying chain, if we bear in mind Lacan's reading of Freud's *The Interpretation of Dreams* (1991 [1900]), in which he argues that the dream-work follows the laws of the signifier, working on the basis of metaphor and metonymy.[8] A similar view of memory is also displayed in the later 'En un playón solitario'

---

6   For an alternative interpretation of Montejo's engagement with and apparent recuperation of the past, not least through memory, see Francisco Cruz Pérez (1992). Cruz Pérez writes lucidly on Montejo's work, but does not see any inherent or theoretical problematics in such an envisaged recuperation.

7   Montejo's technique here recalls that of Borges in stories such as 'La intrusa', 'El encuentro', and 'El otro duelo' from *El informe de Brodie* (1997b [1970]), where the author begins by affirming the confused and uncertain nature of the events of which he is about to write, altered by time, memory, and successive retellings, before proceeding to recount the events in some detail.

8   See Lacan (1966: 509–23). Bowie (1991: 68–71) offers a good overview of this analysis.

(*TB*, 107–18), where Montejo, talking about Joseph Conrad's novel *Nostromo* (1947 [1904]), focuses on the town around which the novel is centred, Sulaco, which was based on the novelist's recollections of the Venezuelan coastal town Puerto Cabello. Unlike Puerto Cabello, however, Sulaco is dominated by a snow-capped peak. It is an addition which memory, in a person now far from Puerto Cabello, has brought about over time:

> En verdad, son necesarias varias millas de distancia y no pocos años de ausencia para contemplar, desde cualquier sitio de Puerto Cabello, algún cerro nevado. (*TB*, 111)

Finally, we are left with the image of a place utterly detached from the town of which it is apparently a memory:

> Todas las visiones de lugares y gentes debieron de entremezclarse en los recuerdos del novelista, hasta confundirse en un solo pueblo reconstruido por la memoria y las lecturas. (112)

But these two essays are not merely further examples of Montejo's disclosure of the problematics of memory. Rather, the specific terms they use to describe memory provide us with the keys to seeing both how Montejo seeks to move beyond the implications of his own poetics and how that move is itself frustrated by its very realisation. The pivotal references are to memories as reconstructions or re-creations based on artistic representation: the 'cuadro, digamos de Vermeer' (*VO*, 181) and 'las lecturas' (*TB*, 112), that is, literature. These two notions of re-creation and representation prove to be recurrent in Montejo's work and constitute a framework for defining what memory produces, given that it cannot be taken as a re-presentation of an actual past.

To understand the importance of re-creation in Montejo's theoretics of memory we must first return to the poem 'Metamorfosis' (*MM*). The poem opens by describing memory as a spider scuttling around things within one's thought:

> Como rápida araña la memoria
> deambula a nivel de las cosas
> dentro del pensamiento. (*MM*, 25)

This ties in with Montejo's depiction of objects as memory-stores, both metaphorical and actual. But it also returns these images to the locale of the mind, enabling us, in the process, to reaffirm the essentially linguistic nature of memory as it slips and wanders from one signifier to the next. The resultant *recuerdo* would thus be produced by this playing around of and in signifiers.[9] As we have seen in our reading of 'Otra lluvia' (*MM*), then, memory (*memoria*) works not to re-present something past, but to produce something from its own play. It is a conclusion supported and extended by the very next lines of the poem:

> Como rápida araña se recrea,
> el sueño es su único paisaje
> y de su melodía se suspende. (*MM*, 25)

Once again, the reference to dreams links memory with dreams or the unconscious and, hence, with language. But more important here is the use of the verb *recrearse*, placed in the same position in the verse as 'la memoria' three lines previously. The verb carries the idea of the memory-spider amusing itself, entertaining itself, hinting at the play involved in its linguistic, weaving construction of memory. Yet, in producing the *recuerdos* of which it consists, it is also 'recreating itself'. The difference between re-presentation and re-creation is crucial here. The former implies a pre-existent something, which was once present, now being repeated or brought back. The latter, however, involves a re-beginning from scratch, discarding the prior creation, or, in this case, in the face of its absence and any way of knowing it. And it is here that Montejo sees a potential solution to the problem of the loss of the past. Rather than bemoaning the unknowability and irrecuperable loss of the 'actual' past, positing memory as a re-creation from nothing offers the chance of eschewing the very notion of there being a past to be presented. Moreover, as the references to literature and art in 'En un playón solitario' and 'Un recuerdo de Jean Cassou' respectively show, the type of re-creation which memory is seen to be is a (space of) quasi-artistic re-creation. Likewise, in 'Metamorfosis' the re-creation takes place in the field of music, the music of the unconscious mind as it dreams ('de su melodia se suspende'). The locus of re-creation in Montejo's poetics, the locus where memory must assume and affirm its identity as re-creation, appears, then, as the artistic space of the poem itself, as one is reminded of Mallarmé's poetic re-creation of a flower which is: 'l'absente de tous les bouquets' (1945: 368). In effect, and returning to my introduction, we see how Montejo's valorisation of myth over history with regard to religiosity plays itself out in relation to the past and memory: in affirming the space of the poem as where the past is recreated rather than re-presented, the past is understood as mythic, and as being from and of the present of the poem, that is, liberated from the effects of time's passing and poeticised.

---

[9]   Likewise for Lacan, meaning (the signified) 'is a mere effect of the play of signifiers, an effect of the process of signification produced by metaphor. In other words, the signified is not given, but produced' (Evans 1996: 186).

Significantly, such an affirmation both of memory as re-creation and of the
poem as the locus for such a re-creation emerges explicitly from Montejo's
reading of two of the Venezuelan poets he most admires, José Antonio Ramos
Sucre and Vicente Gerbasi. Writing on the former, Montejo talks of Ramos
Sucre's 'fabulación, el don de recrear un estado lírico a partir de un dato
histórico o literario que súbitamente rescata del olvido' (*VO*, 78), clearly
aligning the re-creation and 'fabulation' of Ramos Sucre's poetry with the
act of saving from 'el olvido', and, thus, reappropriating his own use of
the term 'fabla' to describe the language in and of his own poems (*É*, 37),
with the sense of lie, or, more pertinently, myth implied by this term now
affirmed. Moreover, what is rescued by this (affirmation of) re-creation in
Ramos Sucre's work is revealed to be infancy, precisely the era that Montejo
has sought throughout to make present: 'la invocación de las aves [en los
poemas en prosa de Ramos Sucre] recreará entonces tal vez el tiempo de una
infancia alimentada de presagios' (*VO*, 80). Likewise, in his later essay on
Vicente Gerbasi, 'La luz de "Los espacios cálidos"' (*TB*, 159–65),[10] Montejo
describes Gerbasi's collection *Los espacios cálidos* (1952) as simply a
'recreación del tiempo mágico de la infancia' (*TB*, 163).[11] Following these
examples, within Montejo's own poetics it is in the early 'Mi vivir es araña
en la tela del poema' (*É*) that we see just such a re-creation begin to be
played out. The spider in question is that of the later 'Metamorfosis' (*MM*),
the spider of memory, of language, weaving and creating not memories as a
representation of something else, but (memories as) life itself, the very being
of the poet, prior to which there is nothing:

> Mi vivir es araña en la tela del poema
> devano en obsesión oscura
> hilos de vida y de muerte [...]
> [...]
> salto de lo vacío y enhebro el recomienzo. (*É*, 37)

It is an idea taken up again in 'La araña veloz' (*AS*), which talks of how:

> veloz se mueve la araña que nos teje
> [...]
> veloz fabrica la piel, la voz, los nervios

---

[10] This essay is present in the first edition (1983) of *El taller blanco*. Montejo has also
written on other works by Gerbasi (for example, Montejo (1977)).

[11] Poems such as 'Te amo, infancia', 'La casa de mi infancia', and 'Rostros campesinos'
in *Los espacios cálidos* appear to have influenced Montejo's own early poetry, with Gerbasi's
poems working around images such as the childhood house, horsemen, the coffee of the past,
and 'los muertos'. For a good discussion of Gerbasi's work as a whole, see Pérez Perdomo
(1986).

[...]
sobre el papel está moviéndome la mano. (*AS*, 43)

Across these three poems, then, memory, poetic writing, and (the creation of) being are brought together and equated.

And yet such an affirmation of the memory-poem as re-creation is beset by a seemingly inescapable problematic. For, as announced by the references in 'En un playón solitario' and 'Un recuerdo de Jean Cassou' to this re-creation or reconstruction as being based on literature and art, any (artistic) re-creation is, inevitably, immediately bound within representation. This inevitability is clear in the poem 'El girasol' (*MM*), where the poet affirms that:

> Sigues contando en la memoria sus pétalos,
> sientes las pinceladas de Van Gogh
> sobre la tela de los sueños. (*MM*, 29)

An object's re-creation in and as memory may not be the representation of a pre-existent *thing*, but it is, nonetheless, inevitably caught up in a chain of representation, as these lines disclose the re-creation of the sunflower to be a re-presentation of Van Gogh's *Sunflowers*. In other words, the sunflower can only ever be perceived as a representation of a representation. Memory, then, like art, like language, sets itself up in Montejo's poetics as a re-creation of what we can never know, but where that re-creation is always already an artistic representation of an artistic representation. Indeed, even initial perception and experience is shown to be subject to the same process in Montejo's work, perhaps most explicitly in 'Madona en el metro' (*MM*), where the poet immediately perceives a woman he sees on the metro in relation to the countless images of the Madonna and, in particular, a painting of the Virgin Mary by Titian.[12]

It is, then, in this struggle between re-creation and representation that Montejo's poetics of loss situates itself. As played out in 'Mi vivir es araña en la tela del poema' (*É*), Montejo affirms the (mythic) artistic re-creation of the past, of infancy, as being the role of the poetic space of and as memory. And yet each re-creation is immediately language (*écriture*), immediately caught up in representation, 'conv[ertida] en otra cosa' ('De sobremesa', *AM*, 202), and immediately subject to alteration, loss, and change of meaning, even as a representation with no claim to be re-presenting the 'actual' past. It is an inevitability reflected in 'Mi vivir es araña en la tela del poema'. Echoing the repeated failure implied within 'Sobremesa' (*MM*), the writing – the

---

[12] The painting in question is probably the *Assumption of the Virgin (Assunta)* (1518) (see http://www.abcgallery.com/T/titian/titian16.html [accessed 1 January 2009]).

re-creation – of the poem must always begin again, rejecting the representation it immediately becomes and calling the spider to *recrearse* once more:

> lo que urdo con seda y orgullo
> [...]
> otra mano lo borra hasta que expíe la aguja
> y vuelva a cardarme al tacto de la red
> y así por cada hora en el harapo mudo
> salto de lo vacío y enhebro el recomienzo. (*É*, 37)

It is, finally, a cyclical process of endless inscription in language with which,
by the title poem of Montejo's last collection *Fábula del escriba*, the poet
appears to have grown weary, as he closes his engagement with this thematic
thread with a call to the spider to remain silent: 'Que no se valga la araña de
mi mano | y permanezca sola en su silencio' (*FE*, 18).

Poetic recuperation and snow

Three elements stand out at the end of this analysis of language and memory
in Montejo's poetics of loss: language, which provides both the structure and
the mechanisms of memory in Montejo's work; the notion of the break as
the unbreachable barrier beyond which all is lost or unknowable (and unre-
presentable), itself synonymous with the move into language (*écriture*); and
silence as the only apparent alternative. These are, of course, concerns which
pertain to a general linguistic and poststructuralist debate, as is indicated
by the references I have made to Heidegger, Lacan, and Derrida and by the
resonance which Montejo's work has with the thought of these figures.

Beyond these more general, philosophical ambits, however, Montejo is
also bound up in a particular focus on the local. As we saw in chapter 1,
the stage on which his early poetry of loss is played out is that of the poet's
homeland, Venezuela, both in terms of his personal experience of it, with
regards to his now-lost childhood and relatives, and in terms of a more
national experience, as implied by the allusion to the white horse of Bolívar.
Accordingly, both the general (philosophical) and the local must form part
of Montejo's poetic disclosure of and response to the problems of language
that I have been outlining, and which I shall term the problems of 'temporolinguistic loss'. And it is around the central leitmotiv of snow that just such a
poetics is constructed, taking in almost the entire span of Montejo's output,
from *Muerte y memoria* to *Fábula del escriba*.

One of the most striking aspects of Montejo's use of snow, and, given
the setting of the Venezuelan tropics, also one of the most logical, is that it
appears predominantly as a lack, and it is this lack of snow in Venezuela and
the tropics generally with which Montejo is primarily concerned, coming

to occupy a central thematic in his work which burrows its way through
his poetry like a trail of absence: in *Algunas palabras* we are told that 'No
conocen la nieve nuestras casas' ('Nuestras casas', *AP*, 25), for example,
and in *Trópico absoluto* the Ávila mountain which provides the backdrop to
Caracas is twice described as 'sin nieve' ('El Ávila', *TA*, 25). It also emerges
as a particularly central motif in *Partitura de la cigarra*, not least in the
opening poem 'Tal vez', which begins:

> Tal vez sea todo culpa de la nieve
> que prefiere otras tierras más polares,
> lejos de estos trópicos. (*PC*, 9)

Quite what the blame is for, here, is never made entirely clear. Montejo
suggested in interview that when he talks in this poem of how:

> Nuestro viejo ateísmo caluroso
> y su divagación impráctica
> quizá provengan de su ausencia, (9)

he is referring to the ferocity of the heat leading to a harsher view of the
world, less ready to hold religious beliefs and less prone to forgiveness.[13]
But it is the following three lines which prove most illuminating, suggesting
that what is at stake is precisely the fall into loss and the absence of the past:

> de que no caiga y sin embargo se acumule
> en apiladas capas de vacío
> hasta borrarnos de pronto los caminos. (9)

The lack-of-snow, piling up, accumulating *like* snow, symbolises and describes
the break between the present and the past, as is also suggested in the earlier
poem 'Visible e invisible' (*AS*), which talks of those who are dead or absent
as being 'aislados por la nieve del camino' (*AS*, 44). The lack-of-snow covers
the paths, writing them out, just as language and memory effect a writing out
of every path back to what they seek to re-present. A similar image is also
found further on in *Partitura de la cigarra*, in 'La puerta', where the erased
path of 'Tal vez' and 'Visible e invisible' is supplemented by the image of
the blocked door:

> Nada de nieve en esta puerta,
> sólo calor [...]
> [...]

---

13 See Cruz (2006: 369–71).

> ... Y la puerta atascada
> de tanta nieve no caída
> que siempre sigue no cayendo
> hasta que este calor se vuelve frío. (*PC*, 19)

In many respects, then, the lack-of-snow in these late poems acts as a revised version of Montejo's rain – the same substance in different form. But, whereas rain is used primarily to describe the gradual loss over time and successive representations, these later poems speak very much more unequivocally of a complete break, a nothingness or vacuum which absolutely cannot be traversed: progression is impeded, and a return to from where one has come is prevented. Snow-as-lack, that is, serves to symbolise more fully the initial break implied by rain.

Notable in Montejo's use of lack-of-snow both as a description of the Venezuelan tropics and as a symbol for the separation between past and present (or its apparent re-presentation) is the extent to which it is depicted in terms which show it acting like snow: in 'Tal vez' the lack of snow piles up layer upon layer and in 'La puerta' it turns the tropical heat cold. Its coldness is also made explicit in the earlier poem 'Hombres sin nieve' (*TA*). On the one hand this poem affirms the lack-of-snow as equating to a lack of cold, stating that:

> Sobre estas tierras no ha nevado en muchos siglos,
> esquiamos en la luna, desde lejos,
> con largavistas,
> sin helarnos la sangre. (*TA*, 8)

But it then goes on to describe how:

> Aquí el invierno nace de heladas subjetivas
> lleno de ráfagas salvajes;
> depende de una mujer que amamos y se aleja,
> de sus cartas que no vendrán pero se aguardan;
> nos azota de pronto en largas avenidas
> cuando nos queman sus hielos impalpables.
> Aquí el invierno puede llegar a cualquier hora,
> no exige leños, frazadas, abrigos,
> nos [*sic*, 'no']¹⁴ despoja los árboles,
> y sin embargo cómo sabe caer bajo cero,
> cómo nos hacen tiritar sus témpanos amargos. (8)

The lack of snow and winter in the tropics is linked with a coldness which is even more pernicious, apt to strike at any time, not following the yearly cycle

---

14 In subsequent publications, 'nos' is corrected to 'no' (see, for example, *AM*, 137).

of the seasons. It is felt not with the arrival of physical snow or cold winds, but precisely with loss: a loved woman who goes away and from whom no letters will come, as all possibility of contact is erased. It is a coldness, an ice, and a snow synonymous with the sense of absence, as the ubiquitous loss of Montejo's early poetics is here crystallised as an essential and profound coldness. As with the poems from *Partitura de la cigarra*, the abiding image is one of layers of cold nothingness, of absence, separating forever the speaker from what is past.

The use of lack-of-snow as synonymous with and, as is evident from the poems cited, possibly both the cause and effect of the irretrievable absence into which everything falls, suggests that snow itself is, potentially, the opposite to this: capable of preserving the past, that which is dead or distant. One of the earliest mentions of snow and the related ideas of ice and the coldness of winter occurs in 'Cementerio de Vaugirard' (*MM*), cited above in full. Here, we are given a scene where what is described is not the absence of snow, but its presence in the 'tierras más polares' of France. What emerges, however, is far from a eulogy on the substance whose lack is felt so painfully in Montejo's work. The poem begins with Montejo talking of 'Los muertos que conmigo se fueron a París' (*MM*, 7), who 'vivían en el cementerio Vaugirard' (7). He then goes on to describe this cemetery where the 'muertos', precisely those who have been a focal point of his poetics of loss up until this point, were 'living' in Paris:

> En el recodo de los fríos castaños
> donde la nieve recoge las cartas
> que el invierno ha lacrado,
> recto lugar, gélidas tumbas, nadie, nadie
> sabrá nunca leer sus epitafios. (7)

The snow, then, *is* linked to preservation, in the twin images of letters gathered up by the snow, preserved intact by a lacquer of cold, and the tombs of the dead: frozen, covered, we imagine, with a layer of encasing ice. But this preservation, far from signifying a presencing of what it preserves, in fact serves both to effect and mark its loss: the letters are sealed off by the cold, just as the layer of ice on the tombs prevents any possibility of even reading the epitaphs, let alone getting to the body inside. In effect, the *presence* of snow and cold is shown to lead to and symbolise exactly the same move into absence and loss as the *lack* of snow and cold. Indeed, both are depicted in the same terms, with the description of the lack-of-snow and winter in 'Hombres sin nieve' as full of 'ráfagas salvajes' and 'témpanos amargos' (*TA*, 8) being anticipated in the description of the 'helado aguaviento' in 'Cementerio de Vaugirard' as 'soplando sobre amargas ráfagas' (*MM*, 7). Montejo bemoans the lack-of-snow, then, but snow itself is shown to be nothing but (a marker of) loss and absence. Put simply, what is being lamented is the absence of (an) absence, the lack of (a) lack, as, no sooner is snow apparently made present than it is no longer capable of being the presence or 'presencing element' it was imagined to be. The lack can only potentially be filled; it can never actually be filled.

But the importance of the use of snow/lack-of-snow as a motif only really becomes clear once we see that Montejo uses the lack-of-snow in Venezuela and the tropics not just as a cipher for the process of loss, of time passing and leaving people and places behind forever, but, as the title of 'Hombres sin nieve' indicates, to define both the region and its people. In interview in 2002 Montejo is explicit in bringing out the centrality of snow-as-lacking in determining both Venezuela and what it is to be Venezuelan, at least insofar as this is synonymous with being from the tropics.[15] He states that:

> Para el hombre de los trópicos la nieve es algo con cuya carencia, sin resignarse del todo, se acostumbra desde niño a dialogar, pues no son pocos las leyendas y cuentos infantiles donde ella es parte esencial del paisaje. Ese diálogo prosigue a lo largo de la vida, aunque ella falte en nuestra geografía, pues constituye un apócrifo complemento de nuestro imaginario. (Gutiérrez 2002)

Snow, that is, is at the heart of the formation and understanding of the self in Venezuela. In other words, it is bound up with an ontological questioning, and one concerned explicitly with being in Venezuela and as a Venezuelan. Bearing in mind our discussion thus far, two important elements emerge from Montejo's words here. The first is that the *formación del ser* described is centred around precisely what is absent in Venezuela, whose *paisaje* is immediately conceived of by the growing Venezuelan as lacking: 'Venezuelan ontology' is built, then, upon a central lack. Secondly, this ontological hollowing out in the Venezuelan tropics is also tied up with the idea that the absent past and the dead are a constitutive part of the (present) self, as I explored in chapter 1, in that the lack-of-snow in Montejo's verse is a cipher for just such a loss or absence of the past.

However, what is crucial here, both for an understanding of the nature of the Venezuelan self thus formed and for an appreciation of what is at stake in the snow/lack-of-snow symbolism more generally, is the fact that Montejo should locate the earliest and formative encounter with snow in

---

[15] The question as to how far Montejo is referring to the tropics generally here or to Venezuela as a tropical country more specifically is often left hanging. I shall comment more on the importance of this uncertainty in chapter 4. Certainly, given the specificity of references to 'nuestras casas' (*AP*, 25) and to the Ávila (*TA*, 25), at the very least Montejo seems concerned with Venezuela as a specific case in point of a wider tropical reality. This ambiguity should be borne in mind throughout the following analysis.

literature or story, and describe both the initial and the ongoing ontological process as a dialogue. These references disclose the centrality of language in Montejo's engagement with snow, and, taken together with the notion of the lack-of-snow which needs to be filled, point up what is a highly resonant and revealing alignment of Montejo's snow with the Derridean supplement. For Derrida, there is a lack at the heart of language which one needs constantly to supplement. Put simply, each signifier's meaning is never fully contained within itself, but is endlessly deferred down the signifying chain, needing, that is, to be supplemented by other signifiers as its meaning is sought. In short, this lack constitutes the very nature of language itself: it is (the condition of) language. Within Montejo's poetics, the attempt of filling the lack(-of-snow) (which 'behaves' like snow) by snow (which 'behaves' like the lack-of-snow) mirrors precisely the workings of Derrida's supplementarity, in that, as Robert Bernasconi puts it, 'what is added to take the place of a lack or default is itself a lack' (1992: 145), that is, the supplement is merely another signifier shot through by absence. More pertinently, given Montejo's declarations above, the implication is that being is hollow, made possible and defined by lack, because, put simply, being is language.[16] Indeed, this is what Montejo appears to be saying when he describes the Venezuelan self as being formed and maintained through dialogue.

The specific role and identification of 'snow' in this schema becomes clear when one looks at how the fundamental lack in language is conceived of by Derrida as that of the 'transcendental signified', an anchoring 'centre' whose meaning is fully present and outside of this play of *différance*, and whose absence thus 'étend à l'infini le champ et le jeu de la signification' (1967b: 411), that is, makes (the play of) meaning possible. For Derrida, the only way of stopping the play of *différance* – the chain of supplementarity – is by attaining this transcendental signified. But this is an illusion: it is never knowable outside of language. Indeed, the point is that it can only be referred to as language: it is the 'présence centrale [...] qui a toujours déjà été déportée hors de soi dans son substitut' (1967b: 411), be this substitute the term God, transcendence, existence, or whatever other word one wishes to use. In Montejo's poetics, 'snow' is the term used as this substitute. As with Derrida's 'transcendental signified', what is lacking is knowable only as a name ('snow'), since the snow which is 'ever-present' in the literature is, of course, precisely not 'present'; it is a word or signifier, a substitute, which, as such, is hollow, shot through by the absence of what it seeks to

---

[16] We might also recall here Lacan's understanding of the signifying chain. As Evans puts it, 'no matter how many signifiers one adds to the signifying chain, the chain is always incomplete; it always lacks the signifier that could complete it. This "missing signifier" [...] is constitutive of the subject' (1996: 96).

represent. Moreover, the fact that the Venezuelan child only perceives the lack when (s)he sees it named or represented in texts – and, significantly, in myths of origins ('leyendas') – underscores that the lack(-of-snow) has indeed 'toujours déjà été déportée hors de soi dans son substitut' (Derrida 1967b: 411), that is, into the word 'snow'. In sum, it is not just that the Venezuelan child sees his or her world as lacking because of an essential difference between it and the world of the literature (s)he reads, but that the literature represents the child's 'becoming' as a linguistic being.

The realisation that snow is the condition of both language and being in Montejo's work, that is, that being is language, also implies a profound reevaluation of the relationship between the dead and the living in his poetry, and, thus, of what it is that he seeks to recover. In chapter 1 we saw how the side of the living is made synonymous with the side of language in Montejo's early poetry concerned with the dead/living divide. The attempt to do away with the difference between the two sides and thus end loss is fraught by the inevitable presentation of the dead in language, thus placing them firmly on the side of the living or present, losing their essence as dead. But, in the absolute alignment of being with language, we see that it is not so much that the dead cannot be brought out in their essence in and as language, but that neither the dead nor the living can. The point is that the only existence – or being – of *both* the dead *and* the living is in and as language. In this way, the living are no more present, no more 'whole' than the dead, revealing an alternative way of understanding the portrayal in 'De sobremesa' (*AM*) of the indistinguishable nature of the voices of the dead and the living which bounce around the table.

This bringing together of the living and the dead as language is made particularly clear in Montejo's use of *hojas* as a recurrent leitmotiv. As we saw in chapter 1, in poems such as 'Otoño' (*MM*), 'En las hojas' (*AM*), copla VIII from *Guitarra del horizonte*, and 'Las sillas' (*AS*), Montejo focuses on the moment of death, the autumnal moment when the leaves, or lives, on the tree flutter down to the ground, to be left – dead – as *hojarasca*. But the very act of aligning *hojas* (with its double meaning of both pages and leaves) with lives discloses the wholly linguistic nature of life as well as existence in the world post-death, the leaf serving, as with Montejo's understanding of the memory-store, as a blank sheet on which are written the life, experiences, and character of the individual before falling to the ground, dead. In this way, the deathly or hollow nature of the dead in their appearance in language (as memories) is no different from the hollowness or deathly nature of the living. This, ultimately, is the significance of being as language, and its consequences can be seen in the tone and imagery of numerous poems throughout Montejo's corpus, from the reference to how 'Y no es que me olvide de morir cada instante | junto a las hojas, los árboles, el viento' (*AS*, 48) in 'El tiempo ahora' (*AS*) to the final lines of the last orthonymic poem of *Fábula del escriba*, 'Final sin fin', which, in suggesting a more ambiguous understanding of death, disclose the ghostly nature of life:

> – Nos iremos sin irnos,
> ninguno va a quedarse ni irse,
> *tal como siempre hemos vivido*
> a orillas de este sueño indescifrable,
> *donde uno está y no está* y nadie sabe nada. (*FE*, 67, italics mine)

Of course, in aligning the living and the dead in and as language, Montejo, in one sense, succeeds in collapsing the difference between the two. But, far from representing a theoretical or poetic success, such a move merely serves to cast the problem under a different light. What was a lamenting of the lack of full presence of the dead, in particular in *Élegos* and *Muerte y memoria*, is now understood as a concomitant lamenting of the lack of full presence of the living. The idea, then, of the recuperation of the dead or absent is firmly placed within the ontological ambit as a recuperation of the loss or lack at the heart of the being of both the dead and the living, which is itself synonymous with a recuperation of the lack at the heart of language. The concern for the end of loss effected by (sequential) time, then, is once more seen to go hand in hand with – indeed, to stand for – an end to ontological hollowness.

By using (lack-of-)snow as the metaphor in which such ontological lack is played out in his work, and thus engaging with the Derridean theory of the supplement, Montejo, as we have seen, announces the ineffectiveness of simply replacing the lack-of-snow by snow, of adding the lacking supplement. Yet there is also a crucial difference between Montejo's and Derrida's schemas, and it lies in the relationship between Montejo's choice of symbol (snow) and the geographical concerns and specificities in which it is placed in his work. Forking off from Derrida's line, the ineffectiveness of the supplemented snow in bringing about an end to the lack is accompanied by an important caveat: the supplemented 'actual' snow which does not work is a European snow. In 'Cementerio de Vaugirard' (*MM*) the snow whose presence merely leads to the same sense of a closing off, of and from the past, is that of colder climes, the snow of Paris. *This* snow, Montejo's work reveals, ultimately offers no solution to the ontological and linguistic problems of loss and lack in the tropics of Venezuela. But that does not mean that the search for a snow which *can* preserve without preserving as loss, a snow which can (keep) present is abandoned. Rather, Montejo seeks to move beyond both this simple process of filling the lack with what is lacking and the appeal to the sort of snow found in places like Paris which this implies, refusing to 'resignarse del todo' (Gutiérrez 2002).

Quite how he attempts to do this is disclosed in 'El ángel indeciso', from *Terredad*. Here, Montejo offers a review of his poetry and its dominant thematics, pointing out many of the apparent contradictions it contains. The 'ángel' in question appears as a sort of poetic superego guiding Montejo's thoughts and work. It is significant, then, that Montejo declares that this 'ángel' 'busca la nieve de los trópicos' (*T*, 66). It is a crucial line in Montejo's poetics of snow. Rather than the snow of 'tierras más polares' (*PC*, 9), which seems often to be what Montejo works towards, here he makes it clear that his poetry is ultimately a search for a *tropical* snow. The inability of the snow of Paris to be the potential snow he seeks, a preserving and presencing snow, is inextricably linked, then, to its not being a snow of and for the place from which Montejo is writing his poetics centred in and around the experiences of Venezuela in general and of himself as a Venezuelan.

The question then arises as to what the nature of such a tropical snow is; how it is different from other snow; and just how it preserves as presence, thus restituting linguistic and ontological wholeness. It is a question addressed in 'Islandia' (*AP*), where Montejo talks of:

> Esta contradicción ecuatorial
> de buscar una nieve
> que preserve en el fondo su calor,
> que no borre las hojas de los cedros. (*AP*, 41)

What is described here is the need for a snow which *does* preserve, like the snow in 'Cementerio de Vaugirard', but which does not seal off or freeze that which it envelops. Rather than being synonymous with death, it is a snow which uses its cold to retain and preserve what I shall term the 'life-heat' or 'heat of being' of that which it covers, the same ontological heat that Montejo presents as lacking in Venezuela in poems such as 'Hombres sin nieve' (*TA*). What is more, that such a snow is precisely the desired 'nieve de los trópicos' (*T*, 66) is made clear in the way that these lines do not just represent a description of a snow which preserves the life-heat in abstract terms. Rather, the 'calor' which is preserved is also the very *calor tropical* of Venezuela. In other words, the snow of 'Cementerio de Vaugirard' not only seals off and freezes past lives, but, in the process, announces itself as diametrically opposed to the heat of the tropics. In Venezuela, and in Montejo's 'Venezuelan' poetics, the 'authentic' snow sought acts both to halt loss, to make present and whole, and also to preserve the nature and identity of Venezuela, as an authentic and whole being is inextricably tied up with the place of being of the people in question, its climate and topography.

Given the intricacies of this engagement with snow and heat, it is perhaps unsurprising that Montejo should give us an ambiguous, if not contradictory, presentation of heat and coldness in his work, where he both *laments* the burning heat (for example, in 'El sol en todo' (*FE*)) and talks of 'la falta que nos hace [la nieve]' ('Tal vez', *PC*, 9) and yet elsewhere proudly *affirms* the heat of Venezuela and declares that '[a nuestras casas] no les hace falta [la nieve]' ('Nuestras casas', *AP*, 25). Clearly, the ambiguity and seeming impossibility of the task the poet has given himself are concordant with Derrida's thought. But the focused development of the snow leitmotiv, not least in terms of the valorisation of a tropical snow, also represents both a greater willingness to persist in the search for a beyond of the problematics of *écriture*, and a deliberate refusal to be bound by the European, either in terms of the meaning and use of symbols, or in terms of the philosophical and poststructuralist strands brought into play in the course of his quest for an end to loss and lack. What is more, this dual engagement and rejection of *lo europeo* is made particularly evident in the alignment of Montejo's snow with another of Derrida's formulations for the workings of language to which I referred briefly earlier, namely cinders. And it is in this alignment that we see the extent to which European theoretical models are alluded to in Montejo's work in order both to aid the thinking of what is at stake and to serve as examples of what must be rejected in favour of autochthonous metaphors and formulations.

As I have noted, for Derrida, cinders, as language, are 'ce qui garde pour ne plus garder, vouant le reste à la dissipation' (1991: 35), where, as Ned Lukacher puts it, 'cinder names [...] that burning within language. To hear, to speak, to write, is to feel the heat, the retreat of the fire as the cinder falls, yet again, to ash' (Derrida 1991: 3). The burning within language is written out *by* language, by the cinders which point to its absence. This, of course, echoes the coldness of Montejo's snow, which freezes or writes out both the life-heat and the tropical heat which it envelops. Turning to the poem 'El Ávila' (*TA*), we see this convergence of Montejo's snow and Derrida's cinders made explicit. Here, looking at a 'fotografía de nuestros padres' (*TA*, 25) (in the generic, national sense, rather than a photograph of any one set of parents in particular) in which the snow-less Ávila forms an immovable backdrop, Montejo asks:

> ¿No será nieve esa lenta ceniza
> que ahora cae de sus rostros?
> Y ese frío que sentimos al verlos
> entre los marcos clavados sobre el muro,
> ¿no es el invierno al que llegamos tarde? (*TA*, 25)

These lines reaffirm what I have noted regarding the 'heladas subjetivas' of Venezuela, the coldness arriving not with an actual winter, but with the contemplation of an image of what is irretrievably in the past. And they also enact precisely the process Derrida describes, as the cinders, revealed as being snow by another name, fall from the faces of the now-dead as cold ash, as the irreducible mark of their absence.

This bringing together of Derrida's cinders and Montejo's snow is helpful in casting further light on what the latter tells us about the nature of language in Montejo's poetics. Continuing the quotation above, Derrida states that 'c'est là la cendre: ce qui garde pour ne plus garder, vouant le reste à la dissipation, et ce n'est plus personne disparue laissant là cendre, seulement son nom mais illisible' (1991: 35). Cinders, that is, are both language and, in some sense, the lack of (legible or meaningful) language. And this is exactly what is seen in 'Cementerio de Vaugirard' (*MM*), where the snow seals the 'cartas' and the 'epitafios', making them, like Derrida's 'nom mais illisible', illegible. Once again, we see Montejo defining lives as language, but we now come to see it as, in an essential sense, illegible language. Indeed, this is also the case in the poem 'En las hojas' (*AM*), where the autumn leaves/lives are 'llenas de nervaduras ilegibles' (*AM*, 165). Lives are language, leaves on which the being of the self is written. Yet this language is at the same time a crossing out of itself, a rendering of itself illegible. It is this move which Montejo's snow describes and enacts, naming that which cannot be read.

The question remains, then, as to what it is that language names unintelligibly; what is this 'inner burning', in Derrida's terms, or the life-heat in Montejo's poetics, which snow-language covers in an incomprehensible naming? The answer lies in a differentiation between this snow-language, language-as-we-have-it, and the idea of the *essence* of language. That is, if snow in Montejo's work is language *per se*, then the tropical and ontological life-heat comes to be seen as the *essence* of language (and, hence, being), Derrida's 'lacking presence', and that which language seeks to present, but can, as a supplement, only supplant. And it is here that Montejo's snow reveals its advantages over Derrida's cinders, on both a general, theoretical level and a local level. On the theoretical level, cinders, as language, are the remnants of a fire, but represent the turning cold of its essence. As such, they act as a symbol for the process of loss, of absenting which the movement into language effects. But Montejo's snow portrays more effectively and in a more consistent way the problematic nature of language and being I have been exploring in both Derrida's and Montejo's work. Rather than standing for a conversion of essence into non-essence, as do cinders, in Montejo's snow formulation, language does not lose its essence. Rather, it never has it, which would seem to be more in line with Derrida's own thinking. Beyond this, Montejo's snow has the further distinction that it is not just a description of the process; it also describes an attempt at recovery, at preserving the heat which is – inevitably – lost. It is a crucial shift in focus, which emphasises the role and nature of language not just as a move into the endless deferral of *différance*, but as a repeated – if vain – attempt at overcoming that move. In this way, we see how snow serves as an advance on cinders not just on a local level, in being a symbol whose lack in the tropical *paisaje* underscores its nature and effects, but also as an intellectual advance, in being a representation both of the process of loss in language and of how that process can be viewed simultaneously as an attempted overcoming of itself, just as Montejo views it in poems such as 'Islandia' (*AP*). Indeed, it is notable that in 'El Ávila' (*TA*) Montejo affirms in anticipatory fashion the primacy – and advance – of his particularly Venezuelan formulation over Derrida's (European) one, as he asks: '¿No será nieve esa ceniza?' (*TA*, 25). Montejo's snow, that is, supersedes cinders both locally and theoretically.

The effect of this use of (tropical) snow as a symbol is, then, to highlight that Montejo's quest is not just generally for a type of snow, or language, which will be an authentic, whole language, escaping the problematics of the hollow, lacking language which we have now and in which we find our being, but that it is a search more accurately described as being for a new, 'authentic(ally Venezuelan) language', which would bring about the recovery of the past and the halting of the slide into absence as experienced within this locus, and which, in the process, would remove tropical Venezuela and its people from the inauthentic or 'hollow' being in which they find themselves.

But there is one further implication to be drawn from the contrast between Derrida's cinders and Montejo's snow. Cinders, as I have noted, mark the difference between (essential) heat and (linguistic) coldness, and do so through the metaphor of a one-way process of decomposition: the irreversible breaking down of the essence, the 'unnameable thing', as its own heat reduces it to cinders and ash. Snow, however, constitutes – chemically and physically – a tight and ordered structure, enabling us to see how, in moving from rain/water to snow, Montejo's poetics hints at the idea of a more affirmatory view of language, accentuating its cohesiveness rather than any process of disintegration, as in the early reference to the 'ceniza de un vano parloteo' ('Tan ululante vuelve y no verídica', *É*, 13). Moreover, whilst snow can be melted or broken down, it can just as well be re-formed. In short, Montejo's formulation is neither irreversible nor is it a disintegration into less order or cohesion. By presenting the search for a new language as a search for a new (tropical) snow, then, Montejo's work not only announces a refusal to be inscribed in a theoretics of language where there is no possibility of a recovery of loss/what is lost, thus affording itself a glimmer of hope, but also points to the new language as ordered and constructed, signalling that this quest is to be an active construction of a new language in and for tropical Venezuela, a construction in which the poet will be central.[17]

---

[17] This particular topos of the poet as architect or constructor of the poem is dealt with in detail in chapter 4. It might here be noted, however, that both in signalling the idea of the new language as a construction and, as we shall see in the remainder of this chapter, in foregrounding the role of the poet in bringing about this construction, Montejo's work once more seems indebted to a certain Heideggerean strand of thought, for whom, likewise, the essence of language was something that poetry alone could enable to be seen (see Pattison (2000: 173–4)).

Flour as 'nieve natal'

In the search for an authentic (Venezuelan) snow, capable of preserving as presence, Montejo settles on one key possibility: flour. This identification is worked through in two key pieces: the poem 'La cuadra' from *Trópico absoluto* and the title essay of the collection *El taller blanco*, first appearing in 1983 (*TB*, 127–34). In the latter, Montejo talks about his childhood, during which he spent a great deal of time in the 'taller blanco' of his father's bakery, watching the bread being made during the night. It is 'el taller que cobijó buena parte de mi infancia' (130), in which are grounded 'mi arte y [...] mi vida' (130). Moreover, it is, for Montejo, an example of the infancy which has slipped into absence, and is symbolic, once more, of a nationwide loss of the past:

> Hablo de una vieja panadería, como ya no existen. [...] Ya no son necesarias las carretadas de leña con su envolvente fragancia resinosa, ni la harina se apila en numerosos cuartos de almacenaje. ¿Para qué? El horno en vez de una abovedada cámara de rojizos ladrillos, es ahora un cuadrado metálico de alto voltaje. (130–1)

Evidently these lines reflect Montejo's Romantic sensibilities as he bemoans the move into ever greater industrialisation and urbanisation in twentieth-century Venezuela, as I examined in the Introduction. I shall look in more detail at this aspect of Montejo's writing in chapters 3 and 4. For now, what is notable is that already here the importance of the 'harina' of this scene is being hinted at, and this is taken up a few lines later in what constitutes the key line for my investigation into Montejo's poetics of snow, as he declares that 'la harina es la sustancia esencial que en mi memoria resguarda aquellos años' (131). The flour is what enables the memories (*recuerdos*) of the *taller* to exist in his memory (*memoria*). Clearly, this could be seen as an alignment of flour with the problematics of memory and thus concomitant with the break. But these lines also contain the suggestion that the flour is the essential substance Montejo invokes so frequently in his work, preserving and presencing this scene for the poet. Indeed, that this is precisely what is implied here is confirmed and stated explicitly in the parallel poem 'La cuadra', where Montejo begins:

> El tacto de la harina en las manos nocturnas,
> nuestra humilde nieve natal
> que Dios nos manda. (*TA*, 20)

Flour is the 'nieve natal', the snow of Venezuela, that is, the tropical snow, which I have identified as constituting the enigmatic centre of Montejo's poetics of loss.

Yet there are problematic resonances here. The way in which the flour works to 'resguardar' the scene as memories is strikingly similar to the description of the lack-of-snow covering all in 'La puerta' (*PC*), or to that of the snow in 'Cementerio de Vaugirard' (*MM*), in that 'su blancura lo contagiaba todo: las pestañas, las manos, el pelo, pero también las cosas, los gestos, las palabras' (*TB*, 131). Indeed, not only is it portrayed as covering all, but it is specifically mentioned to be covering words, echoing the encased and sealed off 'cartas' and 'epitafios' of 'Cementerio de Nangirard'. In short, the flour here is in danger of being seen as the same (lack-of-)snow-language bemoaned by Montejo. Like language, the flour covers that which is gone, keeping it in the memory, but keeping it as language: the shapes of the objects are perceptible underneath the blanket of flour or language, but the things themselves are not, as the actual past is sealed off, silenced. Indeed, in the essay itself all we have left is linguistic memories which inscribe what is remembered in loss and absence, a fact highlighted towards the end, as Montejo laments: 'Ya no veo, es verdad, a los panaderos ni oigo de cerca sus pláticas fraternas; en vez de leños ardidos me rodean centelleantes líneas de neón' (*TB*, 133). In this sense, the echoes of Mallarmé are once more strongly felt. The repeated use of snow and flour – images of whiteness – certainly recalls Mallarmé's more prevalent use of white in images of snow, swans, icicles, sails, paper, not to mention the white spaces of the page in poems such as 'Un Coup de Dés' (1945: 457–77), and the idea of the (white) flour covering all, tracing its outline, resonates with how, in Mallarmé's verse, 'language [...] surrounds the immediate, a zone whose contents are always slipping away' (McCann 1996: 396). So does this mean that flour, despite its affirmation as the 'nieve natal', is to be rejected as yet another failure to preserve without loss and to grant wholeness?

The answer to this question lies in seeing that the flour by itself does not and cannot constitute the desired language and being. Rather, it is the potential for it, (ful)filling the *theoretical* gap and need as Venezuelan, tropical snow. And it is poetry which is charged with turning this potentiality into actuality, as Montejo reveals at the end of 'Tal vez':

> Sí, tal vez la nieve,
> tal vez la nieve al fin tenga la culpa...
> Ella y los paisajes que no la han conocido,
> ella y los abrigos que nunca descolgamos,
> ella y los poemas que aguardan su página blanca. (*PC*, 9)

As these lines show, the snow is the page on which poems are to be written, finally providing, that is, a workable symbolic foundation for poetry to be the solution (the 'authentic' language) we have seen Montejo to envisage it as being in poems such as 'Café' (*AM*) and 'Mi vivir es araña en la tela del poema' (*É*). The image of the *taller* covered in a layer of white flour, then, comes to be seen anew. It is now the white page covering the entire scene, covering every object, word, gesture, with the poet's task being thus to write on it, bringing out what is covered. In effect, we return to the need both to preserve and to bring out the essence or life-heat of language and things. But we can now firmly identify this task as the poetic task: the 'authentic', tropical snow is the symbolic potential for poetry to be the desired presencing language. Indeed, from his earliest essays, Montejo has conceived of this as the poet's task, his engagement with snow bringing out new resonances in his affirmation in 1966 that 'revivir el ardor: he allí el punto más alto del velamen con que parte el poeta' (1966: 21). To bring the life-heat back to life is, then, to write on the white page of this flour–snow, bringing out what it preserves.

Yet, once again, we find that there are shortcomings in this proposal. As with the image of the (lack-of-)snow–language, whose preservative capabilities depend on a freezing of this 'ardor', likewise with flour the very act of writing on it writes over its whiteness, erases its essentiality and that which enables it to be the poetic potential. The logical conclusion is that we are left with just language, just the (lack-of-)snow–language from which Montejo wants an escape. In short, it would seem that, whilst providing the most enlightening and hopeful vista on the problem, flour ultimately falls short: one is left either with the image of a perfect whiteness, finally the 'snow' Montejo has been searching for, the potential page for the writing of the authentic language, but silent, communicating nothing, or with the image of the poet writing on the flour, using it as its base, as its grounding, yet in doing so writing out that which makes it authentic, and ending up once again as (lack-of-)snow–language. Poetry, then, is either silent or it is language. Either way, there is loss and absence.

But that is not the end of the matter. A key aspect of the scene depicted in both 'El taller blanco' and 'La cuadra' is that it is not just a scene from a now-absent place and time from the past which can potentially be made present through the 'sustancia esencial' (*TB*, 131) of flour. It also acts as a model for how the poet can proceed, in that it itself is imagined as *being* a place and time without the absenting and incomplete nature of language and being. This is implied, for instance, by the references in 'La cuadra' to a sense of community and fraternity ('fraternidad de nuestra Antigua sangre' (*TA*, 20)) and to 'el termo de café' (*TA*, 20), both of which link it to the childhood homestead of *Élegos*. It is also implied by the reference to it as full of 'presencias míticas', a mythical, quasi-divine fullness of presence whose lack for the poet writing is lamented:

> Son los seculares procedimientos casi medievales, más lentos y complicados que los actuales, pero más llenos de presencias míticas. [...] En el

taller blanco tal vez quedó fijado para mí uno de esos ámbitos míticos que
Bachelard ha recreado al analizar *la poética del espacio*. (130–1)

A closer look at these lines is called for here. On the one hand, Montejo
appears to cast this locale of his childhood as a somehow more 'authentic'
space and time than the industrialised present. The allusions to the medieval
period signal that the *taller* back then was in tune with what Montejo sees
as a more poetic, alchemic, and sacred time, when, as he says of the Middle
Ages, 'los metales, el fuego, los caballos y el sentido de las palabras, parecían
a diario reavivarse en su contacto con la divinidad' (*VO*, 137). Of course,
such a statement represents a highly romanticised and idealised view of the
Middles Ages, and, in positing this space of his infancy as a similar locale,
Montejo's words thus remind us of the deconstruction of such a presentation
of his childhood found, for example, in the death of his brother Ricardo, as
we saw in chapter 1, and in the implications of the essay 'Tornillos viejos en
la máquina del poema' (*VO*), as examined in the Introduction.

There is, however, a further way to read this affirmation of the childhood
experience of the *taller*. We saw earlier how infancy appears in Montejo's
work as a time when one was not aware of time. And we are now in a position to understand quite what is at stake here. The clue lies in the etymology
of the word *infancia*, coming from the Latin *infans*, literally: speechless.
Whilst the childhood period described here and elsewhere in Montejo's verse
and essays is certainly not that of him as a baby, that is, in a time of literal
speechlessness, the fact that he uses the term *infancia* on repeated occasions
as he looks back on this period underscores that infancy appears as a timeless
time because it is, in some essential sense, seen as prior to speech, or, more
accurately, prior to language, as, once again, time is shown to be inextricably
linked to language in Montejo's work. And it is this idea of speechlessness,
and, hence, unlocatability in history, that brings itself to bear on Montejo's
presentation of the *taller blanco*, opening up a less literal interpretation of the
line in 'La cuadra': 'Antes que las palabras fue la cuadra mi vida' (*TA*, 20').
What is most significant, however, is that the central element of this scene is
not its *historical* location in a time of 'procedimientos casi medievales, más
lentos y complicados que los actuales' (*TB*, 130), but the fact that it is *mythic*
('presencias míticas', 'ámbitos míticos'). In emphasising its mythic characteristics, then, Montejo's words recognise that the *taller blanco* is, above
all, an unlocatable space of re-creation. In short, it announces it as a poetic
space, beyond (historical) reality, as indicated by its alignment with the poetic
'ámbitos míticos' described by Gaston Bachelard in *La poétique de l'espace*
(1958 [1957]), where he comments of this (re)creation of childhood spaces
in (poetic) memory, that 'c'est sur le plan de la rêverie et non sur le plan des
faits que l'enfance reste en nous vivante et poétiquement utile' (33). This is
the plane on which the *taller* is found in Montejo's work, as it aligns itself

with Bachelard's description of the space of the 'maison onirique, une maison
du souvenir-songe, perdue dans l'ombre d'un au-delà du passé vrai' (33).[18]

Crucially, though, the scene is not poetic, or authentic, because of the
way in which Montejo keeps it in his memory, that is, it is not the poetry
we have before us which allows the scene to be poetic. Rather, it is because
of the scene itself: the work of the *panaderos* making the bread. In both 'El
taller blanco' and 'La cuadra' Montejo focuses on how this place (the *taller*)
at this time (his (timeless) infancy) constitutes his poetic *taller*. Underlining
its role as an 'authentic' model for poetry, both pieces read as a paean to the
bakers' *taller* as that which taught Montejo everything he need know in order
to carry out the poetic task:

> Hablo de un aprendizaje poético real, de técnicas que aún empleo en mis
> noches de trabajo, pues no deseo metaforizar adrede un simple recuerdo.
> Esto mismo que digo, *mis noches*, vienen de allí. Nocturna era la faena de
> los panaderos como nocturna es la mía.[19] (*TB*, 131)

The *panaderos* are figured as working at night to produce for the world the
bread where, upon the completion of their work, 'casa por casa el pan se
repartió' ('La cuadra', *TA*, 20). The image is one of the production of a quasi-
religious Eucharistic host for the world to commune with, in effect aligning
the bread created in the *taller blanco* with a full, divine presence. This also
ties in with the tone of Montejo's writing here, which is one of religious
reverence, the task being carried out by the bakers commanding deep awe
and respect in the watching (and remembering) Montejo. And it is the task
of the bakers itself which thus lends the entire scene its religious, poetic, and
authentic character. Aside from the 'técnicas' and the nocturnal nature of the
task, which Montejo did indeed take on in his poetic writing,[20] we might
observe that it is this sense of religious reverence, both on the part of the

---

[18] As these quotations indicate, Montejo's early focus on the childhood *casa* can also be
seen to reflect an interest in Bachelard's emphasis on the childhood house in this work. Medina
Figueredo has touched upon the parallels between Montejian and Bachelardian thought (1997:
45–59), as has Chirinos (2005: 167–8; 175–6), though an in-depth study of Montejo's work
from a Bachelardian perspective remains a potentially fruitful area demanding future attention.

[19] Montejo is insistent throughout his *œuvre* on the night as the poetic time, the time in
which he is invariably figured as wrestling with his work, trying to bring it to fruition (see, for
instance, 'Nocturno al lado de mi hijo' (*AP*), 'Los gallos' (*T*), 'Labor' (*T*), 'La noche' (*TA*),
'Medianoche' (*AM*), 'Canción oída a medianoche' (*AM*), 'Medianoche' (*PC*)).

[20] In interview with Szinetar in 1982, for example, Montejo states that 'Esa disciplina,
esa responsabilidad del panadero con el alba [...] es culpable de que mi ritmo de trabajo sea
nocturno' (2005: 100). Similarly, he stresses the importance of a sense of fraternity in poetry
when talking about the *taller blanco* in his acceptance speech for the Premio Octavio Paz
(2006b: 299), thus resonating with the 'fraternidad de nuestra antigua sangre' ('La cuadra', *TA*,
20) which characterised the *panadería*.

bakers towards their work and as what is evoked and produced by their *faena*, that Montejo sees as lying at the heart of the (authentic) *poetic* task. Again, it is hard here not to perceive resonances with Heidegger, whose religious reverence towards both the poet and his task and the poetic product itself emerges, via Hölderlin, in his idea that 'the speech of the poet is the intercepting of these signs [the language of the gods], in order to pass them on to his own people' (1968a: 311). But more about the Heideggerean elements revealed here later.

As an apprentice of the *taller*, then, the poet's task is to repeat that of the *panaderos*. Indeed, Montejo sees himself, as poet, quite explicitly as the inheritor of the mantle of the *panaderos*. In 'La cuadra', whereas, initially, Montejo describes the *panaderos* as they 'trabajan para el mundo que duerme' (*TA*, 20), later, when he turns to his own *faena nocturna*, we are told that 'escribo para el mundo que duerme' (20), a task from which he will not swerve ('Siempre seré fiel a la noche' ('Sólo la tierra', *T*, 11)). The *taller blanco*, now in the past, is no longer producing, and its quasi-divine bread, full *of* and full *as* presence is to be replaced, to be reconstituted by poetry and *poetic* production:

> la cuadra ahora está llena de libros,
> son los mismos tablones alineados, mirándome,
> gira el silencio blanco en la hora negra,
> va a amanecer, escribo para el mundo que duerme,
> la harina me recubre de sollozos las páginas. ('La cuadra', *TA*, 20)

And yet the tone in these lines is decidedly negative. The poet's task may be synonymous with that of the bakers, but it has not been successfully carried out. The books aligned on the shelves are *like* bread, and yet they are not bread, they do not represent all the bread did, as Montejo muses in 'El taller blanco': '¿Cuántas veces, mirando los libros alineados a mi frente, no he evocado la hilera de tablones llenos de pan?' (*TB*, 132–3). The dawn is coming ('va a amanecer'), and yet there is a sense that still the poem has not been made, has not been produced for the world. The reason for this lies, I would suggest, in that the bakers' task was figured as being carried out in an authentic or poetic time, a time, crucially, of infancy, of mythical presences, and 'un ámbito mítico': a poetic task in a poetic time and space. In contrast, Montejo's poetic task is a toiling in a time and space devoid of the poetic, a time and a space of loss and lack. In short, Montejo is once more unable to escape the fact of being in language and in the sequential time of adulthood, a fact ciphered in the image of the modern city in which he now finds himself, as he laments how 'la furia de la ciudad nueva arrojó lejos a las cosas y al tiempo del taller blanco' (*TB*, 133). As with his valorisation of re-creation over representation elsewhere, Montejo may affirm the mythic scene and the re-creation of the *taller blanco*, but he is firmly in the temporal and the linguistic. In effect, Montejo paints himself as locked in a catch-22: the poetic task cannot succeed in an unpoetic time and space; but the time and space can only be made poetic or 'full' through the poetic task. Indeed, this contrast between the two loci is conveyed by the fact that the essential silence of the flour–snow, the symbol not just of a pre-linguistic silence, but, concomitantly, of a timelessness, that is to say, the symbol and symbolisation of infancy itself, is present and defines the scene in the *taller* of old, in that:

> *Es* el silencio blanco en la hora negra, (*TA*, 20, italics mine)

but is circling around and elusive in the present of the poem, as this line now becomes:

> *gira* el silencio blanco en la hora negra. (20, italics mine)

Moreover, it also explains why, at the end of the poem, the flour is a covering on the page ('la harina me recubre de sollozos las páginas' (20)), covering the poem there written, or, indeed, itself being the very language of that poem, once more just a sealing off and silencing of what it seeks to preserve and present. Like the snow and ice in 'Cementerio de Vaugirard', the flour once more serves as a symbol of mourning ('sollozos') for what is lost, as we return to the images of tears of *Élegos*.

   Despite this failure of the poetic task, however, a way forward is suggested by a closer examination of *how* the bakers carry out their task and make their product. In the model of language based around the symbol of snow, the idea of layers is dominant: the snow–language is seen as covering both the past and (concomitantly) the essence of language and being, both in Venezuela and on a more general philosophical level; likewise, the poetic task is seen as arising out of the potential offered by the flour–snow, which also acts as a cover, preserving what is underneath, for the poet then to write what is being preserved on top of it, adding another layer which, in this case, covers the essentiality (silence, whiteness) of the flour–snow. And this is why such a theoretics inscribes itself in failure. Looking more closely at Montejo's description of the bakers' task, we see that, rather than layers, what is at stake is a mixing of this essential silence in both the task and the product: the bread is made from and with the flour–snow, the silence of the pre-linguistic time-lessness of infancy, the essential 'lack' or 'transcendental signified', through a process itself imbued with this silence:

> Hay algo de quirófano, *de silencio* en las pisadas y de celeridad en los movimientos. Es nada menos que el pan lo que *silenciosamente* se fabrica, el pan que reclamarán al alba para llevarlo a los hospitales, los colegios, los

cuarteles, las casas. ¿Qué labor comparte tanta responsabilidad? ¿No es la misma preocupación de la poesía? (*TB*, 131–2, italics mine)

It *is* the same preoccupation, as is highlighted by both the title of the earlier poem 'Labor' (T) and its description of the lamps of poets working at night:

> son pocas, pero cuánto resisten
> para inventar la cantidad de Dios
> que cada uno pide en sueño. (*T*, 63)

The bread produced by the bakers and demanded by the people ('que reclamarán al alba') is identical to the 'cantidad de Dios' produced – it is imagined – by the poets and requested by the people, as the identification of the bread is once more affirmed as the Eucharistic host.

And yet, despite the common concern of the poet and the bakers, the way in which the poet approaches his task through the notion of flour/snow is, as we have just noted, at odds with that of the bakers. The appeal to the process of breadmaking, where the flour is mixed as part of the product, reveals that this flour is not simply a preserving covering, a white page on which to write the poem. The reason Montejo sees the flour as the type of snow he has been seeking is not just because it is linked with a poetic time and space, and with a familial and Venezuelan setting from his and the country's past, though these are all important elements. Rather, the flour is the potential silence sought because of how it was used by the bakers. The point is not the covering of the bread and the scene as a whole in flour: this is an effect of Montejo's memory, a keeping of the scene in memory by Montejo, that is, in language. The point is that the flour was used by the bakers as a part of the structure of their product: the bread is not laid out on a layer of flour, like words on a page, thus covering the flour's essentiality; and neither is flour laid on the bread, thus preserving it but covering it, sealing it off. The essential preserving silence, that is, is the structure of the materiality of the bread: in all, throughout all, guiding and structuring all, but without silencing. As Montejo later affirmed in his acceptance speech for the Premio Octavio Paz: 'en aquel ámbito el color impoluto de la harina […] marcaba su presencia *en* todas las cosas' (2006b: 299, italics mine). It is thus that poetry, as the new breadmaking, is called not to try to balance or flip uneasily between silence and language, both of which represent a theoretical and a practical failure. Rather, Montejo calls the poet to produce a (poetic) language which combines both the materiality of language and the structuring of silence. This might be seen as what is implied in 'Café' (*AM*), where the absent coffee of the poet's infancy is the silent structure of the poem, there to be drunk 'entre líneas' (*AM*, 163), the poet thus bringing forth the silent, timeless, pre-linguistic, and quasi-religious essence of the mythic 'time' and 'space' of infancy, without seeking *either* to give voice to it *or* to cover it up. Indeed, such a strategy is referred to by Montejo on several occasions in his writing, at times associating it with Taoist thought, as in the preface to *Guitarra del horizonte*:

> Sirviéndose [Sandoval] de las nociones de vacío y plenitud que los orientales han reivindicado desde tiempos inmemoriales, llega a afirmar que la copla consta de 64 sílabas, 32 de las cuales son expresas y encarnan el volumen perceptible de los sonidos, en tanto que las restantes 32 conforman el vacío, es decir, el silencio de la estrofa. (*GH*, 14)

Elsewhere, he cites the Cuban poet Eliseo Diego's declaration that ' "los espacios en blancos significan tanto para mí como las propias palabras" ' (2006b: 256). And, again, we cannot help but also think of Mallarmé's poetry. Derrida, writing on Mallarmé's images of white and also the white spaces of the page, refers to how 'le "blanc" marque chaque blanc [...], la virginité, la frigidité, la neige, le voile, l'aile du cygnet, l'écume, le papier, etc., *plus* le blanc qui permet la marque, en assure l'espace de réception et de production' (1972b: 285), and focuses on 'le blanc comme blanc entre les valences' (284), which, again, appears to coincide with Montejo's structuring flour–snow as an 'in-between'.

And yet there is a fundamental difference implied by the terms of Montejo's writing. Derrida talks of how 'le "blanc" marque chaque blanc' (285), but in Montejo's work the flour–snow of the *taller* marks everything, not just the images of whiteness: 'la blancura lo contagiaba todo' (*TB*, 131). This image does not work just against the idea of a simple covering, but also against the idea of an identifiable series of blanks or whiteness 'in-between', as does the model of the bakers' bread, where the flour is not discernible from the other ingredients in the final product. And this is what is finally brought out in 'Fábula del escriba' (*FE*), where the idea of the 'between spaces' is roundly rejected:

> Recoge aquí cuanto estos signos puedan darte,
> pero elude las voces de entrelineas,
> las mentiras del mundo. (*FE*, 18)

The flour–snow, the essential lack, is, then, envisaged in a way much more akin to the later Heidegger than to Derrida or to Mallarmé through Derrida. Montejo does not seek to single out the lack, only to identify it as ungraspable, yet the basis on which meaning and language works, but affirms it as an integral part of the language of the poem, the essence of language which can be implied by poetry without naming it or seeking to extract it, what Heidegger referred to as the 'noiseless ringing of stillness' (1971: 420) which is *in* words, not behind or between them.

But what enables poetry potentially to work like the bakers and produce such a poetic 'bread'? The difference between Heidegger and Derrida is revealing here. As the alignment with the former implies, Montejo's poetics underscores the primacy of poetry – with which Heidegger was most concerned – over prose, suggesting that it is in the 'voicing' of poetry that the flour–snow can be incorporated. And this is what Montejo's final 'snow poem', 'Algo más sobre la nieve' (*FE*), suggests, as it describes the falling snow:

> Y cuanto cae es más que pensamiento,
> cae la memoria de las cosas
> y sobre todo esa *materia sónica*
> de menudas *partículas melódicas*. (*FE*, 16, italics mine)

The snow is not voiced by being named, but through the musicality of poetic language. In short, Montejo's engagement with snow ends in this poem by foregrounding something akin to Heidegger's chiming 'ringing of stillness' or Paz's focus on poetry's rhythm (1967: 49–97) in *El arco y la lira*, and, as is implied by Paz's title, by sending us back once more to Orpheus and his lyre. What is more, towards the end of his life Montejo himself spoke of poetry's musicality in exactly this way, affirming it as the essence of poetry, which cannot be separated or picked out from the (language of the) poem as a whole:

> Creo que el poema debe partir de una música que [...] guíe la significación de las palabras, que interfiera en el significado de éstas y lo modifique hasta crear una representación distinta. [...] El aporte musical de un poema ha de ser parte indiscernible de su hallazgo, al punto que no se pueda hablar de una música y un significado en solitario, sino que ambos resulten ser, por obra del poema mismo, una misma cosa.
>
> (Lozano Tovar 2006: 25)

Finally, though, we must bring the discussion back to the central image of the flour in the *taller blanco*. For it is not just that the breads laid out in the *taller* represent the potential way forward for the poetic task, but that they speak specifically of the way forward for Montejo's Venezuelan poetic task. I have argued that they imply an engagement in Montejo's work with the sort of thought found in Paz or Heidegger. But it must be stressed that the essential, silent, structuring element of the poetic language sought here is identifiably Venezuelan in its symbolisation ('nuestra humilde nieve natal' ('La cuadra', *TA*, 20)) and in the mythical infancy it comes both to evoke and invoke (the *taller blanco* of Montejo's childhood). It is *this* flour–snow which is to act not as a foundation or base to be built upon, but as the all-pervading structure of the poetic language, even if Montejo's work itself cannot finally altogether escape the covering of language, the fall into memory, into absenting and loss: 'la harina que minuciosamente recubre la memoria del taller blanco' (*TB*, 134).

3

Alienation and Nature

In the preceding chapters I have focused on the broad sense of temporal loss in Montejo's work, taking such loci as the childhood homestead and the poet's father's bakery as leitmotivs through which the effects of temporal – and temporolinguistic – loss are presented. But the importance of these locales in their own right attunes us to the fact that the overriding sense of loss in Montejo's *œuvre* is played out in terms of place and habitat as well. It is a thematic which is most prominent in the collections of Montejo's mid-period, that is, *Algunas palabras*, *Terredad*, *Trópico absoluto*, and *Alfabeto del mundo*, as well as the heteronymic work *El cuaderno de Blas Coll*, although, as with the temporal, Montejo continues to engage with this topos in his late production.

In order to prepare the ground for an investigation of this general topos of place and habitat, it is necessary first of all to take up where the previous chapter ended: with the image of the poet toiling away at night, following the example of the *panaderos* of old. 'The night' is one of the most persistent motifs of Montejo's work from *Algunas palabras* onwards. In every collection up to and including *Fábula del escriba* it appears as the time of poetic work indicated by Montejo in his descriptions of the *taller blanco*: in 'Nocturno al lado de mi hijo' from *Algunas palabras*, for example, the night-time provides the backdrop for the poet's ruminations on the generational cycle; in 'Labor' from *Terredad*, he focuses on the image of 'los poetas en vela hasta muy tarde | [que] se aferran a viejos cuadernos' (*T*, 63); and in *Alfabeto del mundo* Montejo pays particular attention to the image of the poet working by the light of his lamp, a nod to Montejo's Romantic sensibilities and already alluded to in poems such as 'Dormir' (*AP*) and 'Réplica nocturna' (*TA*), depicting it as 'cansada ya de arder, de tanto estar en vela | frente a la oscuridad del mundo' ('Mi lámpara', *AM*, 161).[1] This long-standing thematic thread, spanning some thirty years, is particularly marked in *Partitura de la cigarra*, not least in 'Noche en la noche', which depicts the poet's entire life, in which he

---

[1]   The Romantic substitution of the lamp for the mirror, as set out by M. H. Abrams (1971 [1953]), represents the move from seeing art as a reflection of the external world to seeing it as the outpouring of the personal. It is a motif which also resonates with Bachelard's 'La lumière de la lampe' (1962: 89–105).

has seen his poetic comrades disappear one by one, as one long night working
alone by his lamplight:

> Noche en la noche. Me alumbra ya a deshora
> el nihilismo de esta lámpara.
> [...]
>
> Mis amigos salieron por un instante al pueblo
> pero ya es tarde y no regresan.
> [...]
> Yo me quedé con el carbón del fuego
> y el nihilismo de esta lámpara.
>
> [...]
> Ya va durando décadas la noche
> y mis amigos tardan demasiado ...   (*PC*, 11)

In the previous chapter we saw how, in the alignment with the *panaderos*
of old, the poet is figured as working at night towards a communal and
communional poetic product or language for the rest of humankind whilst
they sleep, to greet them when they dawn. But the fact of this being specifically a night-time task extends beyond the analogy with the profession of
Montejo's father, revealing much both about the nature of this poetic task
in Montejo's poetry and about how the poet's relationship to the outside
world is conceived. Firstly, in all the poems which tell of the poet working
at night, the resonances with the figure of Orpheus are, once again, stark,
with the loneliness of the poet at night, cut off from the rest of the world,
echoing the Orphic descent to Hades. Indeed, Blanchot talks of Orpheus's
descent in precisely these nocturnal terms.[2] But it is Montejo's preponderant
concern for the description of the poet *en vela* at night which is most crucial,
drawing attention to the notions of sleeping and waking in Montejo's poetry.
In short, it leads to a poetics which, in emphasising the poet's wakefulness
at night, reiterates time and again (the rest of) humankind's being asleep.
This then feeds into and informs the persistent allusion in Montejo's poetry
to life being lived as a dream, that is, where we are never truly alive. This is
found, for example, in the poem 'Sentir' in *Alfabeto del mundo*, where the
poet impresses the need to feel the world and time in which we live, before
ending by calling on us to 'apartar de la carne sus viejos bueyes de opio |
hasta que se despierten' (*AM*, 194).

The references to the poet's being awake whilst others sleep suggests that
the poet is charged with waking up humankind from a permanent night to a
state where they might truly 'be', reaffirming the ontological implications of

---

2   See, in particular, Blanchot (1968: 227–34).

the night-time poetic task. But, despite the apparent differentiation between the poet and the rest of humankind thus implied, Montejo repeatedly uses the poet himself as a prime example of this 'sleeping' state of being. In 'Noche natal' (T), for instance, in describing his own birth, the poet states that:

> Y apenas llegado me dormí
> tan hondamente
> que aún no sé si despierto de esa noche. (T, 50)

The poet, like the rest of humankind, is not truly alive. Yet it is the poet who, at least, is capable of seeing this and who is figured as potentially capable of awakening his race from this ontological slumber, as the motif of the night-time poetic task shows.

This idea of the need for humanity to be awakened provides an initial vista onto Montejo's increasing and persistent reference both in these 'night-time poems' and beyond to the poet's task as being that of a searching for, as Montejo puts it in 'Nocturno' (AM), 'un gallo que simplemente cante' (AM, 187). As early as 'Lejano' (MM), Montejo talks of being in a 'Noche sin gallos, sin un solo gallo' (MM, 38), and the references continue in poems such as 'Los gallos' (T) and 'La noche' (TA), before Montejo brings out the connection with the poetic night task explicitly in Alfabeto del mundo in both 'Nocturno' and also 'Medianoche'.[3] The search for the canto del gallo, then, reflects the envisaged need for (poetry to be) a waking up of humanity, and represents a different way of describing and understanding the poetic task in Montejo's work from the alignment with the panaderos on which I focused in chapter 2. What it shares with the latter, however, is an underlying linguistic concern, with the 'night-time poems' making clear from the outset that the sleeping nature of being from which the poet – and the poetic product – is to wake us is inextricably linked to (the problem of) language. The first of these poems, in Algunas palabras, draw attention to the fact that the night-time scene on which the poet is gazing, and which serves as the backdrop to his labour, is determined and identified by its language, where its words appear as shards of shattered glass, as in 'Nocturno al lado de mi hijo', where the poet talks of how 'Caen ahogados murmullos de vidrio | esta noche en el mundo' (AP, 37). 'Nocturno' then expands this identification of language at night, with the poet emphasising sharp edges and angles as he describes the cityscape, before ending with an image of these shard-words shattering:

> Noche de compasiva geometría
> donde los ecos van y vuelven

---

[3] Alfabeto del mundo in fact begins with a poem entitled 'El canto del gallo', and the presence of the gallo and its song continues to be a recurrent motif in Montejo's later poetry. Aside from the poems addressed here, the gallo is also present in the love poems 'Papiro de la luz' and 'Música de gallo' from Papiros amorosos.

> entre edificios rectos.
> [...]
> Las palabras que flotan en el aire
> con murmullos de vidrio
> a esta hora son peces.
> [...]
> La lluvia las arrastra
> a través de largas avenidas
> y estallan en el viento. (*AP*, 29)

The poem immediately following 'Nocturno', 'El último pájaro', provides a schema for understanding how the night, language, and the sought-after – and poetic – *canto del gallo* fit together. The poem concerns the move into night as the last bird stops singing at the end of the day, and ends with an image of the last trill with which the bird disappears, describing it as glass:

> A la detonación oscura
> con que el árbol se borra del patio
> añade un grito seco,
> un vidrio tenso con que cae
> y se parte. (*AP*, 31)

Given the ontological significance of 'the night', which I have outlined, the image offered here equates to a metaphorical presentation both of the moment of irruption into the world-as-language of the individual and, on a wider scale, of the Fall. As night falls, the *grito* of the bird, a single, tense glass–Word, shatters into the shards and fragments described by Montejo in poems such as 'Nocturno' (*AP*). The *canto del gallo*, which the poet is to locate and, thus, produce, is the poetic language itself, as Carmen Virginia Carrillo T. has noted (2005: 21–5), but it is figured here not as a communional bread–Word; rather, it is a recovery of this now-shattered birdsong: a single and whole, transparent glass–Word, the 'Verbo nuevo que tarda en revelarse' ('Alta noche', *PC*, 24) that Montejo describes the poet as still seeking in his night-time task some twenty-three years later. As 'Alta noche' lays bare, however, such a quest is ultimately frustrated. The poetic task may be to awaken humanity and produce a religious Word, ciphered in the image of the *canto del gallo*, but Montejo's poetry consistently reiterates the poet's inability to complete this task. Even as early as *Algunas palabras*, the poet talks in 'Dormir' of the need to:

> Cobrar el sueño que nos deben
> tantas noches de lámparas,
> tantos rotos poemas, (*AP*, 69)

with the antepositioning of 'rotos' and the anaphora of 'tantas'/'tantos' serving to emphasise the repeated falling-short. Similarly, 'Réplica nocturna' in *Trópico absoluto* underscores this failure, showing the poet vanquished by what has become the bloody torture of the night, his words covered by ash and memory, his lamp of poetic toil and inspiration identified as – to return to the negative images of *Élegos* – 'no verídica' ('Tan ululante vuelve y no verídica', *É*, 13):

> No escribiré más por esta noche,
> el silencio, las sombras,
> cubren mis voces de ceniza y recuerdo.
> Las campanas de pronto son lobos,
> cada palabra se torna un cuchillo
> y me mancha de sangre las manos.
> Además, esta lámpara vieja
> miente demasiado. (*TA*, 44)

What underscores this failure emerges both from the contrast between the literal and the metaphorical levels on which the schema of the night works, and also from the dual symbolism of the night, which represents both the ontological night of humankind and yet also the time for poetic creation and poetic potential. A *canto de gallo*, of course, signals an end to the night and a beginning of the day. On the literal level, then, were Montejo to find a *gallo* to sing, it would coincide with an end to – and so failure of – the poetic task in signalling an end to the night. The *gallo* would usher in the break of the day, an awakening, but only on the literal and not the metaphorical and ontological level. What Montejo requires, rather, is an ontological awakening through poetry, and this can only be achieved *in* the poetic time of the night. The *gallo*'s song, in representing the day as opposed to the night, symbolises the relationships of difference and similarity on which language is founded (again, we are back at Derrida's *différance*). The locating of the *gallo* and the song it produces in the night, then, would represent a collapsing of this and, thus, the attainment in and through poetry of the prelapsarian Word, before its fragmentation into language. But the ramifications of Montejo's schema of the *canto del gallo* are precisely that the literal implications of the *gallo* are inescapable, in that underlying the metaphorical and ontological search is the persistent fact that a *gallo*'s song is linked to the Fall from the night *as the poetic*. That is, whilst the night may symbolise the Fallen or postlapsarian state of humankind, the breaking of the dawn, in ending this period *as the poetic time*, is also itself symbolic of the Fall into relationships of *différance*: into language. In other words, and taking the *gallo* and his *canto* as a metaphor for the poet and his production, as soon as the poet produced his song, he would be doing so in the day, in (postlapsarian) language. Moreover, such ambiguity is to be found in Montejo's most explicit poem on the topos of poetry's role in waking up humankind, 'La poesía' (*AS*). The final lines of this poem read:

> Después [la poesía] abre su mano y nos entrega   8
> una flor o un guijarro, algo secreto,
> pero tan intenso que el corazón palpita
> demasiado veloz. Y despertamos.   11
>
>   (*AS*, 18)

On the one hand, the final two words can be seen to allude to the waking up of humanity to that 'algo secreto', the sacred element found in everything that poetry discloses and which goes hand in hand with an ontological awakening. The caesura in line 11 would thus represent this break from the ontological night brought about by the poetic. This is how Montejo seems primarily to have understood the poem.[4] Yet it equally reads as a statement of awakening *from* the poetic, as if the 'algo secreto' were only glimpsed in a dream (the poetic night), with the caesura thus symbolising the loss of the poetic as the recipient of the poem wakes up into the day once more.

In this schema and its inevitable failure to find the *gallo* and its song, then, we see the extent to which the alignment with Orpheus suggested by the use of the image of the night is carried through, as we find ourselves once again recalling Blanchot's depiction of the Orphic descent and search to retrieve Eurydice. For Blanchot, Orpheus 'ne veut pas Eurydice dans sa vérité diurne et dans son agrément quotidien […] [mais] dans son obscurité nocturne' (1968: 228) But, of course, he would only be able to see her outside of the night. The search for the cockerel's song within the night repeats this problematic, as the poet wants to hear the song in the night, to find and produce it in the poetic work, even though this is only possible in the daytime (language), when the poetic essence which the song is figured as constituting, or containing, is tipped out, lost, just as Eurydice's essence too is lost.[5] What is more, by shifting the focus of the myth from sight to sound, from the seeing of Eurydice to the locating of the *gallo* and its then singing, Montejo underscores the particularly poetic understanding of the Orphic descent to the Underworld which Blanchot, among others, brings out. The failure here is that of Orpheus as poet, and the continuation of the night-time poems throughout Montejo's production shows that it is a descent which must continue, since this *is* the poetic task, condemned never to be completed.[6]

---

4   See Posadas (2002: 310).

5   As Blanchot puts it, 'l'essence de la nuit, sous son regard, se révèle comme l'inessentiel' (1968: 228).

6   One is reminded here of Blanchot's affirmation that 'l'artiste, ne terminant son œuvre qu'au moment où il meurt, ne la connaît jamais' (1968: 12).

Indeed, the Orphic nature of the nocturnal failure described by Montejo in the poetry of this mid-period is further implied by Montejo's revisiting the earlier 'Orfeo' (*MM*) in 'Orfeo revisitado' (*AM*). In effect, these two poems act as bookends around the intervening period in which this 'poetics of the night' is developed. And it is thus significant that the later poem should find Orpheus no better off than in the earlier one. The poetic task itself, inseparable from the destitute Orpheus of the earlier poem, as is demonstrated by its being described with the neologism *orfear*, is portrayed still as broken, alone, and – in all its senses – babbling, firmly in the modern postlapsarian world:

> Orfear, verbo que nos declina su alto sueño,
> verbo en milagro del espíritu,
> cuando tartamudeante y roto y solitario
> paga en cantos su vida. (*AM*, 169)

The modern city, the quasi-rural homestead, and nature

Beyond the ontological meaning and implications of the night-time setting there is a further important element found both within these poems and throughout the collections of this mid-period. And it is here that the link between the poet at night and the topos of place and habitat brings itself to bear. For the poems are not simply set at night, but against a modern, late twentieth-century backdrop. We have already seen the urban scene described in 'Nocturno' (*AP*), with its references to the 'edificios rectos' and 'largas avenidas' (*AP*, 29), and the presence of this cityscape from which the poet is writing is repeated time and again in Montejo's 'night-time poems', from the 'rectos edificios' (*T*, 63) of 'Labor' (*T*) to the 'ruido insomne de los taxis' (*TA*, 44) in 'Réplica nocturna' (*TA*), for example. In certain poems, the presence of this cityscape brings to the fore the violence and social problems of Venezuelan cities, primarily Caracas, against which Montejo was composing much of his poetry of this period.[7] 'Nana para una ciudad anochecida' (*TA*), for example, seems to portray the poet wishing not just to lay down his pen for the night, but to put to bed the sheer urban horror of a city which could

---

7   Following the economic boom of the 1970s, the 1980s in Venezuela were characterised by a continued and vast urban population expansion, combined with drastic economic problems stemming from a reduction in oil prices and chronic political mismanagement. The result was an unemployment rate of around 20% throughout the early 1980s and the inevitable social problems of crime and violence (see Haggerty (1993), especially 'Chapter 1: Venezuela: The Triumph of Democracy'). The culmination of these years was the *Caracazo* of 1989.

well be Caracas, the alliterative plosives (*c*, *g*, *t*) and affricate (*ch*) conveying
the sense of violence and menace:

> adormécelo todo ahora que oscurece
> y haz que duerma yo mismo,
> que me desvelo mirando en cada calle
> un oscuro cuchillo
> y en el cuchillo un grito
> y en ese grito una mancha de sangre. (*TA*, 42)

But the primary effect of the setting of the poetic task within the modern
urban landscape is to suggest it is, on some level, coterminous with the idea
of the (ontological) night, and, thus, implicated in the need for and failure
of that task. In 'Sentir' (*AM*), for example, the poet declares that the only
way to be truly alive is to 'Sentir, sentir a pesar de la ciudad' (*AM*, 194), and
the final lines of 'Ante mis ojos' (*AM*) even imply that the modern setting in
which the poet finds himself actively impedes the poetic task:

> Iba a escribir de ti, de mí, ya no recuerdo.
> Creo que abrí demasiado la ventana
> y penetró una vaharada de mi siglo,
> una de tantas, volándome las páginas
> desde mi cuarto hasta el fondo del espejo. (*AM*, 189)

The reference to the twentieth century here carries with it the suggestion
that Montejo is talking about this era as a whole, understood, that is, as
the post-industrial, Freudian, and Einsteinian age, the age of urbanised and
mechanised progress to which Montejo referred in similarly negative ways
on several occasions, as we saw in the Introduction. But the specific mention
earlier on in the poem of the city scene outside ('De pronto ulula una sirena.
Ruido, portazos. | Se oyen tiros' (189)) intimates that the modern city is to be
taken as emblematic and symbolic of what is meant by 'mi siglo'. Indeed, this
identification of the poetically-problematic post-industrial twentieth century
with the modern city is reiterated by Montejo in interview with Arráiz Lucca
in 1987, around the time of the publication of *Alfabeto del mundo*, where he
declares that 'después de la revolución industrial la poesía no ha tenido el
viento a favor, y ello coincide, entre otras cosas, con el empobrecimiento
ambiental de la ciudad' (1987: 3). It is, moreover, a modern reality which
informs being – and the poet's task – around the world. The scenario set
out in Montejo's verse may be the result of the specific urban expansion of
Venezuela in the second half of the twentieth century, but, as Montejo later
stated, the concern for the possibility of poetry in the increasingly urban
nature of the modern world is 'común al poeta que hoy vive en Sidney, en
Madrid o en Caracas' (Gutiérrez 2002).

The extent to which the modern urban reality is implicated in the fallen predicament of humankind only becomes clear, though, when one realises that the lack of *gallos* in the poetic night is due not simply to its being night, but to the poet's location within the city. Two poems which show this double understanding of the lack of the *gallos* and how the city emerges as a central focus in Montejo's poetics are 'Nocturno' and 'Medianoche', both from *Alfabeto del mundo*. In the former, the poet asks whether '¿No quedará en el fondo de la noche, | [...] | un gallo que simplemente cante[?]' (*AM*, 187), whereas in the latter the poet states explicitly that the modern city with its stones stands in place of *gallos*, as if these stones had usurped them. Once more, the poem climaxes by portraying the city as impeding the poet from working, with the chorus of stones building in a maddening crescendo:

> Ningún gallo cantó para negarme
> ni esperé oírlo: ya no queda uno solo
> a mil leguas siquiera.
> Cantó una piedra, sin plumas, de voz ronca,
> insomne en su alarido. – La primera.
> Después otra, ventrílocua, lejana,
> la secundó en la noche íngrima;
> y al fin todas las piedras despertaron
> cantando sin cesar, ebrias, dementes,
> dando gritos y gritos que subían
> hasta las estrellas. (*AM*, 173)

What is clear from these poems is that this nocturnal cityscape with its lack of *gallos* and, hence, of their song, is set up not as an isolated metaphor, but as a comparative one. The question '¿No quedará[?]' (*AM*, 187) and the declaration, by way of answer to this question, that 'ya no queda uno sólo' (*AM*, 173) implies that this situation represents the loss of a habitat where there were indeed *gallos* to sing. And the habitat in question is that of the quasi-rural homestead of Montejo's childhood and of his earlier poetry. Montejo stated this explicitly in 1999, declaring that 'en mi poesía todavía se oyen los cantos de gallo, pero se oyen porque yo los oí en mi infancia. [...] Pues bien, la pregunta ahora es [...] ¿por qué no cantan los gallos? Porque la ciudad comienza donde termina el canto de los gallos, porque somos cada vez más urbanos' (López Ortega 1999: 11).[8] This statement at once reinforces the identification of the (nocturnal) cityscape as a space of (postlapsarian) language rather than poetry: the *canto del gallo*, symbol of the prelapsarian Word and the authentic poetry sought by the poet, is absolutely no more: it is

---

8   Carrillo T. notes this identification of the *gallo* with the poet's 'infancia en la provincia' (2005: 20).

only present in his poems as a *memory* from this childhood, thus disclosing that it is, as we have seen, essentially linguistic, its essence missed.

Yet, in pointing to the *gallo* as a symbol not just of the poetic Word, but of the quasi-rural childhood past, Montejo underscores the specific nature of the contrast being made in his poetry. Certainly the past as a time when there was the possibility of locating the *gallo* and its song chimes with the existence of the *panaderos* and their workshop in that same past, and emphasises that a poetic language and being has been lost in the move into urban modernity. But in placing the focus squarely on these two habitats – past homestead and modern city – Montejo's poetics presents itself as a space in which all aspects of the two are to be compared. Indeed, it is only by reflecting on all that was then and is absent or different now that the nature of the apparently authentic being which Montejo posits can be fully understood.

The absolute divide between these two times and the respective habitats and ways of life associated with them (crudely, rural and urban) is frequently commented on by Montejo. In interview with Arráiz Lucca, Montejo underlines this difference, aligning himself with the rural, at the same time as the mythic, quasi-rural nature of this past is disclosed, appearing as a sort of willed rurality:

> Yo me siento relacionado con ciertas formas rurales no porque haya vivido gran parte de mi vida en el campo, sino porque mi padre, por ejemplo, es un hombre de formas rurales, y eso desde mi casa me acompaña. Además, [...] por edad, estoy más cerca de vivencias rurales que las generaciones recientes, en general mucho más urbanas. (1987: 4)[9]

The mention here of the *casa* draws further attention to this particular habitat, but the general location of the childhood house is also at stake here, with the contrast with which we are presented also being that of the change which Venezuela's cities underwent in the middle of the twentieth century from (semi-)rural, not least in their way of life, to urban.[10] This is pointed up as part of a wider phenomenon in the essay 'Poesía en un tiempo sin poesía', where Montejo explains that:

---

[9]   Within Venezuela itself, the new, urban reality pointed to by Montejo both here and in his poetry of this period led to the emergence of the urban poetic movements associated with the groups *Guaire* and *Tráfico*, a poetics which dominated much of the eighties in Venezuela. See Lasarte (1991: 13–20) and Gomes (2002b: 1010–12) for brief synopses and Gackstetter Nichols (2000) for an in-depth study of these movements.

[10]   For details of the massive urbanisation in Venezuela in the second half of the twentieth century in particular, see Hellinger (1991: 75–6; 86–8).

Lo que nombramos con la palabra ciudad significa algo completamente distinto antes y después de la aparición del motor, al punto que tal vez no resulte apropiado lingüísticamente homologar, si deseamos llamar las cosas por sus nombres, la urbe moderna con la apacible comarca de otras edades. (*TB*, 13)

The extent to which these past habitats of Montejo's childhood are seen as having been eradicated by the modern city is revealed starkly in 'Caracas' from *Terredad*. The capital city, where Montejo was born and spent his first few years, becomes here the ultimate symbol of the move into a modern urban environment, leading the poet to doubt whether the habitat of his childhood was ever real at all:

> Tan altos son los edificios
> que ya no se ve nada de mi infancia.   2
> [...]
> Rectos andamios, torre sobre torre,
> nos ocultan ahora la montaña.   8
> El ruido crece a mil motores por oído,
> a mil autos por pie, todos mortales.
> Los hombres corren detrás de sus voces
> pero las voces van a la deriva   12
> detrás de los taxis.
> Más lejana que Tebas, Troya, Nínive
> y los fragmentos de sus sueños,
> Caracas, dónde estuvo?   16
> Perdí mi sombra y el tacto de sus piedras,
> ya no se ve nada de mi infancia.
> Puedo pasearme ahora por sus calles
> a tientas, cada vez más solitario,   20
> su espacio es real, impávido, concreto,
> sólo mi historia es falsa.
>
> (*T*, 55)

This poem points overtly to the fact that the childhood past of which Montejo talks in his poetry appears as a mythic time and place. In effect, the modern city here brings home to the poet that the notion of a prelapsarian, authentic past is a false one, or, at least, not real in the same physical sense as the modern *urbe* (lines 21–2),[11] as the Caracas of old appears as distant as the

---

[11] Similarly, Montejo's use of the term 'mi siglo' in 'Ante mis ojos' (*AM*, 189) to describe the *late* twentieth-century cityscape deconstructs his claim of a contrast between the latter and an apparently more rural and 'authentic' past locus. See the Introduction for further examples and discussion of how Montejo's identification of poetic and unpoetic times and places in history are open to a deconstructive reading.

ancient and legendary cities of Thebes, Troy, and Nineveh (lines 14–16), suggesting that it has passed into (mythified and idealised) folklore. That said, within Montejo's poetics, as we have seen, the *figuring* of this quasi-rural past as indeed such a temporal and spatial locale remains in place, and the primary function of this poem is to underscore that it is the entirety of this (subsequently mythified) scene of *la infancia* which is hidden, lost in the modern urban space. A particularly pertinent example of this is the sense of family and community which characterised the past habitat, but which 'Caracas' reveals now to be absent. Rather than the welcoming, communal space of the *casa*, populated by now-dead relatives, as described in poems such as 'Mi ayer es una bizca tía' (*É*), in the modern city the poet is 'cada vez más solitario' (line 20). In effect, the loneliness of the poet writing at night is here seen not just to represent the poet as the solitary figure capable of finding the lost authenticity of being and language, but to point to the loss of the communal and communional nature of the quasi-rural past habitat. Indeed, it is worth remarking here that the parallel 'poetic' task of the bakers in the *taller blanco* was one characterised by fraternal bonds rather than solitary toiling.

Such a loss, of course, does not affect just the poet, and the poem 'Mural escrito por el viento' in the following collection *Trópico absoluto* discloses this wider solitude as the poet talks of how, in the city:

> Sus edificios nos vuelven solitarios,
> sus cementerios están llenos de suicidas
> que no dejaron ni una carta. (*TA*, 16)

The separation between individual people is emphasised in this image of the absence of any letters – or words – from the dead, in contrast to the *cartas* in 'Otoño' and 'Cementerio de Vaugirard' in *Muerte y memoria*. And in focusing on 'suicidas' Montejo at once suggests both the ontological depression of humankind in the modern cityscape and, in the lack of explanatory letters, the sense that there is no one to whom these people felt the need or desire to offer some last words or reasons. In short, these lines are pregnant with the sense of human isolation and lack of community. Moreover, that this is a direct consequence of the modern city is disclosed in the poem's general warning of its alienating and impersonal nature:

> Quien amó una ciudad solamente en la tierra,
> casa por casa, bajo soles o lluvias
> y fue por años tatuándola en sus ojos,
> sabe cómo engañan de pronto sus colinas,
> cómo se tornan crueles esas tardes doradas
> que tanto nos seducen.

> Las ciudades se prometen al que llega
> pero no aman a nadie. (*TA*, 16)

Modern cities may appeal to the eye and entrance with the lustre of the new and of progress, but, for Montejo, they lack the warmth and heart of more rural abodes.[12]

As should be evident, there are distinctly Heideggerean resonances here once again. The valorising of the homely qualities of the rural and of small towns, compared with the impersonal and increasingly technologised urban centres is a distinct characteristic of the later Heidegger.[13] Where Montejo contrasts with the latter, however, is in the particularly prominent role he gives to nature and the natural, as he foregrounds the absence of these elements of the rural past from the modern cityscape. That is not to say that Heidegger's own lamenting of the technological and the urban was not itself connected to a sense of the loss of (contact with) nature.[14] But Montejo's treatment of this theme plays a much more central role, as well as differing in several important ways from Heidegger's thought, as we shall see. Certainly, by the time of *Trópico absoluto* Montejo is explicit in his presentation of the modern city in which he lives as a place not just devoid of nature, but from which nature is repelled. This is exemplified by several lines in 'Mural escrito por el viento' (*TA*). In the first stanza the poet warns us that 'Una ciudad no es fiel a un río ni a un árbol, | mucho menos a un hombre' (*TA*, 16), before ending the poem with the image of nature doing precisely what he is advising we do: leave the city:

> Por eso el río pasa y no vuelve,
> por eso el árbol que crece a sus orillas
> elige siempre la madera más leve
> y termina de barco. (16)

This identification of the modern city as a place separated from and empty of nature is persistent in the collections of this mid-period. Furthermore, it provides a further understanding of the prominence of the *gallo* as a symbol of what is missing from this present. The usurping of the *gallos* by *piedras* in 'Medianoche' (*AM*) thus comes to be seen not just as a statement of the change from the rural homestead and all that is related to it, but as a way

---

[12] Gomes has commented in some detail on the contrast between Montejo's bemoaning of urban modernity on the one hand and, on the other, the optimistic and exaltatory view of the modern city in Venezuela taken by the leading kinetic artists of this period of rapid urban growth (2002b: 1009–15).

[13] See, for example, Heidegger (1973b) and (1994).

[14] For an account of an understanding of Heidegger as a deep ecologist, see Zimmerman (1983).

of drawing attention to the usurping of the natural more generally by the concrete and inanimate. By focusing on the image of the *gallo*, then, Montejo is pointing to the underlying and fundamental characteristic of the figured authentic rural past: its contact with nature.

To be sure, the importance of nature in Montejo's work here cannot be underestimated, with the perceived authenticity of the communional and rural past – and hence an ontological authenticity – emerging as dependent upon its presence. 'El país más verde' (*TA*) is, in this respect, indicative of many poems from both *Terredad* and *Trópico absoluto* in the way it reveals this centrality of nature; it describes a past where there was a oneness of it with the poet and the community as a whole:

Era el país más verde de la tierra,
tal se veía por mis anteojos.
Un verde hecho rumor sobre los pastos
de fragantes celajes.   4
Mirándolo hacia junio,
cuando llovía desde el fondo de las hojas,
cada hombre era un árbol a lo lejos,
de pie ante la feracidad del horizonte.   8
Pero más que color, el verde unánime
era un modo de ser, hablar, reconocernos.
Lo llevábamos tatuado en las pupilas
como un mapa de geografías inabarcables.   12
Podíamos verlo aún en la sequía
emergiendo del sueño o las palabras,
era el tono fraterno de nuestra soledad,
la saudade natal de los ausentes,   16
la vida que iba siempre delante del paisaje
con un boscoso silencio de caballos.
                                            (*TA*, 21)

The greenness of the land and life dominates the poem, in which the rural nature of the scene is highlighted in the reference to the 'pastos' (line 3). The very life and being of the poet and community is seen to be determined by and fused with this natural colour: each man 'era un árbol' (line 7); the green not only shaped, or filtered, how they saw the world (line 11), but also infused and characterised their 'modo de ser, hablar, reconocernos' (line 10), at once suggesting that both life and language were natural, in contrast to the modern city, where, as we have seen, language is 'fallen' from the natural song of the bird. Indeed, this suggestion is repeated in the reference to this natural greenness emerging from 'las palabras' (line 14). Moreover, it is a greenness which signals and binds together the people as 'el tono fraterno de nuestra soledad' (line 15): not the loneliness of the individual in the city, but a 'communitarian solitude', of a brotherly people alone with nature. In short, the separation from nature implied by the modern urban life and setting constitutes and lies behind the separation both from other people and also from one's (authentic) self. That is, the lack of authentic being of both humanity and each individual human being, symbolised in the image of the (ontological) night, is synonymous with a loss of connection with nature, a notion which resonates and yet also contrasts with Heidegger, for whom the move into technology is tied both to a loss of contact with things/the world more generally and also to the idea of the imposition of an enframing of 'usefulness' on nature, whereby the natural world is seen as a vast mine of technological and industrial resources (1966: 50).[15] Such terms are absent from Montejo's discourse.

The image used most persistently by Montejo to convey this loss of contact with the natural is that of the alignment of man and tree, as found at the beginning of 'El país más verde'. Here, in a rural past, each man is a tree, signalling his connective oneness with nature (and an additional use of the man/tree metaphor to that dealt with in chapter 1). And it is precisely this connection which Montejo describes as disappearing. In *Terredad*, for example, the opening poem 'En el bosque' begins by laying down the distance separating the two:

> En el bosque, donde es pecado hablar, pasearse,
> no poseer raíz, no tener ramas,
> ¿qué puede hacer un hombre? (*T*, 9)

These lines set the tone for the collection as a whole, which gravitates around the comparison and contrast of the city and nature, and leads in particular to 'Los árboles de mi edad', where we find a striking description of the separation of the poet himself and trees:

> Los árboles de mi edad
> a quienes igualaba de tamaño
> ya son más altos que mi cuerpo
> y menos solitarios. (*T*, 54)

In these lines we see how this separation is certainly not linked exclusively with the move into the city, as they carry the implication that such an alienation from the trees of his childhood is due to the fact of growing up, the move out of infancy brought about by the passing of time. Indeed, this would seem

---

[15] For a discussion of the enframing of 'usefulness', see Heidegger (1977). That Heidegger is concerned with a more general loss of contact with 'things' is evident in, for example, his discussion of the jug in 'The Thing' (2001: 161–84).

to be the primary cause given the poem's subsequent mention of the trees and
the poet being in the same city:

> al crecer me van dejando solo,
> aunque seguimos en la misma ciudad
> viviendo donde siempre
> nos separan los aires,
> ya no alcanzo el rumor de sus voces
> ni sé qué harán de nuevo en poesía,
> ya casi no nos vemos. (54)

And yet the positioning of this poem on the page facing the following poem
'Caracas' underscores the ineluctable implication of the city in this separation: the trees may be physically in the city with the poet, but the modern
urban locus is, at some level, responsible for an essential or ontological separation between the two, even as the temporal move out of childhood is made
present in Montejo's poetics here once more.

Terredad

In his description of the past in terms of an alignment of man and tree and,
more widely, nature, however, Montejo goes beyond a simple portrayal of a
oneness and contact with nature now absent in urban modernity. As a living
organism rooted in the earth, from which it gains its being in a symbiotic
relationship, the tree points towards the pivotal element in the understanding
of what constitutes (authentic) being for Montejo, namely the earth, both
planet and substance, on which we live. 'Sólo la tierra' (T) serves as a prime
example of its importance in Montejo's poetics, as he links it explicitly to the
idea of a true awoken being:

> Por todos los astros lleva el sueño
> pero sólo en la tierra despertamos.
> [...]
>
> Siempre seré fiel a la noche
> y al fuego de todas sus estrellas
> pero miradas de aquí,
> no podría irme, no sé habitar otro paisaje. (T, 11)

The essential connexity with nature is here expanded to take in an emphasis
on our being-on-the-earth: the poetic night is affirmed once more, but with
the understanding that any poetic approach to being must be based on the
natural, terrestrial home on which we live. And it is this focus which forms

the basis of the formulation of (authentic) being that Montejo develops in
these collections, and for which he coins the neologism *terredad*.

Our introduction to the term and how it both begins with and moves on
from the idea of an essential link with nature is provided by the title poem of
the collection *Terredad*, cited here in its entirety:

> Estar aquí por años en la tierra,
> con las nubes que lleguen, con los pájaros,
> suspensos de horas frágiles.
> A bordo, casi a la deriva,   4
> más cerca de Saturno, más lejanos,
> mientras el sol da vuelta y nos arrastra
> y la sangre recorre su profundo universo
> más sagrado que todos los astros.   8
>
> Estar aquí en la tierra: no más lejos
> que un árbol, no más explicables,
> livianos en otoño, henchidos en verano,
> con lo que somos o no somos, con la sombra,   12
> la memoria, el deseo, hasta el fin
> (si hay un fin), voz a voz,
> casa por casa,
> sea quien lleve la tierra, si la llevan,   16
> o quien la espere, si la aguardan,
> partiendo juntos cada vez el pan
> en dos, en tres, en cuatro,
> sin olvidar las sobras de la hormiga   20
> que siempre viaja de remotas estrellas
> para estar a la hora en nuestra cena
> aunque las migas sean amargas.
>   (*T*, 17)

The focus on the earth is set out at the very beginning, and, as with 'Sólo la
tierra' (*T*), has strong Heideggerean resonances, both in terms of the importance of being-on-the-earth, and in the way both poems formulate this as a
being *on* the earth, *below*, and looking up to, the sky above. The definition
which follows the colon in line 9 then makes clear that this is, above all, a
being in tune with nature and its rhythms and cycles, as Guillermo Sucre has
noted, referring to *terredad* as 'un ritmo, un dinamismo en el que la vida
entera participa' (1985: 311).[16] This, then, is how the contact with nature or

---

[16] In 'Building Dwelling Thinking' Heidegger states that '"on the earth" already means
"under the sky"' (2001: 147), where the earth and the sky constitute two elements of the Four-
fold (earth, sky, mortals, gods). Like Montejo, he goes on to make specific reference to the
temporal cycles and rhythms of both (147–8).

the oneness with a tree of Montejo's presentation of the quasi-rural past must be understood: they are formulations which reflect a profound and essential connection with all that is earthly.[17]

The implications and meaning of the term are then shown to go further, as the poet sketches out, in the uncertainties, possibilities, and doubts of lines 12–17, the characterisation of this being as utterly 'inclusive', once more extending the presentation of the quasi-rural homestead, in this case the 'inclusivity' of the familial and communitarian bonds. These lines, in particular the hypothetical clauses of lines 14–17, recall the parenthetical clauses of 'Orfeo' (*MM*), a resonance further implied by the reference to the 'casa' and the 'voz', which appear in that poem. But here the doubts and concerns found in the earlier poem as regards whether Orpheus exists and sings are not part of a worried pessimism. The concept of *terredad*, rather, embraces all, able to, in Sucre's terms, 'acoger lo material y lo inmaterial, lo concreto y lo virtual' (1985: 311). It takes in, contains, holds together opposites, uncertainty, infinity ('(si hay un fin)' (line 14)), and thus represents the all-encompassing, limitless being symbolised both in Montejo's search for the unified horse of life and death and in the annulling of the difference between the living and the dead in the 'coffee moment'. *Terredad*, as an essential connexity with the earth and the earthly, then, is a way of reaching this essential, inclusive, and limitless being.[18] Moreover, as the starkly Christian imagery of lines 18–23 shows, it is also, once more, conceived of as a quasi-religious communional being: all of nature down to the smallest of creatures is drawn together in this oneness of being, as the poet takes up the sense of holy, communional ritual found in his portrayal of authentic being in the past homestead, both in the form of the *panaderos* making their bread and in the Eucharistic coffee. Indeed, the presence of the religious is felt keenly throughout Montejo's engagement with the concept of *terredad*, coming to the fore in 'Creo en la vida' (*T*), where the poet begins by exclaiming:

> Creo en la vida bajo forma terrestre
> tangible, vagamente redonda,
> menos esférica en sus polos,
> por todas partes llena de horizontes. (*T*, 57)

---

[17] Francisco Rivera describes Montejo's poetics, and, in particular, *Terredad*, as 'poesía cósmica' (1986: 51). Certainly the cosmos is present in Montejo's poetry, not least in these closing lines of 'Terredad', but the focus throughout Montejo's writing is conspicuously on the earth itself, rendering dubious the labelling of his poetry as 'cósmica'.

[18] Underscoring this inclusivity of contrasting elements, Montejo talks in a late interview of *terredad* as 'la celebración de la vida' and yet also an expression of 'la angustia de la nada y la muerte' (Posadas 2002: 302).

In the process, he thus also asserts one of the central tenets of his concept of authentic being, namely that, despite his lamenting the passing of time and his desire for a 'timeless time', life – the authentic life in which he believes as though it were a religious state – must be understood and lived as and in the earthly, temporal, material form which it takes, and which is its only expression, an approach which echoes the later Heidegger's dual focus on the earth and the flowing of rivers, and for whom, as Pattison puts it, 'temporality is now conceived as revealing the possibility of a guarding and a protecting, a shepherding of Being' (2000: 15). Ferrari, then, in describing *terredad* as the 'resistencia y acatamiento al tiempo y a la muerte' (1988: 15), perceives the existence of exactly this ambiguous attitude to time in Montejo's poetics.

Beyond this, a further significant move in 'Creo en la vida' is found in the tacit rejection of the opening appeal to *lo terrestre*. Maintaining the religious mantra which begins each of the poem's four stanzas, Montejo affirms his own term in the third stanza as he recasts the poem's opening line:

> Creo en la vida como terredad,
> como gracia o desgracia.
> Mi mayor deseo fue nacer,
> a cada vez aumenta. (*T*, 57)

In addition to affirming the primacy of Montejo's formulation and its wider meaning than simply *lo terrestre*, these lines also lay bare, then, that this being, this *terredad*, is the same truly 'living' being to which the whole of humankind needs to be awoken. Moreover, they underline that such a being is still very much desired rather than attained. Indeed, whilst Montejo himself later described *terredad* as 'un intento de definir la condición misteriosa de los días del hombre sobre la Tierra' (Posadas 2002: 302), implying that it is simply an attempt to describe life, the terms of his poetics both underscore that such a portrayal of being is very much an ideal way of understanding existence and make clear that it is one which has not yet been assumed, even by the poet and, by implication, even within the (poet's) actual quasi-rural past.

The bird and its song: a model for humankind's *terredad*

Having identified *terredad* as the authentic being towards which Montejo works, we can thus return to the motif with which we started: that of the poet toiling away at night, looking for the natural, religious, rural, and familial *canto del gallo*. In portraying the attainment of the latter as a key to or attendant with an attaining of *terredad*, the poetry I have been discussing evidently suggests an essential connection – indeed, a synonymity – between the two, and this connection is played out in Montejo's work in a persistent focus on birds more generally (*pájaros*) and, in particular, the alignment of birdsong and *terredad*. It is worth stating at this stage that, within Montejo's poetics, there are subtle but important differences between the use and implications of, on the one hand, the *gallo* and its song, and, on the other, the *pájaro* and its song, and I shall be examining these differences in due course. For now, it is sufficient to broaden out the *canto del gallo* to the wider import of the *canto del pájaro* in Montejo's presentation of *terredad*.

The connection between birdsong and *terredad* is made clear primarily in 'La terredad de un pájaro' (*T*). In it Montejo sets out how the separation from nature, the notion of *terredad*, and the specific role and relevance of the bird within this schema fit together. The poem, in its entirety, reads as follows:

> La terredad de un pájaro es su canto,
> lo que en su pecho vuelve al mundo
> con los ecos de un coro invisible
> desde un bosque ya muerto.   4
> Su terredad es el sueño de encontrarse
> en los ausentes,
> de repetir hasta el final la melodía
> mientras crucen abiertas los aires   8
> sus alas pasajeras,
> aunque no sepa a quién le canta
> ni por qué,
> ni si se podrá escucharse en otros algún día   12
> como cada minuto quiso ser:
> más inocente.
> Desde que nace nada ya lo aparta
> de su deber terrestre,   16
> trabaja al sol, procrea, busca sus migas
> y es sólo su voz lo que defiende
> porque en el tiempo no es un pájaro
> sino un rayo en la noche de su especie,   20
> una persecución sin tregua de la vida
> para que el canto permanezca.
>
>   (*T*, 52)

The first line immediately focuses attention on the idea of song and language, and, by implication, poetic production, thus underscoring the synonymity in Montejo's poetry of poetic language and authentic being, or *terredad*. Furthermore, the bird's song/*terredad* is then shown to be explicitly tied in with the themes and concerns of Montejo's earlier poetry, in that the song emerges from the (realm of the) dead, of absence, before being made song through the bird (lines 2–4). The song thus represents both the world and nothingness, life and death, both echoing the retrieval of the bridle of the horse of death in 'En los bosques de mi antigua casa' (*É*), and, in the following lines 5–6, hinting at the desire for the same bringing together of the living and the dead glimpsed in the *momento de café*. But this poem also adds to the earlier poems in the way it develops this communitarian aspect of the song, emphasising not that this represents a common, uniting essence of living and dead, though this is certainly present, but that the song, as *terredad*, is what defines and determines the bird as a species. The life of the individual bird is described, in a clear metaphor for the life of a human, as a fleeting journey (line 9) of work, procreation, and finding one's daily bread (lines 15–17), hinting at a Marxist reading of Montejo's work.[19] But the ends of that life are simply 'su voz' – his song – since, in maintaining this essential being or *terredad* during his life the bird is maintaining the essential being of 'the bird', understood as a quasi-Platonic Idea (lines 19–20). The life of the bird, then, is a constant chase (line 21), trying to keep the song aloft, to hand it on to the next bird 'para que el canto permanezca' (line 22), that is, so the *terredad del pájaro* remains. The life of the individual bird may be fleeting, but it can, in this way, be part of a permanent song or being of 'the bird', a poetic stance which recalls Keats's 'Ode to a Nightingale' (1988: 346–8).[20]

Throughout Montejo's subsequent poetic production this relationship between the individual and the species proves to be a recurrent thematic. In 'Anatomía de un gorrión' (*PC*), for example, Montejo describes how:

El cuerpo [del gorrión] se hunde en tierra cuando muere
y el gorrión permanece:
de un canto a otro va rodando, (*PC*, 37)

depicting the generic sparrow as rolling on from the song of one sparrow to another (the individual, mortal bird being identified corporeally): the song is what keeps the species alive. Likewise in 'Canto lacrado' (*AS*), when Montejo declares that 'No pude separar el pájaro del canto' (*AS*, 26), he is reaffirming that the being of the bird is its song: this is what defines it authentically as a bird. Probably the starkest reference to this schema, however, is found in *Guitarra del horizonte*. Sergio Sandoval's copla VII reads:

---

[19] Gomes (2002b; 2004) has undertaken just such a Marxist reading of Montejo's work. Certainly the focus and lauding of the natural, rural scene, where each man works the land in a society built on shared experience and communitarian values, suggests the validity of such a reading. Moreover, Montejo frequently alluded to his disdain for the modern capitalist world where we live 'espoleados por la prisa que impone la religión del dinero' (Gutiérrez 2002).

[20] Borges, for example, discusses the contrast and relationship between individual and species in Keats's poem in 'El ruiseñor de Keats' (1993 [1932]: 116–19).

> En la copa de una palma
> que un ventarrón sacudía,
> un pajarito cantaba
> y el canto no se movía. (*GH*, 27)

Sandoval then goes on to explain in his gloss that, whilst the palm and the bird are tossed about by the wind, 'sólo el canto permanece inalterable, repitiendo su eterna melodía siempre nueva, y unido a una raíz más profunda que la de ningún árbol de la tierra' (27). The paradoxical description of this song as both 'inalterable' and 'siempre nueva' at once supports the understanding of the song/*terredad* of the bird which I have been outlining: always the same essential being, but in each different bird.[21]

Evidently enough, the birdsong stands as a metaphor for human *terredad*, and the relationship between the individual and the species returns us to the idea of the generational cycle set up in Montejo's earlier poetry. But the notion of the essential song–*terredad* passed on like a baton from one human to the next shifts the emphasis firmly onto the idea of a human *song*, that is, onto a poetry-which-is-*terredad* being passed on. *Guitarra del horizonte* once again provides a clear statement of the straight transferral of the birdsong to its human guise, when Sandoval, musing on the advent of the new millennium, asks '¿Quiénes cantarán entonces la vieja canción que de hombre a hombre va pasando?' (*GH*, 58). However, both this gloss and 'La terredad de un pájaro' also highlight the underlying problem, namely the uncertainty as to whether such an essential song can be produced. Sandoval, for instance, adds: 'Pero quizá de tanto en tanto nos despierten los gallos, y volvamos a oír nuestra canción en otras voces, mientras la tierra gira y las Pléyades pasan' (*GH*, 58). These lines refer ostensibly to the possibility of those of us alive now being 'woken up' when we are dead so that we might once more hear the human song being sung in those of the future, but the doubt is clear in the use of the subjunctive. Likewise, in 'La terredad de un pájaro' the bird is presented as unsure whether his song will live on, thus granting him an authentic being not bound by death and time (lines 12–14). Moreover, a closer look at Montejo's presentation of birds and the birdsong as a whole reveals a critical uncertainty at the level of its very meaning, in that it is used not only as a metaphor for an understanding of our essential being, but also as a double metaphor for the fallen condition of humankind. This is particularly apparent in 'Canto lacrado' (*AS*). Here, we read of the poet listening to the bird singing, but where he cannot make out what the song is ('cosas indescifrables' (*AS*, 26)), nor, crucially, whether it is:

---

[21] A similar point is made in 'El mirlo' (*FE*), where the poet says of the blackbird: 'Y dentro trae un nuevo canto y otro, | el mismo siempre en plumas diferentes' (*FE*, 23).

> un son antiguo
> o si su voz se contamina
> en esta hora llena de máquinas. (26)

The question is left hanging as to whether the bird's song has had its essentiality tipped out by the mechanised modern urban world – as is also implied
in 'Carta de abril' in *Fábula del escriba*, which begins by stating '¡Qué difícil
ser pájaro | en este planeta colmado de ciudades! ...' (*FE*, 32) – or whether it
is in fact authentic, the same as in the past, transforming the modern sounds
into an essential innocence, but where the poet's Fallen condition prevents
him from being capable of identifying it as such:

> Ignoro aún si trasmutaba en su inocencia
> ruidos de goznes, pernos, hélices,
> el zumbido de los taxis que van y vienen. (26)

What both readings convey, however, is the sense that the poet and humankind are presently excluded from an authentic being: in understanding the
modern bird as lacking its *terredad* and thus as a metaphor for the human
condition, we see the human need to produce its own essential song; and in
seeing the lack of the bird's *terredad* as a result of our distance from it and
inability to perceive it, we see the concomitant – and synonymous – need for
a reconnection with birds and nature more generally. In sum, there is the need
for an authentic being-on-the-earth through the production of our essential
song. Inevitably, then, the question posed and confronted by Montejo in his
poetry is how this song is (to be) produced.

Returning to 'La terredad de un pájaro' (*T*), we can begin to see how
Montejo describes the birdsong or its *terredad* as coming forth. The poem
describes the song as emerging from deep within him, from where the dead/
past generations are also found (lines 1–4), before being brought into the
world through his voice. The essence, then, is portrayed here as lying *within*
the bird. And this mirrors how Montejo presents humankind, even in the
inauthenticity of modern being. In *El cuaderno de Blas Coll*, for example,
we read of how Coll declared that the velocity of the earth, that is, natural
rhythms, 'es la mía, la de todos, está escrita en nuestros genes' (*BC*, 82).
Similarly, in his own poetry Montejo frequently uses the motif of blood as a
symbol for the essence of being within us. In 'Una palma' (*TA*), for instance,
the image of the song passed down from generation to generation is replaced
by that of:

> Algo de mis huesos, no sé,
> de la sangre que gota a gota
> y hombre a hombre
> viene rodando desde siglos
> a poblarme. (*TA*, 19)

The resonances with the topos of the generational cycle are evident. But what is added in the image employed in 'La terredad de un pájaro' is the realisation that simply having this essence hidden within is not enough: it must be produced if humankind's separation from nature and, more widely, from its *terredad*, is to be overcome.

The importance of this move is developed in *Alfabeto del mundo*, the collection in which Montejo shifts from concentrating on the *pájaro* towards a more marked focus on the specific example of the *gallo* and its song. The first poem in the collection, 'El canto del gallo', is also the most crucial in setting out the process by which the song emerges. The poem reads:

> El canto está fuera del gallo;
> está cayendo gota a gota entre su cuerpo,
> ahora que duerme en el árbol.
> Bajo la noche cae, no cesa de caer   4
> desde la sombra entre sus venas y sus alas.
> El canto está llenando, incontenible,
> al gallo como un cántaro;
> llena sus plumas, su cresta, sus espuelas,   8
> hasta que lo desborda y suena inmenso el grito
> que a lo largo del mundo sin tregua se derrama.
> Después el aleteo retorna a su reposo
> y el silencio se vuelve compacto.   12
> El canto de nuevo queda fuera
> esparcido a la sombra del aire.
> Dentro del gallo sólo hay vísceras y sueño
> y una gota que cae en la noche profunda,   16
> silenciosamente, al tic-tac de los astros.
>
> (*AM*, 159)

Lines 1–3 bring together both the notion of an essence beyond the individual bird, in which the bird partakes, and that of the bird containing the essence: the song is outside the bird, independent of it, again suggesting that this *terredad* or essential being is common to all of nature, but also gradually fills up the inside of the *gallo*, as though the latter were a water jug, before overflowing and bursting free from the bird–container in an immense 'grito' which reverberates throughout the world. And it is this moment of outpouring beyond the *gallo* and out into the world which is crucial. It is the moment when the essence breaks into the world and takes on form, thus disclosing the cockerel's *canto* as the granting of form to the absent, invisible essence of being. Here, then, we see one of the primary reasons for Montejo's recourse to the specific example of the *gallo*, as opposed to the generic *pájaro*. In focusing on the former Montejo is emphasising the importance of this notion of a breaking forth, an emergence of what is hidden and absent into the visible and present, with the movement of the night breaking out into day represented by the *canto del gallo* acting as an affirmatory and symbolic replaying of the process taking place *within* the bird at this dawn moment.[22]

Nevertheless, even with reference to the *pájaro*, the importance of this bursting forth into form is made apparent in this collection. Indeed, in 'Diciembre' the symbolism of emergence into the tangible is taken further as the poem likens the hatching of a bird's egg to the birth of Christ:

> Aunque diciembre nos cubra de pesebres
> todas las casas,
> ninguno muestra tantas cosas de Dios
> como un nido de pájaros.   4
> Basta mirar cualquiera a la intemperie:
> en su interior José y María,
> con diminutos cuerpos
> resultan siempre más reales,   8
> y en el silencio se entregan a velar
> mientras las ramas mecen compasivas
> el huevo que guarda los cantos.
> [...]
> En vela noche y día,   20
> aguardan que la fuerza que expande la raíz,
> la que muda las hojas y mueve los planetas,
> ascienda por el árbol hasta el nido
> y rompa la cáscara.   24
>
> (*AM*, 192)

The bird to be hatched is understood first and foremost as songs (line 11), essentially seeing it as a producer of the essential song, like the *gallo* in 'El canto del gallo'. Moreover, resonating with Montejo's focus on nature and the earth which we have seen to lie at the heart of his notion of *terredad*, the essence which is to burst out is tied explicitly to the earth and to trees, coursing through all of nature finally to burst (literally) forth in the form of the song-bird (lines 20–4). But, in formulating this moment in terms of birth and, in particular, Christ's birth, this poem underscores the importance of two further, and central, characteristics of the song or *terredad*. Firstly, it points once more to its religious nature: in Christian theology the birth of Christ is the emergence of the divine in earthly form, the Word incarnate. 'Diciembre' thus emphasises the persistent link made by Montejo between the authentic song or language he seeks and the concept of the Logos as it appears in

---

[22] María del Rosario Chacón Ortega offers an alternative reading of the *pájaro* and the *gallo* in Montejo's work, which leaves aside the way in which their respective songs work as part of a single overall schema, declaring that 'Jamás dos cantos han sido tan diferentes' (2000).

Christian thought. Secondly, in the image of birth *per se* Montejo under-lines several key aspects of the song: the emergence of what was absent into presence, nothingness into form; the emergence into (full/waking) life which underscores his presentation of what humankind requires; and, crucially, in the physical breaking of the eggshell, the importance of smashing the boundary between (the) binary terms (in question): dead/alive, absent/present, in/out, recalling once more the attempt to effect such a dismantling of the boundary between these terms in his poems of *caballos* and *café*.

The dominant metaphor for this bursting forth into form nonetheless remains that of the *gallo*, and one of the principal reasons for this is its align-ment with the poet working at night, the time when the *gallo* works towards the production of its task, as we are told in 'El canto del gallo' (*AM*). And it is here that the significance of the central difference between the *gallo* and the *pájaro* in Montejo's work becomes apparent. The *pájaros* are, as we have seen in the quotation from 'Canto lacrado' (*AS*) above, still very much present in the modern urban space, but where they are either no longer perceived as authentic or have in fact lost their authentic song or *terredad*. The *gallos*, however, are absent from the nocturnal cityscape. In effect, the *pájaros* act as metaphors for humankind in general: still here on the earth but devoid of their essential being in the modern world. The *gallo*, on the other hand, represents the poet, the figure who can produce the authentic, poetic song, bringing back the essential *terredad* to all humans. And this figure is absent.

The importance of the poet–*gallo*'s absence is underscored in 'Canto sin gallo' and 'Un gallo' from the later *Partitura de la cigarra*. Picking up the idea found in 'El canto del gallo' (*AM*) that the song 'está fuera del gallo' (*AM*, 159) before dripping into it and then bursting forth, 'Canto sin gallo' describes how this essential song is there even without the *gallo* to give it form:

> Canto sin gallo, pero que se oye,
> canto solo, sin plumas ni animal que lo fabrique,
> canto de un gallo muerto en otro siglo
> que fue dicho una vez y sobrevive
> sin que sepamos dónde ni hasta cuándo. (*PC*, 21)

The poet affirms the mystery of the fact that, even in the modern, urban, capitalist world, empty of the qualities of the quasi-rural homestead, the echo of the song can still be heard:

> No hay campos cerca, sino edificios, ruidos urbanos,
> la religión del dinero con sus máquinas...
> ¿Dónde se esconde el eco de ese canto
> que se quedó sin gallo,
> que no cuenta con patios ni verdores? (21)

The poet does not, then, understand how it can be that there are still echoes, but ends by affirming that this pure song is very much still reverberating around on the earth:

> Canto sin gallo que no requiere plumas
> ni terrestre alimento para su forma,
> que no necesita estrellas para expandirse.
> Canto puro, cortante, con su grito
> venido de más allá del gallo,
> canto que atravesó su cuerpo,
> se valió de su noche, su garganta,
> y con su furia se quedó en la tierra
> emparedado dentro de sus ecos. (21)

The song *did* emerge into the world from the body and throat of a *gallo*, as described in 'El canto del gallo' (*AM*). And that, it seems, is enough, with Carrillo T., for example, seeing the *gallo* in Montejo's verse as 'el elemento de la naturaleza que se niega a morir a pesar del avance de la modernidad' in that 'su canto, más bien el eco de éste, se resiste' (2005: 25). Yet in referring to the song which is left as echoes, the poem also suggests an underlying problematic of this presentation. The image with which the poem ends of the song being walled in by its own echoes chimes with several aspects of Montejo's poetics. For one, it inscribes the authentic song back into an image of being contained, of not breaking the boundary separating it from the outside. Likewise, the fact that the song is present as – and trapped in – its echoes ineluctably taps into the notion of the Fall from the (poetic) Word into language: echoes are an endless chain of signifiers which stand for the absence of that which they signify, the absence of, in this case, the original Logos. Indeed, these final lines of the poem resonate with the image in the earlier 'De Sobremesa' of 'la billaresca charla | de voces que rebotan contra el tiempo' (*AM*, 202), an image which describes precisely how language acts as an echo, standing for the absence of that which it represents, in this case the dead who are seemingly talking in the scene in the poem.

Despite its affirmations to the contrary, 'Canto sin gallo' thus ends by disclosing the insufficiency of a single production of the poetic song. The result of this is simply the entrapment of the song in the echoes of itself, that is, in language. But what the poem does stress is that, even if it is in the echoes of itself, the song *is* there. What it both discloses and explains, then, is the primary importance which we have seen throughout Montejo's *gallo*–night poems not of locating the song, but of locating a *gallo*, that is, a poet, who can take these floating echoes, allow them to go *within* himself in order to then produce them in and as the essential song/*terredad*, just like the *gallo* in 'El canto del gallo' (*AM*). This is, moreover, the central theme of 'Un gallo' (*PC*), where Montejo declares that 'Me queda un gallo por oír – y no ha cantado' (*PC*, 30). It is 'El más oculto, quizás, el más incierto | de los gallos del mundo. Y no ha cantado' (30). The suggestion is that this refers to the hoped-for return of the poetic – Orphic – *gallo*, a suggestion reinforced by the following lines, which talk of how 'Aún no sé para cuándo estaba escrito, | sobre el infolio de cuál noche' (30), and by the poet's later affirmation that 'Es sólo un grito suyo lo que espero, | una gota en el aceite de mi lámpara' (30).[23] This *gallo*, then, would be the poet himself who, working at night, would take on the challenge of the night to grasp the echoing, hidden song of 'Canto sin gallo' (*PC*), and give it form in the flash of the *grito*:

> Me queda por oír un gallo todavía,
> inubicable en la extensión silente,
> un gallo con el peso de la noche en sus alas,
> casi un relámpago. (30)

And yet, as the image of the searching poet underscores, whilst the song in Montejo's '*gallo*–poetry' is there to be internalised and then brought out into the world, the *terredad* thus assumed, the essential problem remains the lack of a *gallo*/poet who can do so. In short, in being 'tartamudeante y roto y solitario' ('Orfeo revisitado', *AM*, 169), Orpheus – the poet – is, in fact, absent in the sense that he is no longer Orpheus. The task, then, is for the poet to be an authentic, Orphic poet – a *gallo* – once more.

Of course, in affirming this alignment of the Orphic poet and the absent *gallo*, it would seem that we are falling back into the problematic outlined earlier on, namely that the emergence of the *canto del gallo* signals the end of the poetic time, and, so, the end of the hope for a more ontological awakening which combines the day and the night, present and absent. That is, it signals not the shattering of the separation between night and day, but simply the move from one side of the binary to the other, in contrast to the emphasis Montejo places on finding '*en el fondo de la noche* | [...] | un gallo que simplemente cante' ('Nocturno', *AM*, 187, italics mine). Yet, beyond both the simple move into the day and the impossible producing of the song in the night, the poems in *Alfabeto del mundo* and *Partitura de la cigarra* that

---

[23] In this mention of the poet's lamp – a recurrent motif in Montejo's poetry as we have seen – as being an oil lamp, Montejo further aligns his use of this image with Bachelard's discussion referenced earlier (1962: 89–105). Bachelard draws a sharp comparison between the electric lamp and the oil lamp, declaring: 'L'ampoule électrique ne nous donnera jamais les rêveries de cette lampe vivante qui, avec de l'huile, faisait de la lumière' (90). The oil lamp is both conducive to the poetic imagination and grants a sense of closeness and company, both with it and with the objects remembered and dreamt of as one sits by its light. The modern electric lamp, by contrast, is capable of none of this. Montejo's mention here, then, of his lamp as an oil lamp both symbolises his reaction against modernity and the neon lights of the city and speaks of the poetic oneness with things – with the world surrounding him – which he desires.

I have been discussing also point repeatedly to the fact that this song is authentic at – and only at – the very moment of irruption, the very moment of the breaking of the boundary, the overflowing into form. After that, as we are told in 'El canto del gallo' (*AM*), there is silence as the *gallo* prepares once more for this instant:

> Después el aleteo retorna a su reposo.
> [...]
> El canto de nuevo queda fuera. (*AM*, 159)

Likewise, then, the final reference in 'Un gallo' (*PC*) to the song as 'casi un relámpago' (*PC*, 30). Recurring frequently in Montejo's verse, this *relámpago* is the key: the momentary spark of inspiration and authenticity which serves both further to link Montejo's poetics to Heidegger's concept of the poet as 'exposed to the divine lightnings' (1968a: 308) and also to centre his work on the *instant* of poetic creation in contrast both to the silence that precedes it and the echoes of (plain) language which follow. Indeed, this is precisely what Montejo's heteronym Lino Cervantes aims at in the appropriately titled *La caza del relámpago*, where, in each of his poems, a single initial line of verse is reduced in each subsequent line until, in the final line of each poem, just one syllable remains. As Montejo says, in this poetic project we see 'la ambición de limpiar los confusos ecos del trueno para darle caza alguna vez al fugitivo relámpago' (*CR*, 183), as the poetry seeks to effect a reversal of the rippling echoes of language.

That this is a central facet of Montejo's vision and understanding of the *canto del gallo* is emphasised by his description in interview in 1999, shortly before the publication of *Partitura de la cigarra*, of just how he recalls the *canto del gallo* from his past:

> De niño, ante ese animal tan extraño, yo me hacía la pregunta de por qué cantaba. Un animal que se despierte de madrugada, dé un solo grito, un solo aletazo, y se vuelva a quedar dormido, siempre me pareció una cosa misteriosa. (López Ortega 1999: 11)

This is the nature of the birdsong of the apparently Edenic and authentic childhood locale: a fleeting, momentary song which is impossible to hold onto. Moreover, the identification of the *gallo*'s song as this ephemeral flash bursting out into form, points to a general understanding of (authentic) being in Montejo's poetics as just such a border moment.

The border moment

In order to appreciate the importance – and nature – of the border at stake in Montejo's presentation of being, we need first to turn to *El hacha de seda*, where Tomás Linden, whose name itself implies the liminal, describes life as an 'errar [...] | entre dos nadas, solo y sin retorno' ('Una vida', *HS*, 23). The 'dos nadas' referred to here are those of pre-birth and post-death, and this formulation constitutes the most explicit summary of how Montejo's own poetry frequently presents our existence. Both of these 'nadas' assume important roles in Montejo's imaginary. In 'La tierra giró para acercarnos' (*AM*), for example, the poet describes the essential, natural rhythms and harmony of the world, alluding, at one point, to how 'Un gallo cantó lejos del mundo, | en la previda a menos mil de nuestros padres' (*AM*, 201). The essential song is here placed in the 'nada' which precedes life, which is where Montejo also locates the essential vision and understanding of the world in the later poem 'Pasaporte de otoño' (*AS*). Here, he defines the perception and living of this essence of nature to which he aspires as a recovery of the (in)sight he had in this *previda*:

> contemplar la profunda belleza de todo;   10
> la verdad de una luz alzando el aire
> donde rostros y seres y cosas flotaran;
> alzándome los ojos para ver un instante
> lo bello intacto en cada gota de materia,   14
> lo bello cara a cara en su fuerza terrestre;
> no sólo en una flor, una doncella, en todo:
> – la profunda belleza de todo,
> con la misma visión que tuve en mi previda   18
> y me alumbró ya no sé dónde hasta nacer,
> como tal vez nunca se alcance en este mundo
> aunque por siglos nos aplacen la muerte. (*AS*, 12)

The 'nada' or absence of the *previda* and, by implication, post-death (line 21) appears thus synonymous with the absent essence or song which Montejo seeks. It is, in brief, the lost essence, the ontological home from which the poet – and humanity – has been torn.

Accordingly, and in contrast to Montejo's desire to bring the dead into presence or to (re)appropriate the absent into the language of the poem, there are several moments in Montejo's poetry where his language reveals a simple desire to return to the absence found in this authentic *previda* home and in the other 'nada' of post-death. One of the most striking poems in this regard is 'Las aldeas' (*AP*), which envisages the return to the quasi-rural habitat of the past as where:

> Vuelven los gallos, los mismos de hace siglos
> a aletear otra vez en el patio
> apagando las llamas del tiempo
> y la noche cae al fondo y me cubre
> con sus cantos donde todo es ausencia. (*AP*, 10)

The process of loss effected by time ends and all is subsumed into the poetic night with its *cantos* (of the *gallos*) located and produced, but where this is equated with a return to absence, that is, to the absence prior and subsequent to life.

This desire to return to absence certainly goes hand in hand with a desire to avoid the problematics of losing the essence in language, in form, as we have seen in 'De sobremesa' (*AM*), where the poet laments that it is 'como si tanta ausencia viniera a decir algo | que la vida convierte en otra cosa' (*AM*, 202). And, in its formulation as, in effect, a return from 'alienated existence to the "resolution" of death' (Franco 1976: 42), it constitutes a reminder of the overtly Romantic characteristics of Montejo's verse.[24] But Montejo's development of the *canto del gallo* motif, with the primacy of what I have termed the 'border moment', undermines this solution, as is made particularly evident in 'Ida y vuelta' from *Alfabeto del mundo*. The poem begins by sketching out a scene of familial and community spirit, a return to 'mi casa' and the quasi-rural habitat of the early poetry. Indeed, it is a scene which, in many ways, portrays the hoped-for bringing together of the living and the dead which I examined in chapter 1:

> Ahora mi casa gira en otro tiempo;
> llegan desde sus soledades los ausentes
> a reunirse en el salón, cerca del patio.
> [...]
> ¿Quién ha traído guitarras y licores
> si no es un día de fiesta? – Llegan más visitantes
> desde la vecindad de las haciendas. (*AM*, 180)

The first of the two stanzas then ends by suggesting that this scene is taking place in the space of the *previda*, as we are told that 'Cuando el gallo cante en su hora infinita | nacerá alguno de nosotros' (180), before the poet describes how 'Aguardo el grito y sin embargo me adormezco' (180). When he awakes, he discovers it was his own birth, with the scene of the first stanza now just 'polvo inasible' (180). Significantly, though, it is not the lost scene of the *previda* which the poet wants to recover, but the moment of birth which he

---

[24] This characteristic of Romanticism as the desire for a return to the peace of death following the separation of life, symbolised by the Fall, is expounded upon at some length in Abrams (1971: 141–252).

missed, and he ends by stressing his desire to be awake for and to live this moment when it next comes:

> Cuando de nuevo cante el gallo
> no sé qué puede sucederme.
> Debo permanecer despierto. (180)

This missed border moment, then, again linked with the *canto del gallo*, is the authentic being and locale which the poet seeks. Moreover, that its next occurrence could be (the poet's) death is suggested in the title of the poem itself: life as the leaving from and moving back towards this border moment of being.

It is, however, in *El cuaderno de Blas Coll* that we see the most important engagement with these ideas. In one of the later additions to the *cuaderno*, we find Coll describing the border moment as an irreducible tension between nothingness and the material, that is, form, stating that:

> El cuerpo quiere disolverse en la nada, no tiene otra salida, va hacia allá. La nada, por su parte, aunque menos aparente nos resulte constatarlo, procura también a todo trance hacerse corpórea, llegar a ser un cuerpo, vestirse de efímera materia. (*BC*, 94)

Onto this image we can map the moments of death and birth respectively and understand how each mirrors the other. But Coll then goes on to explain exactly how we fit into this tension, underscoring in the process that such a border moment is not confined just to these two loci, but is a determinant moment of being *per se*:

> En medio de ambas tensiones tiene lugar nuestra existencia, en medio de ambas nos encontramos, mirándolo todo, contemplando cómo ambas nos toman por escenario, reconociéndonos, en fin, el eje, el punto axial donde estas opuestas corrientes se tocan, nosotros que propiamente no somos ni cuerpo ni nada, sino un fugacísimo punto de cruce. (94)[25]

Our authentic being is neither 'cuerpo' nor 'nada', neither form nor essence, presence nor absence, but a flash where these two cross. This border moment, then, is not simply at birth and at death: it is met – and lost – constantly. That is to say, we are a constant 'fugacísimo punto de cruce'. Furthermore, given that, as we saw in chapter 2, we are (our) language, this notion thus helps

[25] This stands out as probably the most crucial fragment of the book. Significantly, it is also described as the one which Montejo, as editor of Coll's *cuaderno*, had most trouble transcribing, and which, even then, remains 'distante del original' (*BC*, 94). This difficulty underscores the impossibility of grasping this border moment.

provide us with a framework for understanding the glimpsing and then losing of this authentic being in language and in the language of the poet working at his night-time task. Montejo's editorial notes on his transcription of this fragment state that:

> En su raro e intraducible fragmento a la vez que leemos lo que he copiado arriba inferimos también que el lenguaje, representación por antonomasia de la vida, participa de una y otra, al modo de un efímero punto de unión. (95)

The synonymity of the phrases 'efímero punto de unión' and 'fugacísimo punto de cruce' once more stresses the identification of being with language; but, most significantly, it thus discloses that where language is at this authentic 'cruce', so too are we, hence underscoring why the poetic task is to place, assume, and maintain both language and humankind at this border point.

Poetry and nature

Aside from underscoring the importance of the border moment as the point of authentic being, participating in both essence and form, Coll also engages explicitly with the image of the *gallo* and its *canto*, referring in Mallarméan terms to the poet's need to put into effect 'el arte de purificar las palabras [...] devolverlas al relámpago de su primer grito' (*BC*, 83), as he affirms the role of the *gallo*: 'El gallo, el gran purificador de los sonidos de su especie, canta siempre con el mítico asombro de la primera vez' (83). Once again, his words here are illuminating. The idea of the border moment of language as this 'primer grito' has strong echoes of Derrida's discussion of 'une parole [...] [qui] ne serait pas une parole: elle se tendrait à la limite fictive du cri inarticulé et purement naturel' (1967c: 443–4). For Derrida, this theoretical limit–speech is a speech 'sans principe consonantique (1967c: 443), and significantly, in Montejo's work this is precisely how not just the *canto del gallo* is presented, but nature more widely. In 'Práctica del mundo' from *Trópico absoluto* we read: 'Relata el sueño de tu vida | con las lentas vocales de las nubes' (*TA*, 31); in 'Las ranas' from *Alfabeto del mundo*, of the croaking toads the poet states that 'En su alfabeto percibo una sola vocal' (*AM*, 199); and in *El cuaderno de Blas Coll* itself we are told that 'lo más hermoso del viento entre los árboles es que, a su paso, prefiera hablar sin ninguna consonante, que sólo se sirva de vocales azules' (*BC*, 64). Moreover, vowels are also presented as constituting the essential being of ourselves, as, in 'Quita a la piedra que soy' from *Terredad*, the poet expresses his desire to be revealed authentically saying:

> lee las vocales de mi cuerpo
> las palabras que buscan la vida
> al fondo, venidas desde lejos, las que estallan
> en el sueño. (*T*, 53)

And in *El cuaderno de Blas Coll* Coll explicitly links vowels to the other
central cipher for this border time of authenticity: the time of infancy, as
he declares, 'Y nada digamos del mágico color de las vocales, ese vívido
color de nuestra infancia, tan prontamente reprimido' (*BC*, 72). In short, what
Coll's and Montejo's words spell out is that, beyond the song of the *gallo*,
this (vocalic) *grito*, which is the authentic language linked with infancy and
the essence of (our) being, is that of nature as a whole.

Importantly, though, Montejo's work here is not simply referring to the
language produced by nature, but, as befits the conflation of language and
being at the moment of authenticity, is speaking of the whole of nature being
understood *as* a language, as a constant *grito*, a constant authentic border.
This is confirmed on a number of occasions in *El cuaderno de Blas Coll*.
In a fragment dating from the first edition (1981), for example, we are told
of Coll's statement that 'la naturaleza es taquigráfica' (*BC*, 46), and, in a
fragment added in the 1998 edition, that 'la materia conocida y por conocer
constituye en sí misma todo un alfabeto' (*BC*, 93). Furthermore, that this is to
be understood as the border moment is suggested in the earlier poem 'Si Dios
no se moviera tanto' from *Terredad*, where the poet's desire to be one with
nature is described as to 'palpar el paisaje | con el tacto del Génesis' (*T*, 16).

The most important poem in this regard, however, is the title poem of the
collection *Alfabeto del mundo*, with which the later Coll quotation dialogues.
In this poem, our distance from (a oneness with) nature is firmly portrayed
as a separation of our language (and, hence, selves) from the language that
is nature, resulting in the latter's being a language we simply cannot understand. The poet sees this language all around him, but its meaning is lost,
with the modern, urban present once more connected to the separation from
nature-as-language: 'Leo en las piedras un oscuro sollozo, | ecos ahogados en
torres y edificios' (*AM*, 166). The whole world, all that is *materia*, including
people, is a language, but one which the poet cannot read:

> Cuando el tahúr, el pícaro, la adúltera,
> los mártires del oro o del amor
> son sólo signos que no he leído bien. (166)

This presentation of the world evidently taps into the tradition of the world,
or Nature, as a Book, God's Book, found in particular in the Middle Ages,
as well as in writers and thinkers such as Galileo, Novalis, and Descartes.[26]

---

[26] The topos of the Book of Nature has been the subject of numerous scholarly works.

But its appearance in Montejian thought is especially resonant with that of Mallarmé and his famous declaration: 'le monde est fait pour aboutir à un beau livre' (Huret 1999 [1891]: 107).[27] For Montejo, the alphabet of the world is just that: an alphabet, signs, that are to be read, understood, and written by the poet. It is, then, this act of transforming nature into human writing that at once both renders nature comprehensible and incorporates humans/human language into its language and rhythms once more. This is the message which emerges throughout this poem, even as the failure of the poet to do so is declared:

> En vano me demoro deletreando
> el alfabeto del mundo.
> [...]
> indago la tierra por el tacto
> llena de ríos, paisajes y colores,
> pero al copiarlos siempre me equivoco.
> Necesito escribir ciñéndome a una raya
> sobre el libro del horizonte.
> Dibujar el milagro de esos días
> que flotan envueltos en la luz
> y se desprenden en cantos de pájaros.
> [...]
> [...] signos que no he leído bien,
> que aún no logro anotar en mi cuaderno.
> Cuánto quisiera al menos un instante
> que esta plana febril de poesía
> grabe en su transparencia cada letra:
> la o del ladrón, la t del santo
> el gótico diptongo del cuerpo y su deseo,
> con la misma escritura del mar en las arenas,
> la misma cósmica piedad
> que la vida despliega ante mis ojos. (*AM*, 166)

See, for example, Curtius (1967: 319–27). Derrida has also covered this topos from a deconstructionist standpoint both in *De la grammatologie* (1967c: 15–41) and in *La Dissémination* (1972b: 51–67), where he begins by outlining the way in which Nature was thus conceived in Medieval times as 'Livre de Dieu, [...] une graphie conforme à la pensée et à la parole divines, à l'*entendement* de Dieu comme Logos, vérité qui parle et s'écoute parler [...]. Écriture représentative et vraie, adéquate à son modèle et à elle-même, la Nature était aussi une totalité ordonnée, le volume d'un livre lourd de sens, se donnant à lire, ce qui doit vouloir dire à entendre, comme une parole, d'entendement à entendement' (51–2). The presentation of Nature as a book both to be read and heard chimes with its Montejian portrayal.

[27] It is worth noting that Mallarmé, in an earlier letter to Verlaine, describes how he understands this book as 'l'explication orphique de la Terre, qui est le seul devoir du poëte et le jeu littéraire par excellence' (1965: 301). Once again, we see how a metaphor employed by Montejo in the search for an authentic poetic language and being sends us back to the figure of Orpheus.

This idea of the writing down of the language which is nature as a potential way of bringing about the authentic, border song of humanity, and thus returning its *terredad*, proves to be one of the most persistent methodologies for an achieving of the poetic task in Montejo's work. It determines his depiction of the poet's separation from nature not just in 'Alfabeto del mundo', but in the earlier 'Los árboles' (*AP*), and numerous times in texts dating from the first edition of *El cuaderno de Blas Coll*. On each occasion, the desire to write the language of nature is described using the term 'anotar', a verb which thus serves to link these references in a common lexical web. In 'Alfabeto del mundo' the poet talks of the signs of the world that 'aún no logro anotar en mi cuaderno' (*AM*, 166), and in 'Los árboles', the poet hears the 'grito | de un tordo negro', understanding that 'en su voz hablaba un árbol, | uno de tantos', before ending by declaring that 'pero no sé qué hacer con ese grito, | no sé cómo anotarlo' (*AP*, 7). But it is in *El cuaderno de Blas Coll* that we see the most detailed exposition of this notion, and one which provides a key to understanding the problematics which finally befall this attempt at reasserting our place with and as part of nature.

That this act of 'anotar' represents the desire to make our language one with (that of) nature is highlighted by the final fragments in the first edition of the book. The text recounts three separate annotations by Coll written on three different types of leaves: 'una hoja de banano', 'una hoja de almendrón', and 'una hoja de malanga' (*BC*, 64–5). Montejo, in his capacity as editor, informs us that 'también las hojas de las plantas sirvieron a Don Blas para anotar sus pensamientos' (64). By this method, Coll can be seen to be trying to effect a merging of human writing with the writing of nature, in this case the 'writing' of the leaves, that is, the pattern of their veins, and what Montejo later refers to in 'En las hojas' (*AM*) as 'nervaduras ilegibles' (*AM*, 165). Indeed, the suggestion is that something along the lines of this merging has taken place over the course of the years, with Montejo informing us that 'en las [...] [hojas] los trazos de su caligrafía ya muestran con los años cierta opacidad ferruginosa' (*BC*, 64–5). What is more, this merging is also implied by what Montejo tells us about what Coll wrote on the banana leaf:

> Una hoja de banano por ejemplo, doblada en cuadros diminutos, da cuenta, pese al deterioro de su materia marchita, de lo que probablemente fue un largo apunte sobre Humboldt. No he podido esclarecer si se trataba de Alejandro, el sabio que recorrió nuestros trópicos, o de su hermano Guillermo, el famoso lingüista, o bien ambos a la vez. Sólo el apellido resalta nítido en el envés de la hoja. (65)

The significance of this uncertainty as to which brother is talked of on the leaf points to precisely the fusion of nature (as language) and (human) language which Coll, along with Montejo, desires: Alejandro von Humboldt

(1769–1859), the traveller, is inextricably linked to nature, and, specifically, the nature of Latin America, including Venezuela,[28] whereas Wilhelm von Humboldt (1767–1835) is, as a linguist, representative of 'language'. The fact that both brothers, symbolising nature and language respectively, are made indistinguishable, fused into and conveyed by the same single word, 'Humboldt', both mirrors and reveals the significance of the merging of Coll's writing with the (writing of the) leaf itself: they must be one and the same, and the writing found on the banana leaf plays this out on every level.

And yet the opacity of the writing here points towards an underlying failure, not least in its echoes of the illegible *cartas* and epitaphs of the tombs of the dead in 'Cementerio de Vaugirard' (*MM*). The reasons for this failure are both ethical and linguistic. The ethical dilemma is brought out by what appears to be the most affirmative of fragments both in *El cuaderno de Blas Coll* and, more generally, in Montejo's production as a whole as regards this noting down of (the language of) nature. In both 'Los árboles' (*AP*) and 'Alfabeto del mundo' (*AM*) Montejo presents the failure of the poet faithfully to 'anotar' (the language of) nature. But in *El cuaderno de Blas Coll*, Montejo transcribes a fragment in which Coll proclaims that he has managed just such a task:

> ... muchos soles soporté oyendo el viento entre las piedras, el chasquido del agua en los acantilados. Fijaba, antes de irme, un cartel a la puerta de mi tipografía: 'Volveré tarde. Salí a buscar una vocal'. De noche, entre las lluvias torrenciales, prestaba toda la atención posible a los diferentes timbres de las gotas en las hojas, y así por años, sin avanzar un palmo en mi propósito. Fue en el crujido de una palma desolada donde por primera vez la advertí. Me hizo el efecto de la cuerda de un violín sumergido que se rompe. *La anoté al instante* con gran contento de mi hallazgo y *la repetí* durante varios años *hasta hacerla mía del todo*. (*BC*, 49–50, italics mine)

Here, then, Coll *does* manage to note down the sound. But what is the result of this? He repeats it for many years, but not in the same way as the *canto del gallo* is the 'eterna melodía siempre nueva' (*GH*, 27) in its repetition every day, 'siempre con el mítico asombro de la primera vez' (*BC*, 83), recalling the repeated re-creation of the poetic spider in 'Mi vivir es araña en la tela del poema' (*É*) who 'salta de lo vacío y enhebro el recomienzo' (*É*, 37). Rather, he repeats it until it is totally his. In short, the repetition serves to inscribe the sound within a power dialectic, enabling him to master the language of nature, to control it, and to own it, until, finally, it is subsumed into him, made

---

[28] Alejandro von Humboldt was on expedition in Latin America between 1799 and 1804, visiting and exploring several countries, including Venezuela, which was his first port of call on 16 July 1799. He left Venezuela on 24 November 1799.

'safe'.[29] Far from a simple oneness with nature, then, Coll merely asserts the self as he 'humanises' (the language of) nature, leaving behind its essence once again.

Moreover, the repetition which reveals these power dynamics is also tied in with the inherent linguistic problematics of the move to 'anotar', underlining once more that the move into language *per se* involves what Derrida refers to as 'iterability', that is, the possibility of repetition and *différance*. The border moment, then, is immediately lost, subsumed into language, rendered an echo, no different from the echoes of language which populate the city-scape in Montejo's poetry. And this is precisely what emerges from the fate of the vowel which Coll discovers. The symbol that Coll writes down to stand for this sound – an act already laying bare the move into *écriture* and the elision of the sound in and as itself – is, we are told in editions from 1998 onwards, '$\odot$' (Montejo 2006c: 25).[30] But, as Montejo comments, the exact pronunciation of this natural vowel, 'nos es por desgracia desconocida' (49). All there are are vague clues that 'era un sonido oscuro, como el de una "u" nasalizada y algo más aguda' (49). One is left to wonder what the actual value is of the act of writing down the sound of nature – the move so privileged by both Coll and Montejo – when it proves incapable of transmitting anything about that sound, that is, when it is shown instantly to lose that which it seeks to represent. But the ineluctable implications of this writing down are also underlined by the differences between the first and more recent editions of the text. In the first edition the typographical symbol used by Coll is, we are told, '@' (Montejo 1981: 39). Dating from a time prior to the internet and email, for non-English-speakers this symbol had no usage in everyday language. But in the years between this edition and the more recent editions this symbol has been subsumed by language, given a value, overwhelming and drowning out the natural sound it was originally intended to suggest. So Montejo, searching for a sign which has no sound in human language, is forced to rewrite the symbol as '$\odot$', even as the fate of '@' speaks ines-capably of how *any* symbol in being used to denote a sound is immediately rendered (human) language.

Beyond these problematics, however, the terms employed by Coll also point us once more towards a central characteristic of the authentic, natural language sought: the *gallo* sings with 'el mítico asombro de la primera vez' (*BC*, 83), and the discovery of the natural vowel had for Coll 'un efecto mítico' (49). Read from a Derridean perspective, this could be seen as a

---

[29] This ethical move recalls Levinas's depiction of the desire of the Self to kill the Other (1971: 216).

[30] The most recent edition (2007) lacks this sign. It appears to be a typographical error, since the sentence requires some symbol at this point in order to make sense. Nevertheless, its lack speaks eloquently of the impossibility of writing (the essence of) the language of nature.

revelation of the impossibility of the quest to locate – or annotate – the authentic border moment, underscoring that it is just a necessary product (or fiction) of language and our own minds. Yet within Montejo's and Coll's production, as we have seen, its acknowledged value as mythic, as an ungraspable moment (of song) which must be sought in poetry is precisely wherein lies its allure.

4

Venezuelan Alienation
and the Poetic Construction of Home

If a sense of general alienation and separation from nature and the earth forms a central part of Montejo's poetics, it is nevertheless important to note that, as with the concern for temporal loss, the setting against which this lamentation is played out is specifically that of a Venezuelan poet in Venezuelan *paisajes*, with the latter representing tropical and American landscapes more widely. Consequently, there is a need to understand that Montejo's poetics is concerned not simply with the human condition, but also with the specificities of the Venezuelan condition. It is on this aspect of Montejo's work that I shall focus in this final chapter.[1]

Journeys, exile, and Venezuela

Certainly, Montejo's presentation of humankind's distance from the natural world runs parallel to the notion of a distance from Venezuela. In 'Las cigarras' from *Algunas palabras*, for example, Montejo lauds and affirms cicadas and their song before declaring that 'sería terrible morir en una tierra | donde no vuelvan las cigarras' (*AP*, 33). The ubiquitousness of cicadas in the poet's homeland identifies the specific locale in question here and thus points up the fear of being and remaining distant from Venezuela. Yet, despite the fear highlighted in this early poem, from *Muerte y memoria* onwards Montejo's poetry is replete not only with poems which describe the Venezuelan poet as indeed being distant from his land, but also with poems which focus longingly on foreign places. To name just a few examples: we find the poet in Paris in 'Cementerio de Vaugirard' (*MM*); in *Algunas palabras* he provides a solemn description of the River Thames in 'Támesis' and desires to go to Iceland in 'Islandia'; and from *Trópico absoluto* on there are numerous poems placing the poet in, or talking about being in, Lisbon, a place for

---

[1] Some limited elements of this chapter and the conclusion are also to be found in Roberts (2006).

which he displays a strong affinity, including 'Lisboa ya lejos' (*TA*), 'Lisboa' (*AS*), and 'Pavana de Lisboa' (*FE*).

Many of these poems and places link back to Montejo's own experiences: Montejo lived in Paris from 1968 to 1971 and was Venezuela's cultural attaché in Lisbon from 1988 to 1994. The predominant element in these poems, however, is not so much being in foreign places as the act of travelling to and from them, thus tying in with the understanding of life as an 'errar entre dos nadas' ('Una vida', *HS*, 23).[2] Indeed, the journey in question is frequently described as a wandering, and usually at sea, and this serves to bind up this travelling with the notion of exile, a point emphasised explicitly by the time of *Alfabeto del mundo* in poems such as 'Ítaca' and 'Ulises'. In the latter, for instance, the poet declares that:

> Soy o fui Ulises, alguna vez todos lo somos;
> después la vida nos hurga el equipaje
> y a ciegas muda los sueños y las máscaras.
> Mi corazón ya leva el ancla. Estoy a bordo.
> Cuando distinga la voz de las sirenas
> en altamar, al otro lado de las islas,
> sabré por fin qué queda en mí de Ulises. (*AM*, 182)

Each human being replays the exilic wandering of the archetypal Ulysses, even if life causes us to lose sight of the purpose of this wandering: the idea of a return to or reaching of home and an attendant understanding of who we are in essence.

In highlighting these related topoi of journeying and exile, Montejo's *œuvre* emphasises its engagement with the biography and work of a variety of poetic figures from both Europe and Latin America. On the one hand, there are echoes of Saint-John Perse, of Pessoa's heteronym Alberto Caeiro, and, once more, of Cernuda, not least in that all three poets incorporate American shores into their poetry and experience of exile, whilst, within Latin American poetics, the thematics of journeying and exile can scarcely be talked about without at least a passing reference to Neruda, although, in Montejo's case, as will become apparent, it is the Colombian poet Álvaro Mutis whose life and work provides a more immediately pertinent model, in its focus on both (personal) exile and, notably, journeying, in the wandering seafaring experiences of the heteronym Maqroll el Gaviero.[3] Nevertheless,

---

2   Poems of journeying and travelling abound in Montejo's collections from *Muerte y memoria* onwards. To name just a few examples: 'El viaje' (*MM*); 'Trenes nocturnos' (*AP*); 'Mudanzas' (*T*); 'Forastero' (*TA*); 'Viajes' (*AM*); 'Noches de transatlántico' (*AS*); and 'Visto y no visto' (*PC*).

3   Montejo frequently referred to Mutis as an influence (for example, Cruz (2006: 373)) and Maqroll el Gaviero is referred to specifically as a figure in Tomás Linden's life (*HS*, 13), as

the most dominant poetic model of exile is an autochthonous one, in the form
of the Venezuelan poet Leoncio Martínez's 'Balada del preso insomne', on
which Montejo wrote in some detail (2006b: 263–72), identifying its poetic
and historical importance in Venezuela in describing it as 'un poema epocal'
(267). Likewise, as I have suggested, the principal setting for Montejo's
poems which are centred around or describe journeys is one where Venezuela
comes to be identified with the land from which the poet has departed or
to which he returns or desires to return. This is made evident both in the
Venezuelan identity of the journeying poetic *yo* and in the alignment between
the journeys described and those undertaken by Montejo himself. Put simply,
the general terms in which the exilic journey of life is couched in 'Ítaca' and
'Ulises' emerge from a poetics whose presentation of that exilic journey is
built around the example of Venezuela.

An initial glimpse of this is found in 'Altamar' (*AP*), a poem alluded to
in the lines cited from 'Ulises', and which, together with 'Navegaciones' and
'Dormir' from the same collection, demonstrates the early attention given to
sea journeys. The poem concerns a journey on the Atlantic ocean towards
Europe. The impression is of an endless journey at sea where the destination
seems never to be reached: 'Vamos enfermos de llegar, | de no llegar en tantos
días de mar adentro' (*AP*, 17). But the point of origin – America, possibly
Venezuela, one imagines – is also denied and unreachable. In a line pivotal
to the exilic understanding of the journey thematic in Montejo's work, the
'estela' of the boat in which the poet and his companions are travelling is
described as one which 'crece y nos destierra' (17), a trail which peters out
and exiles the poet, leading not to origins, but to the open expanse of the sea.
In short, all knowledge and attaining of the land is denied as the poet ruefully
states that 'nada se sabe aquí del mundo' (17).

In the following collection, *Terredad*, this playing out of the theme of exile
in terms of an exile from Venezuela is then made more explicit. Taking up
where the poem 'Támesis' (*AP*) left off, 'En el norte' (*T*) describes the poet
in England looking out over the Thames, acutely aware of the distance of his
Venezuelan homeland, a distance measured not only in miles but in time and
physical and meteorological contrast:

> Es la noche, resguárdate,
> grita el reloj cerca del polo,
> pero a esta hora mi país de ultramar
> cruza el arco del sol
> y se baten azules las palmas. (*T*, 31)

---

well as providing a possible model for Blas Coll's exilic, wandering journey from the Canary
Islands to Puerto Malo.

Once again, the focus of the poem moves onto the sea which separates the poet from his home:

> Entre estas islas y mi casa
> caben todas las aguas por siglos de este río,
> el gris invierno de paredes rectas,
> los vientos que nos tornan monosilábicos
> y quedan leguas que llenar para acercarse. (31)

In depicting the physical distance covered by the sea as a space filled up by the water which has flowed through the River Thames 'por siglos', Montejo neatly brings together both the temporal loss which he laments in his poetry and this physical exile, demonstrating the interconnectedness of these thematics in his work: being abroad, the homeland (*casa*) is felt as distant in the same way as the homestead (*casa*) of his childhood is mourned as lost. Likewise, just as the poet feels out of place and alone in a mechanised and urbanised modern world devoid of the poetic (*gallos*, the natural, the rural), so too does he feel *desfasado* in this northern land:

> Esta noche soy diurno frente al Támesis,
> no voy a bordo en sus vagones,
> sigo de pie con el silencio de una palma.
> Mi país de ultramar resplandece a lo lejos
> y yo cuento sus horas
> en relojes perdidos más allá del Atlántico.
>
> Su ausencia es mi único equipaje. (31–2)

Perhaps the most significant line of this poem, however, is this last one. It constitutes one of four such references in Montejo's mid-period poetry. In 'Paisajes' (*AP*) the poet talks of the Venezuelan *paisajes* which have surrounded him during his life, declaring that 'son los paisajes que llevo a otras ciudades, | valijas leves, impalpables' (*AP*, 35). Then in 'Las piedras' (*T*) the stones of and around the Venezuelan rivers where the poets used to play as a child are described in a similar way:

> De tarde en tarde la sombra de un avión
> en que partimos
> las atraviesa [las piedras]
> y no saben que van en las valijas
> a bordo, que son nuestro único equipaje. (*T*, 48–9)

Finally, 'Yo también soy Orinoco' (*TA*) has the poet talking of the Orinoco river in Venezuela, and how:

por donde viajo llevo su extenso horizonte
doblado en mis valijas,
lo despliego en remotas aduanas. (*TA*, 35)

The description of these three synecdochic markers of Venezuela as the poet's (only) luggage acts as a comment on the fact that both his personal identity and all that he holds dear when in foreign lands is (reducible to) his homeland. Yet in aligning them with 'su ausencia' (*T*, 32) in 'En el norte' Montejo is not just alluding to how, when away from home, the homeland is carried around as that which is absent and pined after, but, crucially, drawing attention to an inherent characteristic of these markers of home: their absence *per se*.

The implications of this are initially taken up in 'Retorno de las islas' from *Terredad*. Following on from 'En el norte', this poem seems to describe the journey back from the British Isles to Venezuela. Far from presenting a recovery of Venezuela, however, Montejo describes the difficulty of fully assuming this return:

> ¡Qué arduo
> cuando por fin partimos de las islas,
> de sus gélidas costas sin palmeras,
> borrárnoslas del cuerpo!
> [...]
> ¡Qué arduo
> cuando ya nos libera el horizonte
> de las islas amargas,
> de sus monótonas noches sin mujeres,
> volver a ver la tierra en que nacimos
> y sentirla después por muchos días
> delante de los ojos
> sin alcanzarla! (*T*, 46)

Even when back at home, that home is still in some sense absent. But the later 'Viajes' (*AM*) goes further, taking the alignment of the stones, *paisajes*, and river of Venezuela with absence to its logical conclusion. Following this period of poetry in which journeys have constituted such a persistent thematic, Montejo writes here of an end to journeying:

> Viaje tras viaje ... ¿Adónde fuimos?
> Todas las calles son iguales.
> [...]
> El Tajo, el Sena, el Támesis
> tienen las mismas lágrimas.

Hay tantos sellos en mi pasaporte,
rectos, oblongos, triangulares.
Busqué otro tiempo para mí en el mundo
y sólo hallé otro espacio.

¿A qué viajar si ya sabíamos
que éramos hombres sin ciudades?
[...]
Aviones, barcos, trenes ... ¡Para otros!
Adiós, turistas sonámbulos.
Que el tranvía de Lisboa venda mi sombra
por montes y caminos ... Ya no parto. (*AM*, 188)

The poem reads as a compendium of images and thematics from Montejo's preceding poetry: the aeroplanes of poems such as 'La vida' (*AP*); the trains of the journeys of 'Trenes nocturnos' (*AP*) and the earlier 'El viaje' (*MM*); the boats of the numerous sea journeys which I have touched upon; the rivers of the three most dominant foreign locales in Montejo's poetry: Lisbon, Paris, and London (it might also be noted that this concern for and naming of rivers hints once more at a distinct Hölderlinian resonance in Montejo's work);[4] and the alignment of the wandering of life with the notion of an inauthentic or not fully assumed living ('sonámbulos') under which humankind labours. The journeys which the poet has undertaken were attempts to find another time ('otro tiempo'), a further indication of the association of an authentic being-on-the-earth with a previous (mythic) era. But all he found was 'otro espacio'.[5] Each foreign city constituted just another modern space, as the poet emphasises that the loss of the communal, quasi-rural cities of the past is a global phenomenon.[6] All of these images of travelling are, then, rejected with the final determined 'ya no parto'. But the relinquishing of the journey is not the result of reaching the authentic home, an achieving of a full being-in-the-homeland postponed in 'Retorno de las islas' (*T*). Rather, 'Viajes' discloses that the reason for the journeying is, in the first place, that home/

---

4   Some examples of Hölderlin's naming of rivers in his poetry are 'Der Ister' (1992: 362), 'Der Main', (220), 'Der Nekar' (243), and 'Der Rhein' (238).

5   The reference to looking for another time yet finding another space here taps into the thought of Henri Bergson (1945 [1889]). Like Bergson, Montejo seeks to move beyond a spatial understanding of time as measurable and divisible into discrete moments in a linear chain. Yet in Montejo's case, a shift towards a different experiencing of time – what Bergson defined as *durée* – is denied.

6   Montejo's statement here that we are 'hombres sin ciudades' (*AM*, 188) is also found in the essay 'Poesía en un tiempo sin poesía' (*TB*, 14) and is expanded upon in interview with Arráiz Lucca (1987: 3). In this phrase Montejo takes 'ciudades' to refer to the quasi-rural cities prior to the increased urbanisation and industrialisation of the second half of the twentieth century (see chapter 3).

the homeland is itself experienced as exile: journeying represents a search for what is felt as lacking at home. This poem, whilst appearing to affirm the arrival and remaining at the homeland, thus shows the poet's return to home as a return to an exile-at-home, with Venezuela being experienced as the absence with which it is made synonymous in the poems describing it synecdochically as his luggage.

As mentioned above, 'Viajes' reveals the ease with which, by the time of *Alfabeto del mundo*, Montejo's 'journey poetry' opens itself up to a global reading, both in its alignment of cities throughout the world and in its reference to the exilic condition of being as inextricably tied up with the modern era of travel and tourism. Indeed, the shifter 'nosotros' seems to have moved from a parochial or national referent ('Las piedras' (*T*), 'Retorno de las islas' (*T*)) towards a more global one ('Viajes'). But Montejo's insistence on the specificity of Venezuela also makes it impossible not to focus on the more local commentary running throughout this presentation of journeys and exile, not least in *Trópico absoluto*, which takes this thematic and demands it be read not just as an example of a general, global experience, but in explicitly Venezuelan terms. This is particularly the case in 'Esta tierra', which points to the experiencing of the homeland as foreign as a permanent characteristic of the Venezuelan condition of being, stretching back into the country's history:

> Esta tierra jamás ha sido nuestra,
> tampoco fue de quienes yacen en sus campos
> ni será de quien venga.
> Hace mucho que palpamos su paisaje
> con un llanto de expósitos
> abandonados por antiguas carabelas.
>
> Esta tierra de tórridas llanuras
> llevamos siglos habitándola y no nos pertenece. (*TA*, 54)

The allusion in these opening lines is to the arrival of the Spanish Colonisers, with Columbus making his first journey westward in 1492 in three caravels. This event underlines and provides an historical basis for the presentation in Montejo's work of Venezuela as a nation formed in and around the condition of being-at-home-in-a-foreign-land, a land which is not felt to be 'nuestra'. In effect, we can read this poem back into the repeated journeys across the Atlantic to and from Venezuela in earlier poems such as 'Altamar' (*AP*), 'Dormir' (*AP*), and 'Amberes' (*T*), and, in particular, into 'Retorno de las islas' (*T*), where the poet's arrival at Venezuela acts as a repetition and playing out of this original arrival at a (new) homeland-felt-as-foreign. Venezuela, 'Esta tierra' discloses, is forever distant:

> Esta tierra feraz, sentimental, amarga,
> que no se deja poseer,
> no será de nosotros ni de nadie. (*TA*, 55)

The most significant poem, however, in terms of the historical engagement with and presentation of this experience of identity and being in Venezuela is 'Nostalgia de Bolívar', a long poem written in 1976, but not published in a widely available form until 1988 (*AM*, 89–90). Moving forward to the other pivotal founding moment – or figure – in Venezuela's history, this poem likewise reveals the sense of a homeland whose essence is somehow absent from the people and their experiencing of it.

The poem announces itself as a celebration of Bolívar as modern (post-colonial) Venezuela's founder and foundation and, more widely, as the country's historical heritage and identity. It begins by describing how:

> En el mapa natal que tatuamos en sueño
> sobre la piel, las manos, las voces de esta tierra,
> Bolívar es el primero de los ríos
> que cruzan nuestros campos. (*AM*, 89)

Bolívar represents not just the heritage of 'our land' in the sense of a political and cultural entity (*patria*), then, but the essence or fluvial life-blood of its natural characteristics, as the heritage of the homeland is rendered inseparable from the land itself and not simply something which emerged from the vagaries of history. What is being celebrated here is more than just the heritage of the homeland, natural and historical, though. As suggested by the reference to the skin, hands, and voices of the land, it is synonymous with and inseparable from what it is to be Venezuelan. Bolívar, as the 'primero de los ríos', represents the essence and grounding of Venezuela and of all Venezuelans, as is implied by the rest of the stanza, which portrays each river and brook of the country flowing into this one river, 'Bolívar':

> El Orinoco lo sigue en la llanura,
> el Meta, el Caroní nutren sus aguas,
> y todos los arroyos que serpean
> por montes y por pueblos
> llegan al mar unidos en su cauce. (89)

Yet the opening stanza also hints at the true nature of this ontological homeland and essence, with the river 'Bolívar' not being an 'actual' river, in contrast to the Orinoco, the Meta, and the Caroní. Bolívar, that is, represents the essence of the Venezuelan land and people, but is beyond the country's physical actuality, even as he is affirmed as its Ground of Being.[7] This is played out in the way in which the poem is unable to maintain the affirmations made in the first stanza, breaking down into a series of questions which leave little doubt as to the unknown nature of 'Bolívar' and the essence which that name represents:

> ya no se sabe adónde va, de dónde viene,
> quién es Bolívar,
> qué trae en su caudal a cada uno, qué reparte.
> Ya nadie sabe si todos en su oleaje nos fundimos. (89)

On the one hand, the repetitious 'ya no'/'ya nadie' here suggests that the essential homeland and being of Venezuela and Venezuelans was once present, known, and assumed, but has since been lost, tying the terms of the poem in with the historical fact of Bolívar's no longer being alive and identifying the period where the essential heritage and being were indeed present as the early nineteenth century. But, just as the name 'Bolívar' here goes beyond the historical personage, so is the nature of this (period of) apparent wholeness of being described not, primarily, in historical terms. Rather, it appears as a transcendent, quasi-religious experience, with Bolívar recast as a Christ-like figure in whom a oneness not just with Venezuela but with the entire cosmos is found:[8]

> A su orilla [del río Bolívar] los hombres en fila se congregan,
> lo oyen hablar a solas con la tierra,
> con el sol y los altos espacios siderales. (89)

Thus, the presentation of the essential homeland, heritage, and being of Venezuela and its people, ciphered in the name and figure of Simón Bolívar, shows itself to be infused with exactly the same religious and, specifically, Christian imagery and frames of reference as the other ciphers for a lost ontological essentiality, be it the rural homestead and the rite of coffee, the father's bakery, or the natural world.

The fusing of the historical and the religious in the poem continues in its

---

[7]   The term 'Ground of Being' is attributed to the theologian and philosopher Paul Tillich (see, for example, Tillich (1952)).

[8]   Simón Bolívar is sometimes referred to as a second Jesus Christ in Venezuelan popular tradition, notably in the second stanza of the song 'Viva Venezuela' released in 1992 by the folk group Un Solo Pueblo. Tellingly, the Caracas-based newspaper *El Universal* tells of how '"Viva Venezuela" […] se convirtió en un verdadero himno desde que salió en 1992. Un himno realmente sentido y querido, que no ha sido impuesto por nadie y que todo el mundo canta, rebosante de optimismo' (*El Universal*, 24 July 1997, http://buscador.eluniversal. com/1997/07/24/esp_art_24317AA.shtml [accessed on 1 January 2009]).

subsequent depiction of the loss of Bolívar. Immediately following a celebratory affirmation of Bolívar's divine position as 'un espejo donde los ojos se miran en llamas, | una ventana que incendia su paisaje' (90),[9] the figure of the *Libertador* assumes his historical guise as a soldier, laying aside for the moment his symbolic, fluvial identity, as Montejo describes him falling into ever greater hardship and marginalisation:

> después se va quedando desnudo,
> sin caballo,
> sin sombra,
> sin nada ... (90)

These lines reflect how Bolívar ended his life in 1830 in poverty, alone and destitute, and with an order of exile from the then Venezuelan President José Antonio Páez hanging over his head.[10] It is an image and a fate which, on the one hand, resonate with the rejection and scorn of Christ which the Gospels impute to those who had cheered him triumphantly as he rode into Jerusalem and whom, in Christian theology, he had come to save. More significantly, these lines, together with the historical elements of the poem 'Esta tierra', also underscore the consistent presence of exile in the key founding moments of Venezuela and *la venezolanidad*.

Returning to the image of Bolívar as a river, the poem then describes his subsequent death in terms which imply the realisation of the order of exile, with the Venezuelan land being emptied of Bolívar's presence as the elusive river moves towards and disperses into the sea in an inexorable slide into loss:

> Cuando sale al océano ya se encuentra muy pobre,
> casi llega en harapos.
> [...]
> Cae en su noche,
> en su naufragio,
> ya no se ve, sus huesos se esparcen por el mundo,
> su alma titila en estrellas lejanas. (90)

In the face of this loss, as in Christianity, the poem depicts the Venezuelan people as being left with rituals and rites which, whilst reaffirming the identification of Bolívar as a Christ-like figure, also announce him as a presence which can only be invoked through faith: 'en cada mesa se parte el pan en nombre suyo | en cada voz resuena su palabra' (90). As in the failure of

---

[9]   The idea of the divine mirror in Christian theology originates in the Letter of James, where the author describes the Word of God as a mirror in which one sees one's true self (James 1. 22–5).

[10]   José Antonio Páez was President of Venezuela 1830–35, 1839–43, and 1861–63.

the repetition of infancy in the generational cycle, the failure successfully
to bring together the living and the dead in the religious rite of Montejo's
'coffee poetics', and the failure successfully to write a poetry which might be
a realisation of the communional bread of the old bakers, the religious rituals
of Montejo's poetry here tell of the absence of that which they represent and
seek to invoke. Indeed, this is exactly what the poem describes, depicting
Bolívar as not just lost, but irrecuperable, with Montejo writing the erasure
of Bolívar's wake as he disperses into the sea:[11]

> Frente al azul final desaparece,
> más allá sus estelas se borran en el mar,
> no hay pasos que lo sigan,
> no hay barcos. (90)

These lines repeat the image found in 'Altamar' from *Algunas palabras*,
written two years before 'Nostalgia de Bolívar', of the 'estela que crece
y nos destierra' (*AP*, 17), and lead to a variety of readings when taken in
conjunction with this earlier poem. On the one hand, Bolívar here repeats the
ineluctable distancing from the homeland which the poet – and Venezuelans
in general – are figured as repeating both physically and metaphorically. Yet
the image in this later poem also reverses the roles, showing (the essence of)
the Venezuelan homeland and Venezuelan being deserting or being exiled
from the land and the people. This provides a further reading of the perceived
need to travel in search of what is missing from the homeland: a search for
the departed Bolívar. It also underlines the sense of the land which is experienced at home as being distant.

   But even as Bolívar – and, by implication, an authentic or full experiencing of Venezuela and Venezuelan being – is affirmed as having been lost,
'Nostalgia de Bolívar' once more reminds us of the underlying mythic identification that we have seen to be associated with all past motifs, eras, and
locales to which Montejo appeals, in that Bolívar holds 'las llaves de El
Dorado' (*AM*, 90). Montejo's poetry, that is, once more disavows the idea
that such a past was ever present, as is further suggested by the declaration

---

[11] This reference to Bolívar dispersing into the sea, leaving a wake, a path which dissolves
and cannot be followed, echoes Bolívar's own description towards the end of his life of his
attempted permanent creation of Gran Colombia, which he had spearheaded in his final years.
In a letter to General J. J. Flores dated 9 November 1830, Bolívar states that 'el que sirve a
una revolución ara en el mar' (1976: 321). The path towards what Bolívar considered the homeland, the place of true being and belonging of the people of modern-day Venezuela, Colombia,
Ecuador, and Panama, then, was as impossible to follow as that which leads towards himself as
the homeland or true being of the Venezuelan people in Montejo's poetry.

towards the end of the poem that 'nadie recuerda *si todos fuimos él* | o lo seremos' (90, italics mine).[12]

What emerges from 'Nostalgia de Bolívar', 'Esta tierra', and the other mid-period poems discussed here, then, is that Montejo not only places the exilic condition of being in Venezuela at the heart of his poetics, but, in various poems, indicates that this is an *inherent* characteristic of this being. Moreover, these poems lay bare the extent to which Montejo's engagement with the thematic of home, exile, and journeying as a whole operates on at least three distinct levels – often simultaneously – as detailed in Table 1.

Table 1

Cause/Nature of Exile	Home	Levels on which Exile Operates
Life	(Pre-)birth/(Post-)death	Human (general/ontological)
Separation from nature	Oneness with nature/ *terredad*	Modern (20th-century) condition; Venezuelan 20th-century urbanisation; Personal experience of the latter
Homeland as exile	Distant/Unlocatable	Venezuelan; Latin American more generally

Put simply, the general postlapsarian condition of humankind is a constant presence in Montejo's work. Yet his poetics consistently gravitates around the particularities of how this is experienced and dealt with in Venezuela and as a Venezuelan, where 'the Venezuelan' necessarily intersects with both the Latin American and the twentieth-century human condition.[13]

With this focus on the specificities of the poet's location in mind, I shall now examine two pivotal aspects of Montejo's poetics of exile and place, namely local *paisajes* and constructed habitats. My aim is to explore how both of these topoi emerge from this particular concern for a lost sense of place and being in Venezuela, and how they enrich and nuance how we view both the general topos of place and being-on-the-earth, as discussed in chapter 3, and the possibilities for a poetic language and response to these thematics within

---

[12] These lines point up the echoes here of Heidegger's reading of Hölderlin's rivers. For Heidegger (1996: 11–15) the reference in Hölderlin's poem 'Stimme des Volks' to rivers as 'vanishing' ('Schwindenden') and 'full of intimation' ('Ahnungsvollen') signals that rivers 'abandon the Now, whether by passing into what is bygone, or into what lies in the future' (15). This locating of the river as always lost in the (mythic) past or deferred to an (unattainable) future resonates sharply with Montejo's presentation of the (ontological) river Bolívar here.

[13] Chirinos comments on the 'falta de patria' (2005: 146) motif in Montejo's poetry, but only inasmuch as he identifies its Romantic antecedents.

both the world and Venezuela, which has emerged as the axial problematic at each stage of my exploration of Montejo's work.

Nature and language: the specificities of place

In describing an essential exile or distance from Venezuela, Montejo refers, above all, to the physical land: its nature, *paisajes*, and climate. The poems which I have been looking at already suggest this, both in the use of the *piedras*, *paisajes*, and horizons of the Orinoco as ciphers for the Venezuelan homeland, as well as in the portrayal of Bolívar as a river weaving its way through the country as the circulatory system of the land itself (literal and figurative) in 'Nostalgia de Bolívar'. Aside from this presentation of Venezuela in the poems overtly concerned with journeying and exile, many of the poems from both *Terredad* and, in particular, *Trópico absoluto* focus on the natural legacy and identity of Venezuela as a part of the Caribbean tropics. One such example is the title poem of the latter collection, which, with its references to the 'palmares azules y blancos', the 'nítido sol marino a orilla de la costa', and 'viento yodado, cuerpos desnudos, oleajes' (*TA*, 12), indicates what is to be found throughout these poems. Indeed, of the first twenty-one of the fifty poems of this collection eleven deal – often in adulatory terms – with the tropical locale of Venezuela. In addition to this, several poems in the collection continue the Hölderlinesque naming of Venezuelan rivers ('Valencia', 'Yo también soy Orinoco', 'El río Chama'), a strand which harks back to 'Nostalgia de Bolívar', as we have seen, as well as to several poems from *Algunas palabras* ('El Orinoco', for example) and *Terredad* ('Yo soy mi río', for example). But if *Trópico absoluto* is where the presence of the Venezuelan landscape is made most dominant, it is the final poem of the previous *Terredad*, 'Un samán', which sets up this emerging emphasis.

Like many others from this collection, the poem is centred around a tree. In this case it represents an imagined monologue on the part of a saman, a tree unique to the American tropics, thus marking itself off from the rest of the collection which talks more in terms of the generic *árbol*. The focus of the tree's discourse is the particular natural environment in which it has spent its days:

> Un samán ya viejo verdea y monologa:
> – solo, sin dar paso,
> en los anillos de mi cuerpo
> anoté mis vueltas al sol de la tierra.
> Se movió el mundo, no mis ramas,
> me quedé tenso ante los días
> como un volatinero.

> Oí muchos pinos hablar de la nieve
> pero no envidié al haya, al abedul
> que pueden conocerla.
> Estoy donde los vientos me dejaron
> sin renegar mis dioses,
> junto a las mansas reses que cobijo
> en la intemperie.
> Jamás he visto un ruiseñor,
> amé otros pájaros,
> cuidé sus nidos inocentes.
> Crecí a la lenta luz del trópico
> mirando las iguanas atar el arco iris
> a mi corteza.
> Con las últimas hojas me ilumino
> levitando en el verde.
> Quise ser lo que soy: un samán de estos campos,
> que el leñador disponga de mis ramas
> para su buena lumbre.
>   Ya no temo los fuegos. (*T*, 67–8)

The poem concentrates on the firmness of the tree and its contentment and pride in the tropics in which it is located and of which it is a part, with no interest in other environs. Within this tropical locale, it talks of a unity and oneness of the various elements of the *paisaje*: the cattle, the birds, the iguanas, all are in a perfectly symbiotic relationship with the saman tree, who then looks forward to his death as merely the continuation of this symbiosis, as the cyclical images from Montejo's earlier poetry return once more, here in an affirmative presentation.

One of the primary effects of the focus on the nature and land of the tropics initiated by 'Un samán' is to bring the themes of exile from homeland and distance from nature together. Both these themes speak of a separation from an ontological authenticity centred around a sense of place or being-on-the-earth, and both are united in the presentation of the distance from the homeland of tropical Venezuela, in that it is a homeland identified with and as its nature. Furthermore, just as the specificity of the example of Venezuela is important for an understanding of Montejo's approach to and presentation of the 'exile-from-home' topos, so too does this concomitant focus on the nature of Venezuela point towards a nuancing of the general problematic of humankind's separation from nature explored in chapter 3.

Before examining such a nuancing, it is important to underline that the poems which gravitate around the nature and climate of Venezuela certainly support and contribute to the overall concept of one's (authentic) being as found in the natural world. 'Trópico absoluto' (*TA*), for example, in describing the 'magia del trópico absoluto' as growing 'en un grito al fondo de mi

sangre' (*TA*, 12), aligns the magic of the tropical setting precisely with the
essence or *terredad* of authentic being. A similar image to that of 'Trópico
absoluto' is also found in 'Una palma' (*TA*). Here the poet talks about the
same essence which is within one's blood ('Algo [...] | de la sangre' (*TA*, 19))
as being contained within the palm tree of the Venezuelan *paisaje*:

> Lo que yo toco en ella [una palma]   20
> con mis ojos
> y miro con mis manos
> es la raíz que nos aferra
> a esta tierra profunda   24
> desde un sueño tan fuerte
> que ningún vendaval
> puede arrancarnos. (19)

And these lines in turn tie in with the final lines of 'Esta tierra' (*TA*) which,
talking of the Venezuelan people, affirm that:

> Ya nuestros cuerpos son palmas de sus costas,
> aferrados a indómitas raíces,
> que [esta tierra] no verá nunca partir
> aunque retornen del mar las carabelas. (*TA*, 55)

What emerges from both these poems, then, is the notion of the 'raíz', the
root which makes the people truly one with the land. 'Una palma' lays bare
that the affirmations at the end of 'Esta tierra', undercut by the rest of the
poem, which talks primarily of an ineluctable distance from the land, rely
upon the identifying and assuming of this 'raíz'. In much the same way as the
poet is envisaged as having to bring out humankind's *terredad*, incorporating
the essence of the world into himself and then bringing it forth in the poetic
song, 'Una palma' tells us that is it the (Venezuelan) poet's job to sense and
locate this (Venezuelan) 'raíz'. And, once more, the difficulty of doing so,
and the need to eschew the norms of human (postlapsarian) language and
logic in order to be able to perceive it, is brought to the fore, here, in the
synaesthesia of lines 20–2.

Significantly, the identity of the 'raíz' in question is made apparent in
a further poem from *Trópico absoluto*, 'Luz de la palma'. The title itself
suggests that the palm tree's light is the essential root that links it and, potentially, the Venezuelan people to their natural habitat. Moreover, the poem both
envisages the poet attaining the essential 'grito' of the 'magia caribe' and,
crucially, has him begin by declaring his goal to be that 'yo seré tu poeta, luz
de la palma' (*TA*, 13), thus identifying the palm's light with that 'grito' and
setting in place a conflation of *raíz*, (essential/poetic/natural) language, and
light in Montejo's poetics. Underscoring the importance of this topos, the sun

or light of the tropics proves to be a key element of Montejo's presentation and understanding of the Venezuelan land throughout *Trópico absoluto* and, to a lesser extent, *Terredad*. As 'Luz de la palma' indicates, it is the essence within the *paisajes*, that which allows this nature to be authentic and poetic, and this connection is spelt out explicitly in the much later 'Una visión' (*HS*) by Tomás Linden. The poem begins by stating that:

> Miraba yo mi amada tierra un día
> con el raigal asombro de estar vivo,
> buscando en su verdor el oro esquivo
> que el viejo sol de lejos le traía. (*HS*, 28)

The sunlight, again sought by the poet just as it is by Montejo in the poems of *Trópico absoluto*, is that which alchemically turns the greenness of the land into an authentic landscape, mirroring the way the poet strives to change humankind and human language, a process which, likewise, is described in vividly alchemic terms in 'El esclavo' (*T*):

> Ser el esclavo, el paria, el alquimista
> de malditos metales
> y trasmutar su tedio en ágatas,
> en oro el barro humano. (*T*, 33)

Finally, however, it is in the poem 'Hombres sin nieve' from *Trópico absoluto* that this presentation of authentic nature through sunlight is linked most starkly to an authenticity of being for the people of this tropical land, as Montejo announces that:

> Nuestra vida está escrita
> por la mano del sol
> en las mágicas hojas de la malanga. (*TA*, 8)

The significance of these lines is particularly evident when one realises that in *El cuaderno de Blas Coll* one of the three leaves on which Coll wrote a part of his work is that of the *malanga*, and that on this leaf we find the statement 'la materia reposa en la nada como el hielo en el agua' (*BC*, 65). What emerges from the conjunction of these two pieces is that 'Nuestra vida' is an essential nothingness which is given form: the boundary of nothingness and form which has returned repeatedly in Montejo's depiction of both an authentic poetics and an authentic ontology, be it in the poetic border that is nature, the *canto del gallo*, or the bread–poem he seeks to write. And it is the sun that writes this essential, border–being on and in the natural habitat of the tropics.

As I have mentioned, despite its resonances with the general ontological questions on which I focused in chapter 3, all the poems discussed here insist on the fact that what is being addressed is very much the nature and light of the tropics, as experienced and found in Venezuela. 'Un samán' invokes the tropical *paisaje* in contrast to that of other, colder climes, echoing and putting in context the affirmations of 'Colores', also in *Terredad*, that 'el trópico fue siempre otro planeta' (*T*, 35). And in the poems of *Trópico absoluto* such an insistence on the particularity of the tropical *paisaje* is equally clear in the frequent references to the fact that what is being described is very much 'la magia del trópico absoluto' (*TA*, 12), abounding in iguanas, palm trees, and colours, a place Montejo often refers to as 'un paraíso', echoing Columbus's comment upon landing at Venezuela's Paria Peninsula.[14] Likewise, the sun or light which bathes the *paisaje* and grants it its essentiality is specifically that of the tropics: the subject of 'El tigre' is not just the sun, but 'el sol de los trópicos' (*TA*, 10), just as in 'Un samán' the tree talks of 'la lenta luz del trópico' (*T*, 67). And all the while the 'colder climes' which are offered up as the primary contrast here are, as at so many other points of Montejo's work, those of Europe. This is implied in the context in which these poems are presented, that is, a poetics which places the exiled or journeying poet in European locales such as London, Paris, and Lisbon, and which has equated snow (against which the snowless Venezuela stands in contrast) with the Old Continent, in Paris, for example, in 'Cementerio de Vaugirard' (*MM*). Likewise, one might point to the reference to life's being eternal only 'en esta orilla del Atlántico' (*TA*, 9) in 'Mi país en un mapa antiguo' (*TA*).

The effect of this emphasis on the specificity of both *paisajes* and light is not just to underscore its natural differences from other (in particular, European) places, but to enable us to see that, if they are different, then the authentic being they represent is also different. Such is suggested in Montejo's depiction of the particular nature of the light in the tropics as affecting how the people see, that is, how they live and experience the world. This is summed up at the start of Montejo's essay 'En un playón solitario' from the collection *El taller blanco* (*TB*, 107–18):

> La luz de nuestro litoral está hecha de una intensa blancura calina que nos contrae las pupilas como en pocas latitudes de la tierra. Los viajeros venidos de países lejanos, sobre todo los que provienen de regiones septentrionales, pronto advierten que aquí el hombre está obligado a mirar de manera distinta. (107)

---

[14] Montejo alludes specifically to this famous comment by Columbus in his essay 'En un playón solitario' from *El taller blanco* (*TB*, 108).

It is a message repeated time and again in Montejo's poetry of this mid-period: in 'Colores' (*T*) he talks of 'las retinas | más contraídas de la tierra' (*T*, 35); in 'Mi país en un mapa antiguo' (*TA*) he draws attention to 'el fulgor de los ojos asombrados | ante la luz de las palmeras' (*TA*, 9); and in 'Trópico absoluto' (*TA*) he comments on the fact that he is experiencing 'el mismo sol que ardía | en las absortas retinas de mis padres' (*TA*, 12), all of which act as examples of the specifically Venezuelan experiencing and articulation of this more generally tropical light.

We thus begin to see the implications of the focus on local nature for Montejo's nature poetry generally. If Montejo talks of the poetic need to make our language that of nature in order to assume a oneness with it and an authentic being for ourselves, then his affirmation of the particularity of tropical nature and, more specifically, of the tropical nature found in and experienced by the people of Venezuela, brings with it an affirmation both of the particularity of tropical and, more specifically, Venezuelan ontology and of the concomitant need for poetry not so much to make our language that of nature *per se*, but to align our language with the nature of the particular place from which we come: in the case of Montejo and Montejo's poetics, that of (tropical) Venezuela.

This notion of a local conjoining of language and nature is also found in *El cuaderno de Blas Coll*, and its articulation here is particularly useful for an exploration of Montejo's wider poetic quest. We have already seen in chapter 3 how Blas Coll desires a natural language, and this is frequently tied in with descriptions of a universal language or 'lengua totalizante' (*BC*, 53) for humankind:

> Quienes en nuestro siglo se han propuesto hacer realidad la utopía de una sociedad nueva han olvidado que ésta tiene forzosamente que acompañarse con la creación de un nuevo idioma, es decir, con una *lingua franca* capaz de coexistir junto a los distintos idiomas de los pueblos comprometidos en el intento. (88–9)

And yet, as in Montejo's own work, Coll is also attuned to the need to match language with (nature of) place. Tellingly, and tapping into the specific Europe/tropics contrast in Montejo's work, for Coll this boils down to the fact that Spanish – a European language – is not 'designed' for and does not match the Venezuelan tropics. Thus he declares that 'la vieja lengua materna, tan abrigada, ya no sirve en estos tórridos climas, y han de ayudarme a desnudarla para que todo pueda ser dicho *más naturalmente*' (42–3, italics mine), here aligning his linguistic project with a more regional concern. Moreover, echoing Montejo, Coll uses the specific example of the lack of snow in Venezuela in his explanation of why Spanish does not fit:

El día que nieve en Puerto Malo, esta lengua de palabras tan largas podrá servirnos a todos, bien lo sabemos, para calentarnos con ella. Nadie desconoce el poder que sus erres y sus jotas tienen contra el frío. Los adverbios terminados en mente, por su parte, constituyen casi una frazada. (73)

In spelling out the problems of this specific disjunction between language and nature in Venezuela, Montejo's primary heteronym throws significant light on several of Montejo's own poems concerning his experience of exilic being in Venezuela and as Venezuelan. Returning to 'Retorno de las islas' (*T*), we see that the difficulty of assuming a being in Venezuela after being abroad for a period is described not just in terms of a reacclimatisation, but as a problem of language, both verbal and corporeal:

> ¡Qué arduo
> después de hacernos forasteros
> recobrar una a una las palabras perdidas,
> curarnos la saudade!
> Cómo los gestos nos delatan,
> cómo demora el cuerpo aclimatándose,
> sacándose las islas de la sangre. (*T*, 46)

Similarly in 'Forastero' (*TA*), the poet describes being in places distant from home primarily in linguistic terms:

> No sé qué extraña lengua están hablando
> en esta taberna.
> Siento que las palabras me rodean
> con sus rápidos saltos de peces
> delante de mis ojos forasteros. (*TA*, 22)

Each land and its *paisajes* emerge as synonymous with its language, and yet, as the condition of being in exile at home implies, this distance from the language of the (nature of the) place is not simply a matter of returning to, in this case, Venezuela and (re)gaining its – and one's – authentic language. And *El cuaderno de Blas Coll* reveals that this is linked precisely to the language of Venezuela being Spanish: a language from another place, a language which is not that of the Venezuelan tropical *paisaje*. This fact, then, underscores, represents, and offers an explanation for the specific and continued distance from the essentiality of Venezuela as homeland and *paisaje* in Montejo's work. Moreover, it also points to the essential problematic at the heart of being and identity in Latin America more generally: its colonial heritage and current post-colonial status.

Coll's texts are, it must be remembered, not those of 'Montejo'. But the connection between the two is palpable here, with Montejo's search for an authentic *poetic* language and being finding many parallels in Coll's search for a new language *tout court*. Primary amongst these is the fact that, as we have seen, just as Coll's linguistic project exhibits both global and local goals, so too is Montejo's poetic project grounded in a search for a poetic language for humankind, but where this poetics must also be of and for the Venezuelan tropics from which he came and in which he lived; it must be a poetics which restores an authentic being-in-Venezuela. Mapping Coll's texts onto Montejo's, the implications for the latter's poetics are stark, for if Coll talks at times of the *linguistic* need to eschew Spanish, a language of Europe not of the tropics, then Montejo's focus on the contrast between the *paisajes* and climate of the Venezuelan tropics and those of Europe leads to an implied need to eschew the leitmotivs and commonplaces of Spanish and, more generally, European *poetic* traditions. This is particularly evident in 'Un samán' (*T*). Aside from the affirmation of the tropical tree, the saman's assertion that:

> Jamás he visto un ruiseñor,
> amé otros pájaros,
> cuidé sus nidos inocentes, (*T*. 67)

carries with it a poetic statement in declaring the nightingale, European Romantic leitmotiv *par excellence*, to be irrelevant: just as the nightingale is not found in America, so is a European poetics, this poem implies, false or inappropriate in the tropics.[15] Indeed, this provides an undercurrent to the later 'Santo y seña' (*AM*), which begins with the poet's surprise at hearing the authentic birdsong somewhere in his blood, despite the urban reality in which he lives:

> – ¡Alto! ¿Quién canta dentro de mi sangre
> en mitad de la noche?
> No hay ruiseñores en mis venas;
> vivo en esta ciudad a leguas de los gallos. (*AM*, 193)

It is an affirmation of the potential for the poet to (re)discover the natural essence, his *terredad*. Yet in their reference to the nightingale these lines also act as a further statement of defiance against the imposition or at least validity of a European song, both natural and poetic, in this Venezuelan setting and poetry.

---

[15] Montejo's engagement with the topos of the nightingale contrasts with that of the Chilean poet Vicente Huidobro who, it was reported, planned to carry some nightingales home from Europe in his luggage, to aid the propagation of poetry in his native land (Balderston 1990: 73).

This affirmation of the validity of a Venezuelan poetics, concomitant with the focus on the Venezuelan *paisaje*, is also brought to the fore in two of the most insistent Venezuelan artistic models on whom Montejo writes in the essays of *El taller blanco*, a collection which itself represents a marked shift towards Venezuelan models, memories, and *paisajes* from the largely 'European' focus of the essays in *La ventana oblicua*, in effect repeating the poetic shift signalled, above all, by *Trópico absoluto*. The two figures in question are the poet Vicente Gerbasi and the painter Armando Reverón, whom Montejo describes as 'dos nombres fundamentales de la expresión artística del trópico venezolano' (*TB*, 160). Writing on each, Montejo is keen to draw attention to the essential Venezuelan light as a dominant presence in their work and that which makes them 'authentic' artistic figures of Venezuela. Of Gerbasi, Montejo comments that 'la luz espejeante y nítida' of Valencia (Venezuela) was 'inseparable de la iluminación verbal de sus poemas' (151–2), whilst he offers Reverón's frequent comments on the white light of the Venezuelan coast as an explanation of his 'enceguecida angustia que lo lleva a pintar a base del blanco' (160).[16]

Yet, just as Coll's final linguistic solution, *colly* – the name he gives to his new language – appears predominantly as based on Spanish, but a radically altered version of it, adjusted to the needs and nature of the tropics,[17] likewise for Montejo the European proves to be an ineluctable part of any Venezuelan poetics, as we are constantly reminded of the European heritage in which post-colonial Venezuelans share. This dual historical legacy is evident in the narratives of origins of Blas Coll, Tomás Linden, and Montejo himself. The details of Coll's life before his arrival in Puerto Malo are, according to Montejo, unclear, but his European connections are implied as we are told that 'según la suposición más aceptable, era originario de las Islas Canarias, pero debió de haber viajado mucho antes de asentarse en esta bahía calurosa' (*BC*, 31), the thematic of journeying once more making its presence felt. Tomás Linden, born in Puerto Cabello (*HS*, 9), another town on the Venezuelan coast, has a Venezuelan mother and a Swedish father (9). And Montejo traces his own family's origins back, like Coll, to the Canary Islands.[18]

Beyond the biographical, the poetics of Venezuela which Montejo and his heteronyms give us is, similarly, laden with the European. Montejo, like his heteronyms, writes in Spanish (with the caveat of Blas Coll's radical version of it, although all Coll's texts are given to us in their standard Spanish version); the use of both coplas by Sergio Sandoval in *Guitarra del horizonte*

[16] For a good overview of Reverón's life and career, including his white period, see Calzadilla (1979: xxviii–xxx).
[17] We are given only a few examples of *colly*, such as the word *brícol*, which is *colly* for *colibrí* (*BC*, 69).
[18] See Arráiz Lucca (1987: 4).

and sonnets by Tomás Linden in *El hacha de seda* corresponds to the use of essentially European poetic forms, even as Linden aims to seek out 'la tierra y la lengua' (*HS*, 10) of his mother's family and Sandoval attempts to write a poetry which might 'seguir la voz natural de su pueblo' (*GH*, 16).[19] And, for all the promotion of leitmotivs and symbols autochthonous to Venezuela, the poetic models and commonplaces of Europe remain present, precisely as they are rejected. This is the case in the affirmation of both a lack of snow and flour-as-snow, as well as in Montejo's implicit rejection of the (European) nightingale in both poetry and nature. Indeed, the presence of the European poetic tradition here is brought out explicitly in copla XXIV of *Guitarra del horizonte*, where Sandoval recounts hearing the song of the *paraulata*, a bird found in the Venezuelan *Llanos*:[20]

> Volví a casa y escuché todavía por mucho tiempo el canto de aquel pájaro [...]. Pensé al punto en la *Oda* de Keats, acaso para comprobar que, por mí mismo, poco había comprendido del poema antes de oír la nocturna profundidad del canto de la paraulata blanca, nuestro solitario ruiseñor. (*GH*, 51)

On the one hand, Sandoval here affirms a Venezuelan version of the nightingale and underlines that a European poetics of nature only makes sense in Venezuela when understood and read through (a translation into) the flora and fauna of this land. And yet these lines also demonstrate an ineluctable comparison with the European and Romantic natural and poetic model, on which the experience and writing of the *paraulata* depend. Indeed, we might comment on the fact that Montejo's overarching notion of the need to locate a (poetic) 'lengua de gracia' for the nation or region described as a 'tierra de gracia' (Posadas 2002: 308) is based upon the initial European valorisation and judgement of that locale (by Columbus).

In effect, in the writing of a poetry for Venezuela we repeatedly come up in Montejo's work against the pull of the linguistic and poetic heritage of Spain and, more widely, Europe, sending us back to the essays of *La ventana oblicua*. In this respect, it is significant that, following both Montejo's and Coll's affirmation of the Venezuelan landscape and a corresponding Vene-

---

[19] The copla form of *Guitarra del horizonte* is certainly identifiable with the *copla llanera* of the Venezuelan *Llanos*, not least given the title of the collection, a reference to the endless horizon of this region. Despite this, the copla's origins date back to the earliest Spanish literature of the *Romancero*, and it is notable that, alongside the emphasis on the Venezuelan *Llanos*, we are told that Sandoval 'veía en ésta la forma por antonomasia de la expresión poética *en nuestro idioma*' (*GH*, 14, italics mine).

[20] The *paraulata* is described by the Venezuelan organisation FUDENA (Fundación para la Defensa de la Naturaleza) as 'tan típica de la sabana y tan dentro del corazón, la copla y la tonada del llanero' (http://200.74.218.204/fudena/contenido.asp?SC=54&SSC=38&CN=279 [accessed on 15 December 2008]).

zuelan poetics and language respectively, these two later heteronyms – Sergio
Sandoval and Tomás Linden – should draw attention to the Spanish traditions
which are found both implicitly and explicitly in Coll's and Montejo's work,
even as they continue the focus on the poetic task carried out, very specifically, in Venezuela.

Yet there is also a further aspect to this problematising of identity, language,
and poetry in both Coll's and Montejo's work, beyond the Europe/Venezuela
dialectic. Coll talks of his envisaged new language as, at different points, a
universal language (*BC*, 88–9), a return to an original Spanish (59–60), a
return to the concision of Latin (48), and a language for the particular place
in which he lives, Puerto Malo (52–3). This range of ambitions certainly hints
at the problematic nature of identity and being in post-colonial Venezuela,
but the specific terms used in the *cuaderno* also draw attention to another
underlying hesitation in Montejo's poetics. For the local *paisajes* and, hence,
desired language, are by no means defined consistently. 'The local' is depicted
variously as America (38), the tropics (72), the tropics of Venezuela (64), and,
specifically, Puerto Malo (52–3). And this same difficulty in identifying 'the
local' is found in Montejo's poetry. As I indicated in chapter 2, the referring
to the primary location at stake in Montejo's work as Venezuela, as I have
done in chapters 2 and 3 and in the present chapter, is both called for, given
the specificity of the (national) historical/geographical, artistic, and personal
allusions made by Montejo in his writing, and yet also deeply problematic,
not least given his focus on the wider term of 'the tropics', which he uses
most frequently in his poems of 'place'. Indeed, whereas the mention of 'mi
país' in poems such as 'Mi país en un mapa antiguo' (*TA*) appears to tie the
location to Venezuela, similar references to 'esta tierra' in poems such as 'Esta
tierra' (*TA*) are more than a little ambiguous: is the land at stake Venezuela,
where Columbus landed, or the tropical region in general alluded to so often
by Montejo, or is Venezuela here being taken as representative of America
generally? Or is it, as seems most likely, all three? The interview conducted
by Posadas is informative here. Montejo alludes to the 'continentalidad' in
his work, 'no en un sentido nerudiano nuevomundista', but where 'yo veo la
continentalidad lingüísticamente. Nosotros hablamos una sola lengua desde
aquí hasta la Tierra del Fuego' (2002: 307). Yet he then proceeds to stress the
linguistic differences between countries and regions within the continent, as
well as speaking of the 'uniformidad geográfica' whilst also underscoring the
geographical contrasts, in that 'si nací en una tierra tropical, esa tierra viene
en primer momento, pero eso no me impide celebrar el paisaje argentino,
mexicano, etc.' (307). Moreover, he then goes on to highlight the specifically Venezuelan identity of place and language in his poetry, in response
to a question about his poem 'Manoa' (*TA*): 'Manoa es importante para los
venezolanos, porque es nuestra Ítaca. [...] Y bueno, en cuanto a la poesía,
nuestra Manoa es la búsqueda de una lengua de gracia' (Posadas 2002: 308).

Certainly, then, all three levels of geographical and linguistic identification (continental, regional, national) are disclosed as being at play in Montejo's work. Yet it is hard not to see Venezuela itself as the primary generating force both in his explicit declarations and implicitly in his poetry and essays, understanding that the country also represents the wider locations of which it forms an integral part, not just the tropics and America, but, as we have seen, the globe too.

A similar schematic can be seen in one of the central stylistic and rhetorical traits of Montejo's poetry, namely its distinctly colloquial tone, where, as he states in the prologue to the second edition of *Algunas palabras*, 'buscaba apenas algunas palabras en las que pudiera reconocerme, en las que me sintiera próximo del habla de nuestras gentes y de nuestro paisaje' (1995: 5). Drawing attention to the European models to which Montejo was particularly indebted, Chirinos alludes to Cernuda's and Machado's move towards a less hermetic poetic language, which was 'un puente entre el autor y el lector' (2005: 135). Similarly, as we saw in chapter 1, Montejo's tone has strong resonances with the colloquial register and rhythms of Vallejo, and, by extension, with many contemporary (post-1950s) Latin American poets influenced by the latter. Yet, closer to home, Montejo himself saw his tone as being a product of a shared philosophy amongst the Venezuelan *generación del 58*, in that 'queríamos hacer un arte en cierta forma más humano, nos interesaba hablarle a un hombre con la misma naturalidad con que se le habla en un café' (Posadas 2002: 305). It is surely the case that all of these aspects contribute to Montejo's poetic register. But each one also represents an ambit in which the linguistic, poetic, and ontological heritage of Venezuela participates more widely, and it is the Venezuelan modulation of these influences on which Montejo appears to focus, just as it is the Venezuelan examples of American tropical *paisajes* and the Spanish language which are generally foregrounded in his work.

Returning to Coll, however, we see that Montejo's heteronym goes one step further than this concentration on the national, in that his primary concern for 'the local' is the town of Puerto Malo itself. The question is thus posed as to where one draws the boundary of the local. For, despite Coll's generalising at times as he talks of the need for a radically new Spanish of America, his focus on the specific case of Puerto Malo demonstrates how there is always a need to be more and more precise: if a language is to be natural and authentic, it must be particular to as concise a number of speakers and as concise a place as possible. The logical conclusion of this reductionist process is signalled by Coll himself when he states that 'la tierra no gira para dos hombres de idéntica manera' (*BC*, 92). Not only does the *paisaje* change constantly, but every *paisaje* is perceived differently by each individual, who, moreover, logically does not have the same experience of (diverse) *paisajes* as any other individual. This would seem to explain the fate of Coll's own language *colly* – which appears at various times to be identified with each of the global and local goals of his project – as it is described simply as 'la lengua solitaria con que [Coll] terminó hablándose a sí mismo' (*BC*, 67). The question is whether Montejo's poetic response and creation can avoid the same pitfall.

The poetic construction of home[21]

In his affirmatory presentation of the Venezuelan land and *paisajes* Montejo focuses, as we have seen, on the Venezuelan land as natural *materia* – foliage, animals, rivers, land – alchemically made golden by the sun/light, which, as essence, writes the very being of land and people into the *paisajes*. Montejo is underscoring here that the language of nature, which poetry is to be, needs to be understood as a meeting-point of a quasi-divine and mysterious essence and its revelation in the form of nature itself. Such a presentation, with its focus on the *materia*, is central not just to our understanding of an authentic being-on-the-earth, but also of how Montejo views the successful realisation of a poetic language and production which might bring this about. The poet, charged with producing an authentic, poetic, and natural language, is not just called, that is, to perceive the essence of the *paisajes* before him and allow it to burst forth from himself. Rather, he must also find a form which allows this to happen, just as nature allows the sun to write itself into it. As Montejo underlines in 'Fragmentario':

> Muchos poemas anticipan su primer soplo en nuestros labios, pero [...] mueren pronto, ahogados por una forma inconveniente. La intuición de la forma llega a hacerse tan necesaria como el mismo hálito inicial que les da vida. (*TB*, 233–4)

We have already seen how the importance of this combination of essential content, or inspiration, and form makes itself felt in the development of the bread–poem, where the silence of the flour–snow must be made into the form of the bread. Similarly, in poems such as 'Café' (*AM*) the question faced by the poet is how to bring into presence (form) the essential/originary coffee of the past. Indeed this double focus is evident throughout Montejo's work, including in the essay 'Textos para una meditación sobre lo poético', in many ways an early model for the later 'Fragmentario' (*TB*) and with which it shares the primary concern of the nature of poetry and the (authentic) poetic act. The first three texts of this essay concentrate specifically on the harmonising

---

[21] An early version of this section is found in Roberts (2004).

of these two key aspects of a poem: the essential, silent content and the form in which this silence is made present and 'revealed'. Montejo states here that 'en el hacer del poema lo **concreto** de su construcción (el lenguaje en estado natural) vale por el vacío de su contexto general (el silencio, las pausas ordenadoras)' (1966: 20). The reference to the language of the poem as natural clearly sets the scene for much of Montejo's later work, and intimates the attendant idea that (the form of) nature itself allows the essence to be brought forth into the world. But it also draws attention to the notion of the *construction* of poetic form, and, in the process, presages the insistent presence of and concern for constructed habitats in the later Montejian corpus, opening up the question of how such an insistence plays into and informs the notion of authentic *poetic* construction. Indeed, whilst the natural environs are a central characteristic of Montejo's presentation of home and the homeland, centred around the personal and national example of Venezuela, Montejo equally formulates both the home(land) and his condition of being in exile from it around images of *casas* and cities: human constructions within that space. In chapter 3, I examined how the modern urban cities and constructions of Montejo's work represent a separation from nature and from the quasi-rural homestead and community of the imagined past of his poetry. But we must now go beyond this initial understanding of these habitats to explore what it is *qua* constructions that makes them not just alienated and alienating from nature, but different from the *casas* and cities of the poet's childhood and Venezuelan's pre-urban past, as presented in Montejo's work.

The importance of the *casa* in Montejo's poetry is suggested from the attention it receives in *Élegos*. The focus here is largely on the *casa* of childhood as now gone, reduced to 'un poco de polvo invencible' ('Un poco de polvo invencible', *É*, 36) and 'piedras ausentes' ('Gira todo vivir por mi reloj ya calvo', *É*, 9). The loss of this habitat returns again as a focal point of Montejo's poetics in *Algunas palabras*, where the childhood *casa* becomes a metonymic symbol for home in a wider sense, signalling both the personal space of the quasi-rural community and the homeland from which the poet – and the wider community – is absent, as this collection engages with the topoi of journeying and exile. The widening of the meaning of the *casa* is shown in Montejo's alternating between references to his own childhood *casa*, 'mis cuatro paredes' ('Las nubes', *AP*, 63), and the extension of this to a more general experience, most obviously in the poem 'Nuestras casas', where the poet talks of how 'Se teme lo peor: morir afuera, | lejos de sus patios' (*AP*, 25).

This extension of the personal *casa* serves as a bridge towards the increasingly dominant motif of the social and national place of the city, especially in the following collection *Terredad*. As we saw in chapter 3, for Montejo there is a clear differentiation between the modern urban space and the authentic city of the past, the 'apacible comarca de otras edades' (*TB*, 13). Particularly

notable is the attention Montejo gives to the *de*struction of the latter, which
constitutes an integral part of the process of *con*struction of the former:

> Están demoliendo la ciudad
> donde tanto viví,
> donde al final, sin percatarme
> los ojos se me unieron a las piedras.
> Están derrumbando sin tregua sus muros,
> los camiones adentro del polvo
> pasan y cargan,
> se llevan ventanas, columnas, portones,
> no cesan,
> no hay nada que salve su caída
> [...]
> sus calles ceden paso a nuevas avenidas,
> los arquitectos miden el futuro,
> verifican sus planos,
> no se detienen. ('Están demoliendo la ciudad', *T*, 40)

The demolition of the old cities, with which the poet feels as one, ties in with
that of the childhood *casa* in *Élegos*, the 'espacio demolido' ('Gira todo vivir
por mi reloj ya calvo', *É*, 9), and is made inextricable from the construction
of the modern habitats of the urban world and urban Venezuela. In short,
what emerges from these poems of *casas* and cities is both an identification
of the authentic home(land) with a now-lost construction, replaced by those
of modern urbanity, and, once more, an insistence upon the dual concern
of the personal and the communal/national in the two types of constructed
habitat on which Montejo focuses.

   Both the personal and the national character of this loss of habitat are also
made clear in Montejo's appeal to a further image of a constructed habitat
in his portrayal of an originary homeland from which he and Venezuelans
are (now) distant or exiled, namely that of a mythical city which is home.
Thus, in 'Mi país en un mapa antiguo' (*TA*), even as he talks of the nature of
Venezuela, he also refers to the early maps of the recently discovered, para-
disiacal Venezuela as showing the legendary cities of Manoa and El Dorado:
'Nunca mintieron; aquí estuvo Manoa | al fin del arco iris que nace en El
Dorado' (*TA*, 9). The importance of these cities in Montejo's work is shown
by the fact that both are also the subject of individual poems: 'El Dorado'
in the previous collection *Terredad* and 'Manoa', the first poem in *Trópico
absoluto*. The former makes clear the identification of this mythic city with
an authentic being and home of the Venezuelan people and presents it as the
envisaged end-point of a wandering journey:

> Siempre buscábamos El Dorado
> en aviones y barcos de vela,
> como alquimistas, como Diógenes,
> al fin del arco iris,
> por los parajes más ausentes.
> [...]
> Perdimos años, fuerza, vida,
> nadie soñó que iba en la sangre,
> que éramos su espejo.
> [...]
> Jamás lo descubrimos,
> no era para nosotros su secreto.
> Los hombres del país Orinoco
> teníamos raza de la quimera. (*T*, 20)

The alignment of the city with the essence of the people ('en la sangre'), together with the reference to those searching as alchemists, serves to tie the search for El Dorado in with the poetic search for the alchemic nature and being of Venezuela found throughout these mid-period collections. Likewise, in the later 'Manoa' this vain quest for the legendary city is repeated, as is the assertion that this city is the authentic being to be brought out from inside. Only here the emphasis is on the specific relation to the individual poet's search:

> Anduve absorto detrás del arco iris
> que se curva hacia el sur y no se alcanza.   12
> Manoa no estaba allí, quedaba a leguas de esos mundos,
> – siempre más lejos.
> [...]
> Manoa no es un lugar   18
> sino un sentimiento.
>
> (TA, 5)

In all three of these poems concerned with El Dorado and Manoa, the point is repeatedly made that they are unlocatable in both time and place: they are at the end of the rainbow, a point which one can signal and move towards, but which recedes as one approaches, 'siempre más lejos'. They underscore, that is, what has been evident throughout this study: that the places and times put forward as authentic, as of a Golden Age, are mythic. But these poems also underline that the ultimate aim of Montejo's poetry is not just to bemoan the loss of these mythic habitats, be it in the image of El Dorado, the Caracas of old, or the poet's own quasi-rural *casa*, but to work towards a (re)discovery or a recovery of this construction of home, just as the natural essence of the country is to be journeyed towards and (re)discovered.

The question remains, then, as to how we are to understand and view these authentic, mythic habitats, both personal and communal.

An initial – and central – vista onto this question is provided by the fact that both *casa* and city are brought together by Montejo in their presentation as inseparable from a *poetic* loss. Following his reference to the replacement of the 'apacible comarca de otras edades' by the 'urbe moderna' (*TB*, 13) in the essay 'Poesía en un tiempo sin poesía', Montejo goes on to affirm, with regard to the lost city, that:

> Hoy podemos advertir, tras la pérdida de ese espacio, de qué modo resulta imprescindible la relación del hombre y la ciudad para explicarnos las obras que nos legaron los artistas del pasado. [...] El París de Baudelaire, la Alejandría de Cavafy, la Lisboa de los cuatro Pessoa, se nos tornan inseparables de sus logros artísticos. (13)

Similarly, in 'Materias del destino' from *Trópico absoluto*, referring to the relationship between poetry and the *casa*, Montejo asks '¿Quién en sus muros grabó mi poesía | antes de ser ésta mi casa?' (*TA*, 49). In short, Montejo is suggesting that the collapse and demolition of the old habitats, on both a personal and a collective level, leads to a loss in poetic creation.

However, it is notable that Montejo's explicit appeal to Heidegger as a philosopher who shared his lamenting of the spaces and technology of the modern era, on which I commented in the Introduction and in chapter 3, occurs immediately before his statements regarding the lost poetic cities of the past in 'Poesía en un tiempo sin poesía'. And it is in Heidegger's work on poetic construction that we find a key to understanding the relationship between poetry and both the *casa* and the city which Montejo's work discloses here. In his essay ' "... Poetically Man Dwells ..." ' (2001: 209–27) Heidegger affirms that 'poetic creation, which lets us dwell, is a kind of building' (2001: 213). It is poetic creation, that is, 'which lets us dwell', not a dwelling which lets us create poetically. Holding this claim in mind, our reading of both the passages just cited changes radically. In the case of Montejo's question as to who inscribed poetry into the walls of the house before it was his *casa*, our critical gaze, guided by Heidegger, becomes fixed on the word 'antes'. Poetry precedes the *casa*. It is what allows the walls to be seen as the authentic habitat which was his childhood *casa*. Poetry is not lost, then, as a result of the loss of the house. Rather, the *casa* is lost because poetic creation has ceased.

Turning to the first quotation, regarding the city, the effects of such a Heideggerean rereading are even more radical. The question is whether Montejo's reference to the Paris of Baudelaire, the Alexandria of Cavafy and the Lisbon of the four Pessoas concerns the actual cities in which these poets lived, or whether, in fact, it is a reference to the cities which are found in and produced by their poetry. Read in this way, the quotation now seems to describe how the artistic achievements of these poets are inseparable from the way in which their poetry creates the *poetic* habitats 'Paris', 'Alexandria', and 'Lisbon'. The achievement in question, then, is precisely the construction of a poetic city, a poetic habitat. This, of course, suggests more than the simple reversal of the relationship between poetry and the mourned habitats of the past posited by my proposed rereading of 'Materias del destino' (*TA*). Rather, it indicates that the authentic city whose loss Montejo mourns is itself nothing but poetry. There is no physical city here; there is only a poetic one. Moreover, this is a reading which turns out to apply not just to Montejo's concept of the city but also to his concept of the personal habitat of the *casa*. This is made manifest when Montejo's poetry on the lost *casa* is read alongside one of his earliest essays 'Aproximación a Ramos Sucre' (*VO*, 67–84), concerning the poetry of José Antonio Ramos Sucre, whom Montejo generally seems to consider to be Venezuela's last great national poetic figure. In this essay Montejo cites a number of lines from Ramos Sucre's poetry which bear a striking resemblance to many lines and images from *Élegos* concerning his old *casa*, as can be seen in the table below:

Ramos Sucre	Montejo
' "Unos *jinetes* bravíos me escoltaban durante la visita al país de las *ruinas* legendarias. [Nos detuvimos a maravillar los arabescos y perfiles de un puente de arcos *ojivales*.]" ' (Cited in 'Aproximación a Ramos Sucre', *VO*, 80. Continuation of the poem, entitled 'El error vespertino', (not cited by Montejo) in square brackets (Ramos Sucre 1980: 193), italics mine)	'De quién es esta *casa que está caída* […] Y el *jinete* de sombras que transpuso en la *ojiva* su ser.' ('De quién es esta casa que está caída', *É*, 12, italics mine)
' "*recorro* sin descanso los aposentos de *mi casa antigua*, rescatada en la esquivez de una sierra." ' (Cited in 'Aproximación a Ramos Sucre', *VO*, 80–1, italics mine)	'En los bosques de *mi antigua casa* […] cuando *recorra* todo.' ('En los bosques de mi antigua casa', *É*, 5, italics mine)

It becomes clear that what is being mourned is, as in the case of the city, not the loss of an actual house, but the loss of a poetic house, a house built by and out of poetry, in this case the poetry of Ramos Sucre, the great national poetic figure, thus reminding us once more of the inseparability of the personal and the national in these poems. It is not just that poetry is seen as potentially leading (back) to an authentic, constructed home. Rather, home and the homeland *are* the construction of authentic poetry.

Importantly, if this authentic poetic construction is aligned with Manoa and El Dorado, and, by extension, mythic, 'siempre más lejos' (*TA*, 5), the details and presentation of the constructed (poetic) habitats in question can, nevertheless, shed light on both the nature of the poetic goal striven for and a possible way in which it might be worked towards. In defining authentic habitat as poetry, Montejo's work echoes Heidegger's description of poetry and suggests that it is by somehow living in poetry that we are truly at home, in an authentic being-on-the-earth. In order to explore in more detail how this is presented in Montejo's work, we must, thus, first tackle the further question raised here of what constitutes the *inauthentic* habitat in which the poet and modern Venezuela find themselves and from which a way out must be sought.

In *El cuaderno de Blas Coll*, Coll tellingly refers to his goal as being to bring hygiene into 'la casa del habla' (*BC*, 40) and later describes language as 'la verdadera piel del hombre' (46). Language, then, is our home, that which we inhabit, as the distinct engagement with Heideggerean thought is disclosed once more, specifically with the latter's declaration in 'Letter on Humanism' (1993: 213–65) that 'language is the house of Being. In its home man dwells' (217). Yet this house is simultaneously described by Coll as our 'cárcel alfabética' (*BC*, 92). For Coll, (alphabetic) language often gives us the 'ilusión de que somos sus dueños, o los herederos de sus ilusorios inventores' (91), but in fact 'la lengua nos habla como la música nos baila' (44), recalling Heidegger's assertion that 'man acts as though he were the shaper and master of language, while in fact language remains the master of man' (2001: 213).[22]

These lines from *El cuaderno de Blas Coll* are pivotal. In short, Montejo's concept of the inauthentic habitat, ciphered in the images of the modern, urban city and the lack of the childhood *casa*, is revealed here as a being caught in language *as* a prison, the 'prison-house of language' to borrow a term from Fredric Jameson (1972) and, ultimately, Nietzsche. Caught inside it, Montejo tells us, its walls 'nos tapian el mundo' ('Final provisorio', *TA*, 66), as the walls of the city enclose and entrap the poet. Put simply, language may be the home of being, but this home is only authentic, or essential, when that language is poetry, as Heidegger underscores when he declares, a number of years after 'Letter on Humanism', that 'poetry is what really lets

---

22   Rodríguez Silva (2005b: 78–81) comments on the Heideggerean echoes here, but prioritises the earlier ideas of Wilhelm von Humboldt which focus more on how each language
pertains to (and determines) a different way of understanding the world. He also points up the
presence of this Humboltian and Heideggerean linguistic tradition in Venezuelan authors such
as Rafael Cadenas and J. M. Briceño Guerrero. Unfortunately his analysis comes to an end
without exploring the avenues he has opened up.

us dwell' (2001: 213).[23] It is to this poetic language that Montejo seeks to 'return', transforming the prison of language into the poetic home once more.

The starkest declaration of this poetic intent arises in 'Una ciudad' in *Terredad*, where Montejo begins: 'Escribo para fundar una ciudad' (*T*, 61). In effect, following on from the Paris of Baudelaire, the Alexandria of Cavafy, and the Lisbon of the four Pessoas, Montejo seeks to create the Caracas of Montejo: a poetic habitat for his countryfolk, where the poet is 'el arquitecto por excelencia' (*TB*, 14),[24] searching for:

> la arquitectura subjetiva
> de puentes, columnas, catedrales
> creada en palabras nuevas
> con el abecedario de las formas fuertes. ('Una ciudad', *T*, 61)

In referring to the words which are to make up this poetic city as 'palabras nuevas' Montejo is drawing attention here to the fact that, despite the impression of his poetry as one which mourns and pines after lost habitats from the past, the poetic habitats in question can only ever be projected into the future. Of course, having thus established that the poetic language out of which the authentic home is to be built is, in fact, projected rather than recuperative, the question still remains as to how this envisaged poetic language and habitat is to escape from being 'plain' language, the prison-house. Crucial in this respect is the persistent recurrence in Montejo's poetry of *piedras*, not least as the constituent pieces of the walls of the demolished *casa* and city. When talking of the now-gone *casa* of his childhood in *Élegos*, for example, Montejo focuses on the 'piedras ausentes' ('Gira todo vivir por mi reloj ya calvo', *É*, 9), just as in the later 'Nuestras casas' (*AP*) he refers once more to the stones which make up the walls of these abodes, talking of the voices of the past generations being 'en sus piedras' (*AP*, 25). Similarly, when alluding to the lost city of the past it is frequently the stones which comprise the walls of its buildings around which Montejo gravitates. In 'Están demoliendo la ciudad' (*T*), for instance, Montejo describes his sense of oneness with the stones of the city being demolished ('los ojos se me unieron a sus piedras' (*T*, 40)), and later in the same collection the poet laments the loss of the Caracas of his childhood, declaring at one point that 'Perdí mi sombra y el tacto de sus piedras' ('Caracas', *T*, 55). Indeed, this preponderant concern

---

[23] The relationship between poetry and language is expounded upon at some length in Heidegger's earlier essay 'Hölderlin and the Essence of Poetry' (1968a: 291–315). Here he identifies poetry with the essence of language and, thus, being; it is 'the inaugural naming of being and of the essence of all things' (307).

[24] The appearance of the poem as an architectural construction in Montejo's work has been discussed at some length by Consuelo Hernández (1993).

for the stones of the authentic constructions extends to the mythical cities
to which Montejo has recourse, with 'Manoa' (*TA*), for example, begin-
ning: 'No vi a Manoa, no hallé sus torres en el aire, | ningún indicio de sus
piedras' (*TA*, 5). In short, both the personal habitat of the *casa* and the lost
communal or national habitat of the city are understood as constructions
of stones. And it is the loss and destruction of these stones which underpin
Montejo's poetics of the loss of authentic, poetic habitat. Indeed, Montejo
offers an overt and distinct contrast between these stones and those which
make up the modern urban constructions, talking in 'Final provisorio' (*TA*)
of how 'Ahora deambulo contemplando las piedras | que se amontonan en
altos edificios' (*TA*, 66), an image of the stones of the dominating modern
buildings whose negativity is clear.

The contrast between the two different types of stones corresponds to
the contrast between the home of poetry and the prison-house of 'plain'
language; poetic words and plain words. The poetic habitat that Montejo
strives to build, then, is to be constructed from these 'authentic' stones. And
in the later 'Escritura' from *Alfabeto del mundo*, some eight years after the
publication of 'Una ciudad' (*T*), this specific nature of the poetic goal and the
poetic construction is finally stated explicitly:

> Alguna vez escribiré con piedras,
> [...]
> Estoy cansado de palabras.
> [...]
> Con piedra viva escribiré mi canto. (*AM*, 179)

The stones or words of the poetic construction are not simply 'palabras', the
plain words ciphered in the piled-up stones of modern buildings, but stones
infused with life, whose echoes are, today, 'ahogados en torres y edificios'
('Alfabeto del mundo', *AM*, 166).

Yet, in between these two poems describing the construction of the poetic
habitat ('Una ciudad' (*T*) and 'Escritura' (*AM*)) there are reminders that such
a poetic construction made of 'piedra viva' is still very much envisaged rather
than actual. 'Las sombras' from the intervening *Trópico absoluto* is key in
this regard, as the poet depicts his writing of poetry as leading not to the
sought-after authentic habitat, but merely to a repetition of the imprisoning
language which he is attempting to replace and avoid:

> No sé por qué ni para quién
> sigo escribiendo.
> Ya mi mano también es una sombra
> y letra a letra me tapia entre murallas. (*TA*, 65)

Once again the condition of Orpheus in the modern world makes its presence felt in Montejo's poetry, as the doubts and questions of 'Orfeo' (*MM*) come back to haunt the poet. The walls created through his poetry may be those of a city ('murallas'), but, far from being the city of 'Una ciudad', written with the stones described so explicitly in 'Escritura', the poet constructs the same prison-habitat, the same inauthentic city as before.

But if Montejo considers the poetic city a construction that he has not yet realised, he also, crucially, feels it as potential, and a potential which the poet must work towards, as is clear in the declaration 'Escribo para fundar una ciudad' (*T*, 61). To understand what is involved in this process, then, we must look to understand the nature of the poetic stones: what makes them poetic, authentic, and different from those of modern habitats, that is, from 'plain' words.

Whilst the characterisations, descriptions, and definitions of *piedras* in Montejo's work could themselves form the basis of a study of some length, we can, nevertheless, identify several key traits of the stones with which one imagines Montejo attempting to write his poetry. One of the most important texts in this regard is the essay 'Las piedras de Lisboa' (*TB*, 135–42). Here Montejo depicts Lisbon as the sort of authentic habitat which he feels is now gone in Venezuela, focusing on how stones are used in its streets and buildings. These stones are 'signos con los que algo sabido o no sabido viene a decirse' (137). And they are, in Montejo's eyes, to be aligned with the use of the third person *o senhor/a senhora* in Portuguese to refer to the second person, in that they grant 'una zona neutra, un ámbito indefinido […] menos concreto' and 'cierto atributo intemporal' (138). The stones used in the construction of this authentic city, then, are linked with the unknown and an unlocatability in both space and time. In short, they are mythic in character, just as I have identified the authentic poetic dwelling to be for Montejo. But the lines cited here also underscore the identification of the authentic habitat made from these stones with the notion of the border to which we have seen Montejo return repeatedly in his poetics: as signs which indicate 'algo sabido o no sabido' and grant an 'ámbito indefinido […] intemporal' (138), the stones are imbued with the characteristics of the liminal moment between nothingness or essence and form, the very 'punto de cruce' (*BC*, 94) to which Blas Coll refers. This is further suggested by a key line in 'Las piedras' in *Terredad*. Talking of stones which are 'más profundas que la infancia | y de más sólido paisaje' (*T*, 48), Montejo refers to them as 'madres pétreas' (*T*, 48). This phrase resonates with the Spanish terms *madre patria* and *células madres*, at once emphasising the engagement with the idea of national essence here and also that the stones in question in Montejo's poetics are to be originary, providing the mould from which not just all stone but all material is formed. In this sense they appear aligned with the stones or, significantly, letters out of which God created the world according to the

kabbalic tradition of the *Sefer Yetzirah*, or *Book of Creation*:[25] they are originary, essential, and both prior to form in things or language, and yet also the
point of initiation of form itself, echoing Heidegger's affirmation that poetry
is not 'building in the sense of raising and fitting buildings', but 'the primal
form of building' (2001: 224–5). Moreover, one of the last fragments to be
added to *El cuaderno de Blas Coll* implicitly taps into precisely this understanding of the stones. In a note published, we are told, in the apocryphal and
significantly-titled Puerto Malo-based journal *La piedra*, Coll writes that 'las
verdaderas palabras [...] carecen de letras [...]. [S]on propiamente formas
del Verbo cuya presencia nos antecede en la tierra. Con tales palabras se ha
de escribir el poema' (*BC*, 99–100).[26]

Clearly Montejo's engagement with stones here in his portrayal of the
envisaged poetic habitat points to a general philosophy of poetry. And, indeed,
he wrote much which addressed the importance of the form of poetry from
just such a broad anthropic position.[27] But we must also hold present that
the terms within which this question of (constructed) habitats is presented is
largely that of his personal *casa* and the communal and national habitats of
Venezuelans more widely. Hardly surprising, then, that the stones from which
the authentic habitat of this poetics is to be constructed are also identified as
those of Venezuela itself. This is implied in 'Las piedras', both in the allusion
to the *madre patria* contained within the reference to the *madres pétreas* and
in the fact that these stones are aligned with the horizons of the Orinoco and
the *paisajes* of Venezuela in their depiction as 'nuestro único equipaje' (*T*,
49), as we have seen. In addition, the poem is also notable for its personal and
nostalgic air and detail, evident in the broader context in which the *madres
pétreas* are mentioned:

> Y son las mismas madres pétreas
> que en inocente desnudez
> al zambullirnos
> se quedaban oreando las ropas. (48)

Beyond this poem, the identification of the stones with which Montejo's
poetics is concerned as specifically Venezuelan is also made in several other
pieces. In *El cuaderno de Blas Coll*, for instance, following Coll's declaration
that Spanish 'ya no sirve en estos tórridos climas' (*BC*, 42–3), the typographer

---

[25] See Eco (1997: 28–32) for relevant extracts from the *Sefer Yetzirah* and comments on
the nature of the stones/letters of this tradition.

[26] The last of Montejo's heteronyms to appear, Lino Cervantes, also published two poems
in *La piedra* (*CR*, 215).

[27] See, for example, 'Textos para una meditación sobre lo poético' (1966) and 'Fragmentario' (*TB*, 229–43).

talks of the new language in the following terms, stressing the importance of the stones or construction materials being those of the local area:

> Yo me iré un día, pero quedarán los cimientos de una fundación que Vds. habrán de proseguir hasta elevarla sólidamente. Es la casa de todos, a la que cada uno debe su ladrillo. Es *una casa hecha con las piedras del lugar, con el barro y las cañas del lugar*, pero no será una casa ajena donde se viva como hasta ahora, de modo tan incómodo y desguarnecido. Será una casa para vivir en paz. (43, italics mine)

Following on from this extract, which dates from the first edition of the text (1981), Montejo himself then emphasises that he is concerned with the stones of Venezuela in the poem 'Mi país baja al mar…' (*AM*). This poem presents a rich tapestry of descriptions and imagery which draws upon several aspects of Montejo's Venezuelan poetics, from the *canto del gallo* to the light found in the tropics. The poem, in full, reads:

> Mi país baja al mar con sus antiguas piedras
> llenas de sol e intactos jeroglíficos.
> No se leen en sus poros el alfa o la omega,
> su alfabeto está hecho de signos salvajes   4
> que aprendemos en sueño, de oídas,
> por el canto del gallo.
>
> La luz cae densa sobre el tatuaje eterno
> que guarda sus silencios. En ellas se demora   8
> con sus lentos anillos, nómada y blanca.
> Ninguna es jónica o corintia, nunca fueron a Grecia,
> detestan los viajes.
> El Partenón no las verá entre sus columnas,   12
> han echado raíces lejos de la nieve,
> donde la tierra gira más despacio.
> Su mar es éste, el que pule sus cuerpos
> con las espumas que jamás Afrodita   16
> palpó junto a sus formas estatuarias.
>
> Mi país las reúne junto a las costas
> en una fila de murallas sentimentales.
> Si hablan a solas será de los antiguos,   20
> de quienes vuelven a veces de la sombra
> y graban sus secretas cosmogonías.
> Si sueñan tal vez sea con la lluvia,
> con el viento que corre y no las mueve.   24
> Han pasado la vida en los acantilados
> mirando los barcos que parten y no vuelven,
> pero nunca los siguen.
> Ya no tienen deseos sino soledades.   28
>
> (*AM*, 190)

Using, once more, the cipher of snow to mark out the tropics of Venezuela (line 13), Montejo affirms the particularity of the stones in question, differentiating them keenly from those of classical European constructions. This marking out of a Venezuelan construction is then underlined in the final strophe, which depicts the stones built up around the country's coast as the city walls of the entire country itself.

Aside from highlighting the stones' Venezuelan identity this poem also demonstrates the connexities between (local) nature and the (local) constructions within that nature which poetry is to bring about. The stones – or words – described are 'llenas de sol' (line 2), endowed with the 'tatuaje eterno' of 'la luz [que] cae densa' (line 7), the white light which has no fixed home ('nómada' (line 9)) and which cannot be captured, but which can be perceived and lived in its writing in the stones. In short, the stones with which Montejo is to write the authentic, poetic habitat are inextricably linked to the nature on which the sun inscribes authentic being, as we saw in 'Hombres sin nieve' (*TA*). As humans, we need a construction in language because, as Montejo's work repeatedly suggests, we are (our) language.[28] But by constructing this home and being from the authentic stones of the Venezuelan *paisaje*, poetry, Montejo's work implies, can build a linguistic construction for the Venezuelan people which is authentic, one with nature, and alchemically endowed with the absent essence of being, ciphered in the light of these tropics.

In fact this conflation of language-as-being and language-as-home is also crucial to our understanding of the stones and constructions, both authentic and inauthentic, in a further way. Within the terms used by Montejo there is an unavoidable spatial and logical tension: on the one hand our being is language, and only in poetic language is our being authentic; yet, on the other, both language and poetry are portrayed as a habitat, that is, a place *inside which* we live. The addressing of this tension is pivotal in the envisaged move from the prison of language to the home of poetry.

In his depiction of inauthentic habitats and being, Montejo describes himself as a part of these inauthentic constructions, as we can see in 'En esta ciudad' (*TA*):

> En esta ciudad soy una piedra;
> me he plegado a sus muros seriales, opresivos,
> de silencios geométricos. (*TA*, 45)

---

[28] Aside from the leaves/lives metaphor in poems such as 'Otoño' (*MM*), this is made clear in the development of the identification of language as our home, that which supports us and allows us to be, from the linguistic spider's web found in 'Mi vivir es araña en la tela del poema' (*É*), 'Fragmentario' (*TB*, 240), copla XIV of *Guitarra del horizonte*, 'La araña veloz' (*AS*), and 'Fábula del escriba' (*FE*) to the 'casa del habla' (*BC*, 40) and 'piel del hombre' (*BC*, 46) of *El cuaderno de Blas Coll*.

Similarly, in 'Las piedras al acecho' (*TA*) the stones of the modern city appear lying in wait as 'se apilan en los muros', ready to 'convertirnos en pálidas estatuas' (*TA*, 43), artistic (stone) constructions devoid of life or 'authenticity'. In short, that this inauthentic habitat of language is our being is affirmed in the image of our and the poet's oneness with it. Turning to his presentation of authentic being there is, likewise, a depiction of a oneness with the stones of both the authentic habitats and authentic artistic production. Describing the demolition of the habitats of old, Montejo begins the poem 'Están demoliendo la ciudad' (*T*) by stating how 'los ojos se me unieron a sus piedras' (*T*, 40) and ends by reaffirming his oneness with the now absent constructions of his past:

> Me duele cada golpe de las picas,
> cada estruendo,
> ahora que mis ojos son las últimas piedras
> que le quedan
> en la casa sin nadie que soy
> a la orilla del tiempo. (40)

And the envisaged *return* to authentic habitats is conceived of in similar terms, as it too engages with the idea of the poet being sculpted like a statue. Only here the statues in question have none of the negative connotations of those of 'Las piedras al acecho'. This is the case in 'Quita a la piedra que soy' (*T*) and 'Presencia' (*TA*), where a mysterious figure sculpts and crafts the poet's body, which is described as both stone and words:

> Quita a la piedra que soy
> lo que le sobra,
> martilla, esculpe, talla.
> [...]
> lee las vocales de mi cuerpo
> las palabras que buscan vida. ('Quita a la piedra que soy', *T*, 53)

> Siento sus manos noche y día
> a sol y sombra en mi carne, trabajando.
> A través del sueño o la vigilia
> nivela, ajusta, no me abandona,
> martilla despacio, intensamente
> con los golpes exactos.
> [...]
> siento sus golpes intensos todavía
> pero no sé quién quiere que yo sea,
> su afán no ha terminado. ('Presencia', *TA*, 61)

The figure in these poems can be identified with Orpheus, poetic inspiration, a lover, or the absent essence, and perhaps its polyvalency points to its being this (absent) centre or essence of language and being, to which, as Derrida has pointed out, we give a variety of names (1967b: 409–11). What is clear, though, is that this sculpting of the poet's body represents the work of returning to authentic art and poetry, away from both the dead stones and language and the 'pálidas estatuas'. It is concomitant, that is, with a return to authentic being and an authentic construction.

Yet, despite these similarities in the depiction of both types of stone/ language as our *being*, there is a central difference between the two in the way in which they are presented as our *habitats*, one suggested in the total confla- tion of the (poet's) body and the (artistic) construction in 'Quita a la piedra que soy' (*T*) and 'Presencia' (*TA*). Whilst poems such as 'En esta ciudad' (*TA*) may at times depict the poet and the people as one with the inauthentic stones of the modern city, the overriding sense of entrapment *within* its walls is inescapable: the prison to which I have referred. Thus, in 'Las piedras al acecho' (*TA*), whilst referring to us as 'pálidas estatuas', the focus is, in fact, on how the stones of the city 'nos amurallan con rectos edificios' (*TA*, 43), resonating with the reference to the city walls in 'Final provisorio' (*TA*) which 'nos tapian el mundo' (*TA*, 66). And even in 'En esta ciudad' (*TA*), the iden- tification of the poet with a stone in the walls of the city buildings is tied to a menacing sense of oppression and containment ('sus muros seriales, opre- sivos' (*TA*, 45)). By contrast, and as the statue poems suggest, the oneness with the authentic stones both of the habitats lost and of those which poetry is to construct is one where the self is not contained or bound by its walls, but is simply and wholly the stones of the constructions themselves: the 'casa sin nadie que soy' (*T*, 40), with no one contained within that house.

This change in positionality is central to the theoretics and ethics of Montejo's proposed poetic construction. The focus on the stones and walls of the construction or habitat ties in with the focus on the border in Montejo's work, and in placing the poet at this border Montejo effectively rejects any location which falls into one side of the implied binary: in/out; life/death; *materia*/nothingness, with the poet in a position where both terms are brought together. But the key to Montejo's poetic solution here is found in the way in which two terms – absent essence and the *materia* of the walls/poet/words – are envisaged as interacting at this border point, with the most eloquent poem in this respect being 'El esclavo' from *Terredad*, a poem whose meaning and significance can only be appreciated when the surrounding and following poetics are read back into it. The poem describes the poet's nocturnal and alchemic task, but, significantly, begins by defining the poet in the following way:

> Ser el esclavo que perdió su cuerpo
> para que lo habiten las palabras.

Llevar por huesos flautas inocentes
que alguien toca de lejos   4
o tal vez nadie. (Sólo es real el soplo
y la ansiedad por descifrarlo). [*sic*] (*T*, 33)

The poet's form is words, and on this border construction, where the poet's
body is one with the walls of his (linguistic) home, the essence (the wind,
the divine) is invited to play him like a musical instrument, producing thus
the harmonious *canto del hombre*, humankind's authentic *terredad*. Indeed,
this is picked up on some nine years later by Sergio Sandoval, who describes
the horizon of the Venezuelan *Llanos*, a further image of an ungraspable,
unlocatable border, as a musical instrument:

Cuerda larga y sin clavija
que suenas de monte a monte,
¡quién te tocara algún día,
guitarra del horizonte! (Copla IX, *GH*, 29)

Likewise in copla XXXVII, Sandoval talks of the traditional adobe houses of
Venezuela as being synonymous with the authentic, natural, poetic construction, in that 'puesto que son de barro sus palabras, nada que los aparte de la
tierra podría interesarles' (*GH*, 67). And, like the horizon and the body–words
of the poet in 'El esclavo', their being is spoken by what flows and passes
through them, including, once more, the wind, with its inevitable connotations of the divine essence, as we are told that 'ninguno hablará de sí mismo;
eso lo dejan a la lluvia y al viento, o a la fila de hormigas que de tanto en
tanto recorre sus grietas' (67). It is what Montejo refers to in his own poem
'El buey' (*AM*) as 'el habla porosa de las piedras' (*AM*, 168).

Returning to the earlier poem, 'El esclavo' further reveals that the effect
of this relationship between form and essence is a complete breaking not
just of the idea of containment, but of any notion of being as restricted and
locatable. The idea of sides, of inside and outside, breaks down entirely in
the logic of the poem: the being of the poet appears to exceed its form, as
the words – his body – are now described as inhabiting him ('para que lo
habiten las palabras' (line 2)), suggesting a freedom in which being thus goes
beyond words but is only visible in words. That said, the poem also serves
as a reminder of the continuing uncertainty in the presentation of this poetic
solution and construction, in that the essence which is to play the body–words
of the poet is denied as soon as it is affirmed: no sooner is it 'alguien' (line
4), than, immediately, it appears as 'nadie' (line 5), underscoring the impossibility of permanently apprehending the absent essence in language, as the
poem stresses the *continuing* desire to do so (lines 5–6).

One of the most significant aspects of 'El esclavo', however, is its ethical dimension, and here too it feeds into and off Montejo's wider and continuing development of this poet-as-border schema. The move from prison to home constitutes a stark ethical move in its rejection of the prison guard/prisoner, master/slave relationship. The desire expressed by Montejo and Coll to *anotar* the language of nature or nature as language masks a desire to reverse rather than overcome this ethics, making this essential language 'mía del todo' (*BC*, 50). Hence its failure. But the move towards being one with language as the walls/border of one's habitat carries with it a different approach. Coll describes the controlling nature of language by referring to how 'la combinación de letras y significados pone en juego, tan pronto aprendemos a emplear su mecanismo, a un organismo autónomo que nos convierte en pasivos usuarios de su casi infinita posibilidad de variaciones' (91). Repeating the power relations of the prison-house, humans here are passive, dominated by language. And this seems to be the case in Montejo's own declaration regarding *poetic* language and the *poetic* construction in 'Fragmentario' too:

> Lo que el poema exige es debilidad para invadir, por eso el poder de la razón casi siempre lo obstaculiza. El poeta auténtico aprende a desmontar la resistencia (y no a armarla, como aconsejan los manuales literarios); crea mecanismos y reflejos de indefensión para que el poema lo invada. Así pues, pasivamente femenina es la creación, y mientras más pasiva, más hondamente contribuye a gestar la voz poética. (*TB*, 233)

Yet there is a fundamental difference between these two sorts of passivity. Rather than being 'pasivos usuarios', unaware of the way in which, as Coll puts it elsewhere, 'la lengua nos habla como la música nos baila' (*BC*, 44), what is at stake here is what I shall term 'active passivity', where the poet must actively assume a passive role, actively moving to the border, free from the constraints of language and reason, to allow the essence (of being, language) to pass through him, to 'play' him. In interview with Cruz, Montejo reiterates this idea, whilst underscoring the debt he owes here to the thought of Paz, as he talks of how 'como afirma Octavio Paz, terminamos por convencernos de que [el lenguaje] es el verdadero autor de un determinado poema. Su armonía, su naturalidad, provienen de la destreza del poeta para hacer posible que hable a través de sí' (2006: 378). Indeed, going back further, we might also link this move to Heidegger's presentation of the poet opening himself up as a conduit for the language of the gods (1968a: 291–315). In each case, the simple ethical binary appears as deconstructed. And yet, in its very title, 'El esclavo' reminds us of the separation between the theoretical move and the attempt to bring about its realisation. Just as the problems of language appear insuperable in this poem, so too does the ethical straitjacket: the poet depicts his position as that of a slave, in effect marking the uncompleted or unrealised nature of the poetic task set out by the poem, as the poet feels enslaved both by the very fact – or necessity – of being a poet called to assume this position and by the self-perpetuating nature of this failure.[29]

But the question of ethics surrounding this (task of) poetic construction does not stop there, in that the entire topos of the constructed habitat is riven by an ethical tension which, ultimately, remains unresolved. The habitats lost are both personal, in the form of the *casa*, and societal or national, in the form of the city. As we have seen, these two forms of construction are often made interchangeable or blurred in their presentation by Montejo. In 'Están demoliendo la ciudad' (*T*), for example, the poem begins by talking of the demolition of the old city, with whose stones the poet's eyes have become one ('los ojos se me unieron a las piedras' (*T*, 40)). But the poem ends with Montejo repeating the alignment between the poet's eyes and the stones, only, this time, they are the stones of the *casa*:

> ahora que mis ojos son las últimas piedras
> que le quedan
> en la casa sin nadie que soy
> a la orilla del tiempo. (*T*, 40)

This merging of the two sorts of habitat is not simply an expression of their both being the same sort of authentic construction, only on different levels. Rather, it represents a highly significant conflation: the city which Montejo seeks to construct is also his – the poet's – personal *casa*, a conflation paralleled and, it might be argued, glossed by Blas Coll's description of the house he wishes to build as 'la casa de todos' (*BC*, 43). The *casa* of the poet is just such a house, then: the house of both the wider city of the community/nation, and, by analogy, and more widely still, that of humankind. Certainly, this is suggested by Montejo's overarching concern for being *per se* and is also further implied by the final line of 'En esta ciudad' (*TA*): in being 'a la orilla del tiempo' the lost poetic house that is the poet presents itself as the cosmos as a whole: the border of time (and space) itself.

The ethical problem with this conflation of the poetic *casa* and the wider habitat of both Venezuelans and, implicitly, humankind, is that it is only the poet who makes the move to the walls of the construction. He may be one with the walls of language, transforming the prison into a poetic home, where he is open to the through-flow of the essence, but the rest of the nation/humankind is bounded by the poet, still bounded, that is, by the walls of language. Against this problematic, in his essay on 'Balada del preso insomne' Montejo refers to Martínez's poem as speaking not just for the nation, but where the

---

[29] In an interview conducted four years after the publication of 'El esclavo' (*T*), Montejo repeated that, as well as being 'una especie de isla de salvación [...] también la poesía se siente como maldición, como esclavitud de las palabras' (Szinetar 2005: 96).

nation also assumes the more active role of speakers themselves, as he talks of artistic works who 'están al servicio de una vehemencia iluminada por la que comienza hablando el propio artista y terminamos hablando todos' (2006b: 267). And yet this declaration does not exclude the idea that the masses are simply accepting that the poet speaks for them, in the way implied by the reference to the Orphic poet as a ventriloquist in 'Orfeo revisitado' ('con trucos de ventrílocuo' (*AM*, 169)). Moreover, the religious overtones of Montejo's presentation of the poet further underscore this ethical impasse. Frequently, the Orphic poetic figure appears as a salvational God–man, both in terms of the latent and constant presence of the pagan Orpheus himself and in the repeated allusions made to a Christ-like understanding of the envisaged poetic figure, from the presentation of Simón Bolívar in 'Nostalgia de Bolívar', where the 'divine' *Libertador*, in being conflated with an authentic home, thus aligns himself with the poet-as-home, to, for example, Montejo's Christological depiction of Pessoa in 'La estatua de Pessoa' (*AM*) with his call 'Démosle vino ahora' (*AM*, 178). The primary figure to be depicted in this way, however, is that of the poet of Montejo's own poetry, working away at night to transform language alchemically, to produce the communional bread that is the poetic product and which, as we have seen in poems such as 'Quita a la piedra que soy' (*T*), is also portrayed as his own body. The envisaged solution of the poetic home in Montejo's poetics is caught up, then, in an ethics of subordination and subsumption, of a quasi-Christological separation between the God–man poet and others which simultaneously writes out its success in keeping the rest of the people bound by and dependent upon the walls of the poet's language. As López Ortega, speaking of the Venezuelan nation, says of Montejo's poetry: '[es] un signo que de tan amplio y abarcante nos consume y define' (2005: 16).

With this in mind, we can see how Montejo's poetry falls into the same trap as Blas Coll in creating a (poetic) language which is only assumed by its creator. Concerned with a mythical habitat, a habitat on the border of time and physical space, the poet is shown ultimately to be unable to effect a change for his people within the history and spatial reality of his country. In short, the poetics of construction, of the poet as the poetic home, affirms the opening lines of 'Orfeo revisitado' (*AM*), where Montejo declares that 'Orfear aquí tal vez el hombre puede | sólo para sí mismo en la hora atea' (*AM*, 169), revealing that, even with the envisaged successful construction of the poetic *casa*, 'la casa de todos' (*BC*, 43), the poet would still only be able to write *himself* into an position of authenticity of being and language. Indeed, it is perhaps significant that the image of the poetic figure at home on the coastline – the border – of Venezuela, but alone, should appear so frequently in Montejo's later work in particular, from the figure of Blas Coll throughout the eighties and nineties, to those of the painter Armando Reverón and the poet Teófilo Salazar, as recounted in the essays 'La luz de "Los espacios cálidos"' (*TB*, 159–65) and 'En un playón solitario' (*TB*, 107–18), respectively.

Home as homecoming: construction as process

There is, however, a caveat to be added to Montejo's presentation of the construction of an authentic poetic home, and one which offers a potential way out of its ethical impasse. One of the central reasons for Montejo's persistent engagement with the topos of stones in his poetics of construction is that they represent a permanence which provides an end to temporal loss, an end to death, and the fulfilment of the desire for 'el canto [que] permanezca' ('La terredad de un pájaro', *T*, 52). Put simply, these poetic stones remain when our fleeting lives are gone:

> Ellas quedarán por nosotros,
> ellas se lavarán en el diluvio
> profundas, porosas, inocentes. ('Por el tiempo que quede', *AP*, 83)

Yet, echoing the importance of temporal experience found in the notion of *terredad*, Montejo also affirms the movement of (transitory) life, our earthly passage, within this schema of the stones, in that, alongside the description of the poet as the stones of the authentic habitat or the statue being crafted to perfection, Montejo also declares himself to be a river, a river which contains and is inextricably linked to stones. This is the case in several poems, such as 'El Orinoco' (*AP*), 'Yo también soy Orinoco' (*TA*), and 'Dame tu mano' (*TA*), and ties in with the depiction of both Bolívar and Venezuelans in general in 'Nostalgia de Bolívar', as well as with the overarching concern for rivers as a topos in Montejo's work. One particularly explicit example is 'Yo soy mi río' (*T*), which contains distinct echoes of 'Nostalgia de Bolívar' and sets out the basis of the relationship between the stones, which I have been discussing, and the concept of the self as river. The first nineteen of the poem's twenty-six lines read as follows:

> Yo soy mi río, mi claro río que pasa
> a tumbos en las piedras.
> Me circundan las horas y las ondas,
> no sé adónde me arrastran,   4
> desconozco mi fin y mi comienzo,
> voy cruzando mi cuerpo como el arco de un puente.
>
> Las nubes me siguen por los campos
> con cálidos reflejos.   8
> Entre los árboles derivo, entre los hombres,

sólo traje a la tierra este rumor
para cruzar el mundo,
lo he sentido crecer al fondo de mis venas.   12

Estas voces que digo
han rodado por siglos puliéndose en sus aguas,
fuera del tiempo.
Son ecos de los muertos que me nombran   16
y me recorren como peces.

Yo soy mi río, mi claro río que pasa
y me lleva sin tregua. (*T*, 24)

The river is that of life itself, and the stone-words of the poet are both found
within it and polished by it. Life itself, then, is the gradual etching of this
smoothness on the stones, producing, that is, a writing which is nothing,
finally taking the lost writing of the branch of life on the wind to be blown
away and lost in 'Otoño' (*MM*) and reformulating it as this same absent
writing, but on the permanence of the *piedras*. This is how life can live on
when the individual river has gone, as Montejo states in the later 'Yo también
soy Orinoco' (*TA*), referring to how 'lo que he amado quedará entre sus
márgenes [del Orinoco] | tatuado en alguna de sus piedras' (*TA*, 36).

Two initial considerations emerge from this presentation of the river.
Firstly, the alignment of the poet with the river seems to stand in contradiction to the oneness of the poet with the stones. However, this dual alignment of the poet with both the inscriber and the inscribed in fact serves to
underline that the goal towards which the poet is working is precisely the
unlocatable and paradoxical border moment where form and essence are in
harmony. Moreover, such an apparently impossible harmony is tied in once
more with the desired poetic figure of Orpheus, who, in Montejo's poetry,
is both craftsman ('Quita a la piedra que soy' (*T*); 'Presencia' (*TA*)) and yet
also the 'estatua rota' ('Orfeo', *MM*, 19), awaiting its transformation into the
perfect(ed) artistic construction.

The second consideration is that, in depicting the river as that which
inscribes or crafts the stones, Montejo conflates the symbols of the river,
the sun, and the Orphic poetic figure/craftsman working away at the poet.
All three are portrayed as the essence which inscribes (itself into) the form
of the stone. On the most basic level, this discloses the inseparability of the
(absent) essence from the movement of life. But it also serves to highlight
a key aspect of Montejo's understanding of the former, in that, specifically,
all three ciphers appear as symbols which correspond to an overarching and
abstract essence in which each individual life partakes: the light of the tropics
is what, the poet declares, 'me compendia la vida y la muerte' ('Trópico absoluto', *TA*, 12), but it is also that of the nation as a whole, and each individual
Venezuelan can declare the same; the Orphic figure, working at the individual

poet in 'Quita a la piedra que soy' (*T*) and 'Presencia' (*TA*), likewise comes to take the form of a deity who shapes *all* people, as Montejo describes in the later poem 'Mi Hacedor' (*PC*); and, most significantly, the poem 'Yo soy mi río' is weighed down by seemingly conflicting images of the relationship of the poet to the river: he is the river (line 1), and yet its waves 'me arrastran' (line 4), the river 'me lleva sin tregua' (line 19), as well as having its 'rumor' located within him (line 12). The poet, that is, has the river within him, is the river, and is contained by the river. The river-that-is-the-poet, then, comes to be seen as a river within the wider river that is life as an abstract, echoing the relationship of Venezuelans to Bolívar in 'Nostalgia de Bolívar'. And it is this endless river of all people, of all lives, which has polished the stones, as is implied by the reference to the stone–words having been polished 'por siglos' (line 14), recalling both the notion of humankind's song being passed down through the generations and Montejo's concept of words as containing the inherited being of all those who have spoken them before (2006b: 292). Thus, when the poet declares of this Venezuelan river-of-all that:

> De tanto seguirlo me confundo con él,
> yo también soy Orinoco
> – escribo para serlo, ('Yo también soy Orinoco', *TA*, 36)

he can be seen to be vocalising a desire to be the Christ-like figure, Orpheus, the essence of *all*: that is, to be the Venezuelan nation and its *terredad*, rather than simply one poet, one *pájaro*, aiming to fashion the stone–words in and for his time as part of a never-ending work of polishing or inscribing with smoothness. Yet it is in the acceptance of this individual role within a wider process – an acceptance found in 'Yo soy mi río' – that the ethics of subsumption are to be avoided.

The primary effect of Montejo's poetics on both fronts – the stones and the river – however, is to underscore that the move towards the apparent goal of permanence and oneness with both a universal essence and form is, above all, a process: the statue which is the Orphic poet is constantly being fashioned, as each individual poet is merely one brick or stone in the wider poetic work or habitat, just as the river of life is travelled on and in by countless lives, all of which will, themselves, end. And it is this process, this movement towards the goal, which is consistently valorised by Montejo. In short, rather than being lamented, the journey of life – as an exilic journey towards (the) home(land) and as the course of a river inscribing the stones of that poetic home with smoothness – is affirmed as the only essential way in which a home and an authentic being can be found and forged. In this respect, Montejo's work once more engages with a distinctly Heideggerean mode of thought. For Heidegger, the journey which begins in exile constitutes the necessary process of any poetic attempt at a becoming homely, in that one must 'first become homely in the return from the foreign' (1996: 125). Indeed, more resonant still with the wandering terms in which the journey is frequently portrayed by Montejo, Heidegger also affirms that the return which is homecoming 'is only possible for one who has previously, and perhaps possibly for a long time now, borne on his shoulders as the wanderer the burden of the voyage' (1968a: 278–9).

Yet what is at stake in Montejo's poetics goes further. The home to be constructed does not, crucially, appear as separate from this process, this movement: as we have seen, the stones are unthinkable without the process of inscription, just as the homeland is unthinkable without the sense of the need to approach it, even when one is physically in it. This, then, is the reason for my proposing the term *construction* rather than *construct*: the (poetic) product is inseparable from the (poetic) process, to the extent that an authentic being and poetics *is* the approach to it. This is implied by the very terms Montejo uses: 'escribo para serlo [el Orinoco]' (*TA*, 36); 'escribo para fundar una ciudad' (*T*, 61); the bird, like the poet, sings 'para que el canto permanezca' (*T*, 52). The authentic being is a process of construction, a continuation of the building carried out by previous generations, and a laying down of the foundations upon which the following generations will work, reflecting Montejo's dual concern for tradition and *actualización* which I identified in the Introduction. Certainly a similar approach is found within Heidegger's texts, notably in *What is Called Thinking* (1968b), where he argues that ' "being" means something in being, and the act of being' (220). But Montejo's schema here also differs from Heidegger's in its incorporation of the sense of fixedness that comes with the idea of (the) home (of/as being). In interview in 1999, Montejo talked of his desire 'de viajar y no viajar al mismo tiempo, [...] de ir y volver simultáneamente, [...] de encontrar una forma de partir mediante la cual uno logre quedarse' (Márquez Cristo and Osorio 1999). He comments that this is the journey 'que más me seduce porque trata de reunir los contrarios' (Márquez Cristo and Osorio 1999). Yet his work itself reveals that this is not just another example of his desire for harmony; it is the *central* harmony sought in his work, in that it is a way of expressing the sense of being – or remaining – *at* home in the process of the never-ending movement *towards* home: it is what poetry seeks to be. Thus, we can see how the final lines of Montejo's final poem speak not just of the ghostly nature of life, as I argued in chapter 2, but also of this constant process of the approach to home as being home itself.

> – Nos iremos sin irnos,
> ninguno va a quedarse ni irse,
> tal como siempre hemos vivido
> a orillas de este sueño indescifrable,
> donde uno está y no está y nadie sabe nada.
>
> ('Final sin fin', *FE*, 67)

In many ways, then, Montejo's work chimes with Rodolfo Kusch's reading and interpretation of Heidegger and, in doing so, emphasises once more the constant need for this to be an American poetics and a Venezuelan poetics. For Kusch, the 'Ser' of Heidegger's thought does not fit being in Latin America. In the Americas, 'nuestro vivir está [...] más en el nivel del estar' (1976: 155), and in Montejo's poetics it is in the place of the Venezuelan tropics, the remaining at (this) home, the constant movement of the journey, the poetic process of writing and rewriting, and the flowing of the river, all of which are contained in the idea of the *estar* of life. As Kusch goes on to add: 'nuestro modo de vivir se concreta en un "estar siendo"' (156), which is the 'única posibilidad [para] nuestra autenticidad' (158). And it is just such a poetics of the authentic being and home as a constant *estar siendo*, and, perhaps to convey better the nuances at stake here, an *estar, siendo* that emerges from Montejo's work.

Conclusion

In tackling both temporolinguistic loss and the loss of an essential home or being-on-the-earth and in Venezuela, I have shown how Montejo repeatedly ties the space of the poem to the apparently authentic times and places to which he appeals: his childhood *casa*, the bakers' *taller*, the *terredad* of the natural *canto del gallo*, and the poetic construction of home. It is the authentic poetic space that appears as the mythic, timeless locale for which Montejo strives in his work, and it is, thus, through the work of the poet that such poetic authenticity is to be (re)found and (re)forged. Consistently, the problem facing the poet in his task is characterised by a latent and ineluctable tension which permeates Montejo's writing. Inextricably linked to the nature of language itself, this often appears as a tension between life and death, presence and absence, in particular the contrast between temporal, fleeting life and a permanence free from and beyond death. In his early work this tension manifests itself through the dominant and recurring images of the *caballo* and the *casa*, images which continue to surface into his later poetry, where they are joined by the poetics of journeys and homeland, river and stone. In each case the poet attempts to locate and bring about the authentic construction or space for himself, his country, and humankind, a space found at the chimeric and mythic border at which both terms of the tension meet, and a space identifiable both with the impossible centre which is free from the play and rupture of *différance* in Derridean terms and with the moment of irruption into being, on the level of both the individual (birth) and the world. This envisaged space of the poem is, then, where the tension between the terms might be turned into harmony, the harmony which Montejo repeatedly declares himself to be seeking ('mi alma | que siempre sueña la imposible armonía' ('Las avispas', *AM*, 196)). Nevertheless, that such a feat is unrealisable is underscored in one of Montejo's later poems, 'Contramúsica' (*PC*), which also emphasises that the tension which Montejo seeks to harmonise is that found within language itself:

> En vano intento que escritas en mis versos
> las palabras no riñan unas con otras.
> [...]
> Tan pronto llegan, las palabras se retan,

se baten, se combaten, no cesan,
viven en guerra como los átomos del mundo,
como los glóbulos de sangre. (*PC*, 18)

The envisaged harmonious space of the poem also takes us back to the
question of a renewed Venezuelan poetics imbued and in tune with the
national poetic tradition, a central dual concern of Montejo's writing and
thought. As each of the chapters of this study has shown, Montejo's poetics
often works around certain symbols: *caballos*, *café*, the flour–snow of Venezuela, its *paisajes* (rivers, stones, light/sun), the birds which sing – or used to
sing – in it, the *canto del gallo*, and a poetic home. In effect, Montejo built up
his own symbology, constructed around symbols and synecdochic markers of
Venezuela which he presents not as pertaining to any one time or place within
the country's history, but as national symbols which can represent and thus
unite its people, past, present, and future. Indeed, this is precisely the implication of the alignment of each of these symbols with an atemporal, mythic
locale. Moreover, in bringing all of these symbols together in the space of
the poem, Montejo's poetics thus posits itself as the very metatraditional
space to which I referred in the Introduction, a space which, in incorporating
and containing the overarching markers of the nation, thus also takes in the
national figures associated with it, both poetic/artistic and historical: Bolívar
(*caballos*, river), Gerbasi (*paisajes*), Reverón (*luz*), Ramos Sucre (*casa*). In
short, Montejo's own response to the times in which he lives, both generally
in terms of the modern questioning of language and nationally in terms of a
perceived untying of natural, communitarian, and familial bonds amongst the
people (and with their land), is not so much to seek a return to a particular
past era, but to attempt to create this metatraditional poetic space which is
not bound by any time or place.

But within this construction of a symbology for his Venezuelan poetics
there is also a further tension, beyond those of ontolinguistics. As discussed
in chapter 4, and as implied by my analysis of, for example, *caballos*, *café*,
snow, and the role of the bird in Montejo's poetry, there is a persistent tension
between the use of and appeal to European thought, traditions, and symbols
and the underlying desire for Montejo's poetics and the poetic space or
construction it is to bring about to be specifically of and for the tropics of
Venezuela (a locale which, we should recall, also participates in the wider
focus on the tropics and (Latin) America more generally). As we saw at the
end of the discussion in chapter 4, here too the concept of harmony is key,
with Montejo's understanding of authentic being as a process of approach to
home chiming with Kusch's American reading of the European Heidegger.
The point is, then, not that the European is to be rejected, but that it must
be reappropriated within the nature, symbols, and, hence, assumed ontology
of America, the Caribbean tropics, and, more specifically, Venezuela, adding

to the linguistic charge and meaning of inherently European terms, thought, and poetics.

Beyond my exploration of this process with regard to the symbols already mentioned, this 'reappropriation' is exemplified particularly well by the increasing presence of the *cigarra* in Montejo's work. On several occasions the *cigarra* appears as an indicator of Venezuela, as nature and as home. This is the case in 'Las cigarras' (*AP*), 'Trópico absoluto' (*TA*) and 'La iguana' (*TA*), and 'La carta' (*AM*). Paramount in the poet's mind in this use of the *cigarra* is the contrast between nature and being in tropical Venezuela and nature and being in Europe. This is brought out most explicitly in a rereading of Aesop's fable of the ant and the grasshopper in both *El cuaderno de Blas Coll* and *Guitarra del horizonte*. In the former we are told how 'en contra de Esopo y de los fabulistas del Mediterráneo, conviene no perder nunca de vista que en el trópico – *solía advertir Blas Coll* – es la cigarra, y no la hormiga, la que tiene razón' (*BC*, 72). What is meant by this is expounded upon in the later heteronymic work, where Sergio Sandoval explains in the gloss to copla XLVIII that:

> En el álbum sentimental de nuestra coplería, la chicharra aparece como el insecto que más seduce a la imaginación de los cantadores. Nada puede contra ella la acrimonia de Esopo, que moraliza a partir de su supuesta ineptitud para el trabajo y el ahorro, virtudes éstas que atribuye a las hormigas. El coplero reconoce que también el canto es un trabajo sutil e indispensable, y se identifica con su destino. De tal forma, sin saberlo, más que al sordo Esopo, su instinto lo acerca al melodioso Homero, cuyos hexámetros tanto deben a los sonoros élitros de estos insectos. Por lo demás, la nieve nunca llega a nuestra tierra, de modo que las hormigas no tienen ocasión de solazarse con el rencor que les endilga la esópica moraleja. (*GH*, 82)

These extracts speak of a fundamental difference in being between Europe and the tropics and link that difference to climate, once again making reference to the heat and lack of snow. But they also provide an important indicator of the role which the *cigarra* comes to play in Montejo's work, in particular in the longest poem of Montejo's career 'Partitura de la cigarra' (*PC*).[1] Building on the extract from *Guitarra del horizonte* just cited, 'Partitura de la cigarra' represents the culmination and explicit declaration of a prioritisation and affirmation of the *cigarra* over the *pájaro* as a symbol of nature, the poet,

---

[1]   Miguel Gomes (2002a; 2002b: 1015–22) has undertaken the most detailed analysis thus far of 'Partitura de la cigarra', but it remains a poem which demands significant future study, not least of its treatment of the various aspects and images of Montejo's work which have been discussed in this present work.

and his production of *terredad*. In 'Un samán' (*T*) and 'Santo y seña' (*AM*) we saw how the European poetic and natural trope of the nightingale was found to be wanting in the tropics and its poetic verse, since, in the tropics, there were different birds. But this late poem confirms that it is not so much an autochthonous bird as the autochthonous *cigarra* which is to take its place in this Venezuelan poetics. It is the *cigarra* who 'está cantando en un árbol' (*PC*, 54) and who 'custodi[a] los tonos sagrados | del insondable enigma de las cosas' (57), taking on the role of both the individual bird which dies, to give way to the next:

> Queda en el viento su ceniza cantora
> que se dispersa ya inaudible
> hasta que su rumor regrese en otro cuerpo,
> en otro vuelo de sus alas, (47)

and also of the generic 'bird' as an overarching poetic figure, reducing Orpheus to the role of the individual poet ('la maestra de Orfeo, la reina maga' (54)).

The irony in Montejo's recourse to the *cigarra* throughout his poetry might seem to lie in the fact that, despite his valorisation of Venezuelan Spanish[2] and affirmative references to the prioritisation of local terms in the Venezuelan poetic tradition,[3] the term *cigarra* is itself a word more commonly used in Spain than in Venezuela, where *chicharra* is the more *criollo* term, as used by Sergio Sandoval. But, perhaps more significantly, the cicada is itself a well-known commonplace of Ancient Greek culture and poetics, an association from which Montejo's use of the animal cannot escape.[4] And yet, given Sandoval's reference to the cicada's influence on Homeric verse, this is also an association from which 'Montejo' appears quite happy not to escape. What is key here, then, is the idea of the remodulation of the European. Montejo accepts and incorporates the European poetic symbols and traditions to which he is indebted, yet, placed within an American (Venezuelan) poetics and the tropical Venezuelan landscape, their meaning changes. Just as in the case of the horse, the snow, and nature in Montejo's work, the *cigarra*, like

---

[2]   See Montejo's acceptance speech for the Premio Nacional de Literatura (2006b: 391–4), for example.

[3]   See, for instance, Montejo's discussion of the *generación del 18* and their use of autochthonous terms (López Ortega 1999: 10) and his reference to Leoncio Martínez's use of *exilarme* rather than *exiliarme* in his poem 'Balada del preso insomne', the former being 'la forma del verbo comúnmente empleada entre nosotros' (Montejo 2006b: 265).

[4]   See Egan (1994). The recourse to the cicada also ties in with the persistent influence of Oriental thought on Montejo and his work. In 'Partitura de la cigarra', Montejo refers to the fact that this is the 'cigarra que conoce el camino del Tao' (*PC*, 53). The cicada is also a commonplace in Chinese folklore, as discussed in Riegel (1994).

being itself, is charged with the autochthonous and the personal, as Montejo discloses, for example, when describing 'la voz de mi padre que está en su silencio | y regresa en el canto de la cigarra' (*PC*, 58). In this way, as he declares the *cigarra* to be a metaphor for the poet ('Yo y mis ojos de palo | yo y la sonora cigarra de mi sangre' (68)), looking for 'un órfico grito que manda la tierra | y en su carne de insecto se queda sonando' (61), we can thus see how Montejo is at once affirming his debt to the European and announcing that both the poet and (poetic) being in America and tropical Venezuela are (to be) a renewal and a rewriting of these terms and traditions.

The increasing role given in Montejo's work to both the *cigarra* and heteronyms is also key in pointing us towards the question of the poetic figure himself. Throughout this study we have seen the centrality of the poetic figure as the one whose task it is to bring about an authenticity of being on a personal, national, and global level, with Montejo positing the poetic journey as one which works – endlessly – towards the authentic border space where the poet would be one with the poetic production/construction: the poetic Word and the poet as Word. In this way, just as this envisaged border space and moment is riven with tension on the level of the poem, so too is the poetic figure himself. We have seen how the moment of writing, the moment of entry into language on the part of the poet, as for anyone else, is an entry into fragmentation, the single, glass Logos shattered into the shards of the play of *différance*. This is the ineluctable problematic which underlies the frustration of Montejo's task of grasping this authentic border. And it applies to the poet himself too, as one with this border Word. The very act of writing, of writing in order to be the salvational Orphic poet ('escribo para serlo' ('Yo también soy Orinoco', *TA*, 36)), is, at the same time, a fragmentation of this single, Orphic, God–man figure, and this is what is represented by the incursion into heteronymic writing or the writing of *voces oblicuas*. Discussing this mode of writing in the essay 'Los emisarios de la escritura oblicua' from *El taller blanco*, Montejo describes it as 'en cierto modo, [...] una escritura en espejo, [...] un espejo que no sólo invierte los ángulos de las cosas, sino que también es capaz de recrear ángulos nuevos' (*TB*, 183). This understanding of heteronymic writing as a refractory mirror is also in evidence, in a less developed form, in the earlier essay 'Sobre la prosa de Machado' from *La ventana oblicua* and ties in with how the most famous exponent of the practice, Fernando Pessoa, described this writing process as one where 'sinto-me múltiplo. Sou como um quarto com inúmeros espelhos fantásticos que torcem para reflexões falsas uma única anterior realidade que não está em nenhuma e está em todas' (1966: 93). Montejo's heteronymic writing represents this splitting or fragmentation of the single poetic self, the unattainable 'única anterior realidade' which is forever 'anterior'. Indeed, the fact that even the orthonymic author 'Eugenio Montejo' is a pseudonym points to the idea that the voices we have before us are part of a jigsaw-like construction of an unknown, whole poetic self.[5] Moreover, it is a fragmentation which is, ultimately, endless, as demonstrated by the periodic emergence of new *voces oblicuas* in 'Montejo's' work from the publication of the first edition of *El cuaderno de Blas Coll* in 1981 onwards.[6] In short, even as Montejo laments the loss of and desires a return to Orpheus, the Romantic 'yo transcendental' ('Novalis: El fuego ante la noche', *VO*, 30), or what we might see as the humanist and Petrarchan notion of a unitary self, or a 'self struggling to seem unitary' (Greene 1991: 14), his poetry demonstrates its awareness of the impossibility of such a self, an awareness tied in, as we have seen, with the effects of poststructuralist thought and with the modern, twentieth-century era in general, the Romantic poetic figure now seen as an effect of play, a mythic space from which there is only the fall into fragmentation, as, to repeat a citation referred to in my Introduction, 'a la deificación romántica del individuo como vértice mítico de la creación, se ha opuesto el monólogo quebrado del yo lírico moderno' ('Poesía y vitalidad en Drummond de Andrade', *VO*, 99).

And yet the *élan* with which Montejo set about producing his *voces oblicuas* also tells of an approach to this fragmentation of the elusive poetic self which was far from negative. In short, just as the diversity of influences – American, European, Oriental – is affirmed in the production of a poetics which pretends to be both universal in its goals and, simultaneously, of and for tropical Venezuela, so too is there an implied – and envisaged – harmony between the idea of a singular (Venezuelan) Orphic poetic self and the fragmentation of the self represented by the multiple poetic voices (heteronyms and orthonym), as indicated by the latter's appearance as a deliberate poetic strategy on Montejo's part, alongside the continued engagement with Orpheus.

The key to understanding how such a paradox functions within Montejo's work is finally glimpsed by returning to one of the central topoi of his

---

[5] The status of the orthonym as being neither more or less privileged nor on a different hierarchical level from the heteronyms is certainly implied by the orthonym's (Montejo's) use of a pseudonym. Seabra, writing on Pessoa, also draws attention to this important characteristic of such writing, stating that 'Na realidade, [...] o poeta ortônimo situa-se ao mesmo nível que os restantes poetas – ele é, em rigor, um heterônimo a que o autor emprestou a sua identidade privada' (1974: 10). Gomes, however, writing on Montejo's use of heteronyms, refers to it as a process whereby 'el rostro ha sido substituido por una máscara evidente' (2007: 19). Such a reading stands in contrast to Montejo's problematisation of identifying or fixing a 'real' self, as found, for example, in the poem 'Dos cuerpos' (*TA*), where he talks of how: 'Solamente la luna | sabe [...] | qué rostros ríen detrás de las máscaras' (*TA*, 46).

[6] José Agosto Seabra, writing on the heteronymic practice in relation to Pessoa, makes precisely this point regarding its potentially infinite nature, stating that 'este processo de construção criadora não é de nenhum modo fechado sobre si, nem se limita a uma pluralidade finita de sujeitos poéticos: ele é potencialmente aberto e infinito' (1974: 15–16).

poetics: his valorisation of and quest to bring out into form the light of the
Caribbean tropics, as found and experienced in Venezuela. Like the Orphic
poetic self, the light acts as a cipher for the essence in which all partake.
And as in the case of the poetic self, there comes a pivotal point in Montejo's
work at which the fragmentation of this light is affirmed. The poem in question is 'La calle de los colores' from *Trópico absoluto*, where the presence
of refracted light leads into a concatenation of images of fragmentation and
dispersal, not bemoaned but revelled in:

> Pasan cuerpos azules, verdes, rojos
> por la calle de los colores.
> Son flotantes fragmentos de ciudad
> donde la luz se encarna melodiosa
> al palpitante rumor de las aceras. (*TA*, 51)

Contrary to his valorisation of the pure white light of the tropics elsewhere,
here Montejo affirms that it is through fragmentation that the light – the
essence – is made flesh, made form, not in the negative terms of the Fall,
but in a poetic musicality and harmony. What is crucial here is the nature
of white light itself. For just as the production of white light following its
prismatic dispersal requires the bringing together of the infinite colours or
wavelengths into which it is refracted, so too, then, does the recuperation of
the common denominator of being, of the essence from which all comes and
which infinitely exceeds each individual, like the concomitant grasping of the
(single, poetic) self and (an originary, poetic) language, *require* the bringing
together of an infinite number of selves and linguistic acts or poetic writings.
It is, thus, paradoxically only in the search for the infinite fragments of the
world and of the (poetic) self, a search made up of infinite poetic works, that
Orpheus can be reconstructed, that is, that a single unity, a single Work, and
a single poetic Word – that which is posited as having been lost – can vainly
be approached. The deathly journey of life which was so lamented in *Élegos*,
then, finally emerges transformed through (the course of Montejo's) poetry
as the endless poetic journey towards a space of authenticity.

BIBLIOGRAPHY

Dates in square brackets indicate the year in which the work was first published (in its original language, where appropriate). In the case of Montejo's works they indicate earlier editions which have subsequently been updated and expanded; in the case of Montejo's interviews, they correspond to the year of original publication or, where known, the year when the interview was carried out, where this is different from the main entry.

EUGENIO MONTEJO AND HIS HETERONYMS (IN CHRONOLOGICAL ORDER)

Montejo, Eugenio. 1959. *Humano paraíso* (Valencia: Impresiones Clima)
—— 1966. 'Textos para una meditación sobre lo poético', *Zona Franca: Revista de literatura e ideas*, 3: 39, 20–2
—— 1967. *Élegos* (Caracas: Editorial Arte)
—— 1969. 'El laúd del visionario', *Imagen*, 45 (March 1969): page reference unknown
—— 1972. *Muerte y memoria* (Caracas: Dirección de Cultura de la UniversidadCentral)
—— 1974. *La ventana oblicua* (Valencia: Ediciones de la Dirección de Cultura de la Universidad de Carabobo)
—— 1976. *Algunas palabras* (Caracas: Monte Ávila Editores)
—— 1977. 'Vicente Gerbasi: Retumba como un sótano del cielo', *Zona Franca: Revista de literatura e ideas*, 3: 3: 69–70
—— 1978. *Terredad* (Caracas: Monte Ávila Editores)
—— 1979. 'En torno a la obra de Fernando Paz Castillo', in Fernando Paz Castillo, *Antología poética* (Caracas: Monte Ávila Editores), pp. 7–25
—— 1981. *El cuaderno de Blas Coll* (Caracas: Fundarte)
—— 1982. *Trópico absoluto* (Caracas: Fondo Editorial Fundarte)
—— 1988 [1986]. *Alfabeto del mundo* (Mexico City: Fondo de Cultura Económica)
—— 1995. *Algunas palabras*, 2nd ed. (Maracay: La Liebre Libre)
—— 1996 [1983]. *El taller blanco* (Mexico City: Universidad Autónoma Metropolitana Unidad Azcapotzalco)
—— 1997 [1992]. *Adiós al siglo XX* (Seville: Renacimiento)
—— 1999. *Partitura de la cigarra* (Madrid: Pre-Textos)

—— 2002. *Papiros amorosos* (Madrid: Pre-Textos)

—— 2006a. *Fábula del escriba* (Madrid: Pre-Textos)

—— 2006b. *Geometría de las horas: una lección antológica*, selection, prologue, and notes by Aldolfo Castañon (Xalapa: Universidad Veracruzana)

—— 2006c. *El cuaderno de Blas Coll seguido de La caza del relámpago por Luis Cervantes* (Caracas: bid & co. editor)

—— 2007a [1981; 1983; 1998; 2005; 2006]. *El cuaderno de Blas Coll y dos colígrafos de Puerto Malo* (Valencia: Pre-Textos)

——2007b. *Poeta en residencia* (Madrid: Residencia de Estudiantes), available at http://cedros.residencia.csic.es/docactos/2695/dossier%20de%20prensa/dossier%20de%20prensa02695003.pdf [accessed 1 January 2009]

Sandoval, Sergio. 1991. *Guitarra del horizonte*, preface and selection by Eugenio Montejo (Caracas: Alfadil Ediciones)

Linden, Tomás. 1995. *El hacha de seda*, preface and selection by Eugenio Montejo (Caracas: Editorial Goliardos)

Polo, Eduardo. 2004. *Chamario: libro de rimas para niños*, preface by Eugenio Montejo (Caracas: Ediciones Ekaré)

Cervantes, Lino. 2006. *La caza del relámpago (Treinta coligramas)*, in Eugenio Montejo (2006c) (see above), pp. 83–127

INTERVIEWS WITH MONTEJO

Araujo, Elizabeth. 2004. ' "Hay que invocar la lucidez" ', *Tal Cual* (Venezuela), 14 July 2004, at http://venepoetics.blogspot.com/2004_07_01_venepoetics_archive.html [accessed 1 January 2009]

Arráiz Lucca, Rafael. 1987. 'La poesía es la última religión que nos queda: Conversación con Eugenio Montejo', *Imagen (Artes, Letras, Espectáculos. CONAC)*, 100: 33: 3–5

Bracho, Edmundo. 2006 [2004]. 'Respuestas para Edmundo Bracho', in Montejo (2006b) (see above), pp. 357–65

Campo, Ernesto. 2004. 'Entrevista a Eugenio Montejo', at http://leonardomelero.blogspot.com/2008/06/entrevista-eugenio-montejo.html [accessed 31 December 2008]

Cruz, Francisco José. 2006 [2001]. 'Entrevista a Eugenio Montejo', in Montejo (2006b) (see above), pp. 367–80

Dagnino, Maruja. 1997. 'Montejo: "La poesía es una verdad" ', *El Universal* (Venezuela), 27 August 1997, supplement: 'Cultura y espectáculos', at http://buscador.eluniversal.com/1997/08/29/cul_art_29314DD.shtml [accessed 30 December 2008]

Gutiérrez, María Alejandra. 2002. 'El diálogo con el enigma de Eugenio Montejo', *Literaturas*, at http://www.literaturas.com/EMontejoLC.htm [accessed 30 December 2008]

López Ortega, Antonio. 1999 [1998]. 'El (pasajero) eclipse de la poesía', in *Recital: Jueves de poesía, Ciclo Poetas en voz mayor, Auditórium. 25 de junio de 1998*, presented by Antonio López Ortega (Caracas: Espacios Unión), pp. 5–13

Lozano Tovar, Wendolyn. 2006. 'Lo eterno vive de lo efímero. Entrevista con Eugenio Montejo', *Literal. Latin American Voices*, 7: 25–36

Márquez Cristo, Gonzalo and Amparo Osorio. 1999. 'El tiempo no me habla de la muerte', *Común Presencia*, 12, at http://comunpresenciaentrevistas.blogspot.com/2006/12/el-tiempo-no-me-habla-tc-el-tiempo-no.html [accessed 1 January 2009]

Martins, Floriano. 1998 [1990]. 'Anotações da permanencia do canto', in *Escritura Conquistada. Dialogos com poetas latino-americanos: Entrevistas, tradução e notas Floriano Martins* (Fortaleza: Letra & Música Comunicação), pp. 245–54

Posadas, Claudia. 2002 [2001]. 'Eugenio Montejo: Hacia una poesía de la gracia', in *Versos comunicantes I: Poetas entrevistan a poetas iberoamericanos*, coordinated by José Ángel Leyva (Mexico: Universidad Autónoma Metropolitana, Ediciones Alforja), pp. 301–10

Rodríguez Marcos, Javier. 2002. 'Siempre necesitamos decir de nuevo las palabras de Amor', *El País* (Spain), 22 June 2002, at http://www.elpais.com/articulo/narrativa/MONTEJO/_EUGENIO/Siempre/necesitamos/decir/nuevo/palabras/amor/elpbabnar/20020622elpbabnar_20/Tes [accessed 30 December 2008]

Szinetar, Miguel. 2005 [1982]. 'La poesía es la última religión que nos queda', in *Eugenio Montejo: Aproximaciones a su obra poética*, ed. Aníbal Rodríguez Silva (Mérida: Universidad de los Andes, Consejo de publicaciones), pp. 95–103

OTHER WORKS CITED

Abrams, Meyer Howard. 1971 [1953]. *The Mirror and the Lamp: Romantic Theory and the Critical Tradition* (London: Oxford University Press)

Aleixandre, Vicente. 1935. *La destrucción o el amor* (Madrid: Signo)

Anderson, Benedict. 1991. *Imagined Communities* (London: Verso)

Bachelard, Gaston. 1958 [1957]. *La poétique de l'espace*, 2nd ed. (Paris: Presses universitaires de France)

—— 1962. *La flamme d'une chandelle* (Paris: Presses universitaires de France)

Balderston, Daniel. 1990. 'Huidobro and the Notion of Translatability', *Fragmentos* 3: 1: 59–74

Balza, José. 1983. 'Orfeo y su cassette', in *Transfigurable* (Caracas: Dirección de Cultura UCV), pp. 109–14

Bello, Andrés. 1985. *Obra literaria* (Caracas: Biblioteca Ayacucho)

Benjamin, Walter. 1992 [1936]. 'The Work of Art in the Age of Mechanical Reproduction', in *Film Theory and Criticism: Introductory Readings*, ed. Gerald Mast and Marshall Cohen (Oxford: Oxford University Press), pp. 665–81

Benn, Gottfried. 1986. *Sämtlicke Werke: Band 1 Gedichte 1* (Stuttgart: Klett-Cotta)

Bergson, Henri. 1945 [1889]. *Essai sur les données immédiates de la conscience* (Geneva: A. Skira)

Bernasconi, Robert. 1992. 'No More Stories, Good or Bad: de Man's Criticisms of Derrida on Rousseau', in *Derrida: A Critical Reader*, ed. David Wood (Oxford: Blackwell), pp. 137–66

Blanchot, Maurice. 1968 [1955]. *L'espace littéraire* (Paris: Gallimard)

Boas, George. 1972. 'Cycles', in *Dictionary of the History of Ideas: Studies of Selected Pivotal Ideas*, ed. Philip P. Wiener (New York: Charles Scribner's Sons), pp. 621–7

Bolívar, Simón. 1976. *Doctrina del libertador*, compiled by Manuel Pérez Vila (Caracas: Biblioteca Ayacucho)

Borges, Jorge Luis. 1993 [1932]. *Discusión* (Madrid: Alianza Editorial)

——1997a [1960]. *El hacedor* (Madrid: Alianza Editorial)

—— 1997b [1970]. *El informe de Brodie* (Madrid: Alianza Editorial)

Bowie, Malcolm. 1991. *Lacan* (London: Fontana Press)

Briceño-Iragorry, Mario. 1983 [1952]. *Alegría de la tierra [pequeña apología de nuestra agricultura antigua]* (Caracas: Edición Especial de la Procuraduría Agraria Nacional)

Brownlee, Marina Scordilis. 1990. *The Severed Word: Ovid's Heroides and the Novela Sentimental* (Princeton: Princeton University Press)

Cadenas, Rafael. 1966. *Falsas maniobras* (Caracas: Universidad Central de Venezuela)

Calzadilla, Juan. 1979. *Obras Singulares del Arte en Venezuela* (Caracas: Euzko Americana de Ediciones)

Carpentier, Alejo. 1967. 'De lo real maravilloso', in *Tientos y diferencias* (Montevideo: Arca), pp. 96–112

Carrera, Liduvina. 1997. 'La narrativa breve de Andrés Eloy Blanco en la confluencia de dos vertientes temáticas', in *El Centro de Investigaciones Lingüísticas y Literarias*, at http://www.ucab.edu.ve/investigacion/cill/lanar.htm [accessed 5 September 2005]

Carrillo T., Carmen Virginia. 2005. 'El gallo como símbolo poético en la obra de Eugenio Montejo', in *Eugenio Montejo: Aproximaciones a su obra poética* (see Szinetar (2005) above), pp. 19–38

Castellanos, Enrique. 1966. *La generacíon del 18 en la poética venezolana* (Caracas: Comisión Nacional del Cuatricentenario de Caracas, Comité de Obras Culturales)

Cernuda, Luis. 1942. *Ocnos (1940–1942)* (London: Dolphin)

—— 1974. *Poesía completa*, ed. Derek Harris and Luis Maristany (Barcelona: Barral)

Chirinos, Orlando. 2005. *Eugenio Montejo: La vocación romántica del poema* (Valencia: Universidad de Carabobo)

Conrad, Joseph. 1947 [1904]. *Nostromo: A Tale of the Seaboard* (London: Dent)

Crespo, Luis A., Eugenio Montejo, and Alberto Patiño (eds). 1981. *El caballo en la poesía venezolana* (Caracas: Acapromo SRL)

Cruz Pérez, Francisco José. 1992. 'Eugenio Montejo: el viaje hacia atrás', *Cuadernos hispanoamericanos*, 504: 67–80

Curtius, Ernst Robert. 1967 [1948]. *European Literature and the Latin Middle Ages* (Princeton, NJ: Princeton University Press)

Derrida, Jacques. 1967a. *La Voix et le phénomène. Introduction au problème du signe dans la phénoménologie de Husserl* (Paris: Presses universitaires de France)

—— 1967b. *L'écriture et la différence* (Paris: Éditions du Seuil)

—— 1967c. *De la grammatologie* (Paris: Éditions de Minuit)

—— 1972a. *Marges de la philosophie* (Paris: Les Éditions de Minuit)

—— 1972b. *La dissémination* (Paris: Éditions du Seuil)

—— 1974. *Glas* (Paris: Éditions Galilée)

—— 1988. *Limited Inc.*, trans. Samuel Weber and Jeffrey Mehlman (Evanston, IL: Northwestern University Press)

—— 1991 [1987]. *Cinders*, trans., ed., and with an introduction by Ned Lukacher (Lincoln: University of Nebraska Press)

—— 1996. *Résistances de la psychanalyse* (Paris: Galilée)

—— 1999. *Donner la mort* (Paris: Galilée)

Eco, Umberto. 1997 [1993]. *The Search for the Perfect Language*, trans. James Fentress (London: Fontana Press)

Egan, Rory B. 1994. 'Cicada in Ancient Greece', *Cultural Entomological Digest*, 4. (November 1994), at http://www.insects.org/ced3/cicada_ancgrcult.html [accessed 30 September 2004]

Eliade, Mircea. 1971 [1949]. *The Myth of the Eternal Return: Or, Cosmos and History*, trans. Willard R. Trask (Princeton, NJ: Princeton University Press)

Eliot, T. S. 1922. *The Waste Land* (New York: Boni and Liveright)

Evans, Dylan. 1996. *An Introductory Dictionary of Lacanian Psychoanalysis* (London: Routledge)

Ewell, Judith. 1984. *Venezuela: A Century of Change* (London: Hurst)

Fabricus, Johannes. 1976. *Alchemy: The Medieval Alchemists and Their Royal Art* (Copenhagen: Rosenkilde and Bagger)

Ferrari, Américo. 1988 [1986]. 'Eugenio Montejo y el alfabeto del mundo', in Montejo (1988) (see above), pp. 9–28

Franco, Jean. 1976. *César Vallejo: The Dialectics of Poetry and Silence* (Cambridge: Cambridge University Press)

Freud, Sigmund. 1961 [1925]. 'A Note upon the "Mystic Writing-Pad"', in *The Standard Edition of the Complete Psychological Works of Sigmund Freud, Volume XIX (1923–25): The Ego and the Id and Other Works*, trans. James Strachey in collaboration with Anna Freud (London: The Hogarth Press and the Institute of Psycho-Analysis)

—— 1991 [1900]. *The Interpretation of Dreams*, trans. James Strachey (London: Penguin)

Gackstetter Nichols, Elizabeth. 2000. *Rediscovering the Language of the Tribe in Modern Venezuelan Poetry: The Poetry of Tráfico and Guaire* (Lewiston: Edwin Mellen Press)

García Lorca, Federico. 1928. *Romancero Gitano* (Madrid: Revista de Occidente)

Gerbasi, Vicente. 1952. *Los espacios cálidos* (Caracas: Ediciones Mar Caribe)

Goethe, Johann Wolfgang von. 1956 [1806]. *Faust: eine Tragödie I und II Teil* (Munich: Goldmann)

Gomes, Miguel. 1990. *El pozo de las palabras* (Caracas: Fundarte)

—— 2002a. 'Montejo: Partitura de una contramúsica incesante', *Everba*, at http://everba.eter.org/summer02/montejo_gomes.html [accessed 1 January 2009]

—— 2002b. 'Naturaleza e historia en la poesía de Eugenio Montejo', *Revista Iberoamericana*, 68: 1005–24

—— 2004. 'Eugenio Montejo's Earthdom', in Eugenio Montejo, *The Trees: Selected Poems 1967–2004*, trans. Peter Boyle (Cambridge: Salt), pp. xvii–xxiv

—— 2007. 'Montejo, la otredad y el tiempo literario', in Montejo (2007a) (see above), pp. 11–24

Greene, Roland. 1991. *Post-Petrarchism: Origins and Innovations of the Western Lyric Sequence* (Princeton, NJ: Princeton University Press)

Guevara, Ernesto. 1997. *Guerrilla Warfare*, with revised and updated introduction and case studies by Brian Loveman and Thomas M. Davies, Jr. (Wilmington, DE: SR Books)

Gutiérrez Plaza, Arturo. 1994. 'El alfabeto de la terredad: estudio de la poética en la obra de Eugenio Montejo', *Revista Iberoamericana*, 60: 549–60

Haggerty, Richard A. (ed.) 1993. *Venezuela: A Country Study - Federal Research Division, Library of Congress* (Washington DC: The Division), at http://lcweb2.loc.gov/frd/cs/vetoc.html [accessed 30 September 2005]

Heidegger, Martin. 1962 [1927]. *Being and Time*, trans. John Macquarrie and Edward Robinson (Oxford: Basil Blackwell)

—— 1966. *Discourse on Thinking*, trans. John M. Anderson and E. Hans Freud (New York: Harper & Row)

—— 1968a [1949]. *Existence and Being* (London: Vision Press)

—— 1968b [1954]. *What is Called Thinking?*, trans. and with introduction by J. Glenn Gray (New York: Harper & Row)

—— 1971. *On the Way to Language*, trans. Peter D. Hertz (San Francisco: Harper & Row)

—— 1973a. *The End of Philosophy*, trans. Joan Stambaugh (New York: Harper & Row)

—— 1973b [1961]. 'Messkirch's Seventh Centennial', trans. Thomas Sheehan, *Listening*, 8: 1–3: 40–57

—— 1977. *The Question Concerning Technology and Other Essays*, trans. William Lovitt (New York: Harper & Row)

—— 1993 [1977]. *Basic Writings from Being and Time (1927) to The Task of Thinking (1964)*, revised and expanded edition, ed. and with introductions by David Farrell Krell (San Francisco: Harper San Francisco)

—— 1994 [1933]. 'Creative Landscape: Why Do We Stay in the Provinces?', trans. Thomas Sheehan, in *The Weimar Republic Sourcebook*, ed. Anton Kaes, Martin Jay, and Edward Dimendberg (Berkeley: University of California Press), pp. 426–8

—— 1996 [1984]. *Hölderlin's Hymn 'The Ister'*, trans. William McNeill and Julia Davis (Bloomington: Indiana University Press)

—— 2000. *Elucidations of Hölderlin's Poetry*, trans. with an introduction by Keith Hoeller (Amherst, NY: Humanity Books)

—— 2001 [1971]. *Poetry, Language, Thought*, trans. Albert Hofstadter (New York: Perennial Classics)

Hellinger, Daniel C. 1991. *Venezuela: Tarnished Democracy* (Boulder, CO: Westview Press)

Hernández, Consuelo. 1993. 'La arquitectura poética de Eugenio Montejo', *Inti: Revista de Literatura Hispanica*, 37–8: 133–43

Hobsbawm, Eric J. 1983. 'Introduction: Inventing Traditions', in *The Invention of Tradition*, ed. Eric J. Hobsbawm and Terence Ranger (Cambridge: Cambridge University Press), pp. 1–14

Hölderlin, Friedrich. 1992. *Gedichte* (Frankfurt: Deutscher Klassiker Verlag)

Huret, Jules. 1999 [1891]. *Enquête sur l'évolution littéraire* (Paris: J. Corti)

Instituto de Investigaciones Económicas y Sociales, Universidad de Los Andes. 2008. 'Población, Densidad y Crecimiento: Censos 1873–2001: Estado Carabobo', available at http://iies.faces.ula.ve/Censo2001/PoblacionDensidadCrecimiento/pob_dens_crec_carabobo.htm [accessed 1 January 2009]

Iribarren Borges, Ignacio. 1987. 'El Orfeo de Eugenio Montejo', *Imagen (Artes, Letras, Espectáculos. CONAC)*, 100: 28: 6–7

Jager, Eric. 1993. *The Tempter's Voice: Language and the Fall in Medieval Literature* (Ithaca: Cornell University Press)

Jameson, Fredric. 1972. *The Prison-House of Language* (Princeton, NJ: Princeton University Press)

Keats, John. 1988 [1973]. *The Complete Poems*, 3rd ed., ed. John Barnard (Harmondsworth: Penguin)

—— 1990 [1820]. *Lamia, 1820* (Oxford: Woodstock)

Kusch, Rodolfo. 1976. *Geocultura del hombre americano* (Buenos Aires: Fernando García Cambeiro)

Lacan, Jacques. 1966. *Écrits* (Paris: Seuil)

—— 1973. *Le séminaire de Jacques Lacan. Livre 11, Les quatre concepts fondamentaux de la psychanalyse, 1964*, text established by Jacques-Alain Miller (Paris: Éditions du Deuil)

Lasarte, Javier. 1991. *Cuarenta poetas se balancean: poesía venezolana (1967–1990). Antología* (Caracas: Fondo Editorial Fundarte)

Lastra, Pedro. 1984. 'El pan y las palabras: poesía de Eugenio Montejo', *Inti: Revista de Literatura Hispanica*, no. 18–19 (Fall-Spring): 211–28

Levinas, Emmanuel. 1971 [1961]. *Totalité et infini: essais sur l'extériorité* (The Hague: Nijhoff)

Liscano, Juan. 1973. *Panorama de la literatura venezolana actual* (Caracas: Publicaciones Españolas)

López Ortega, Antonio. 2005. 'Eugenio Montejo: las voces que confluyen', in *Eugenio Montejo: Aproximaciones a su obra poética* (see Szinetar (2005) above), pp. 13–17

Mallarmé, Stéphane. 1945. *Œuvres complètes*, text established and annotated by Henri Mondor and G. Jean Aubry (Paris: Gallimard)
—— 1959. *Correspondance 1862–1871*, vol. 1, collected, arranged, and annotated by H. Mondor (Paris: Gallimard)
—— 1965. *Correspondance II 1871–1885*, vol. 2, collected, arranged, and annotated by H. Mondor and Lloyd James Austin (Paris: Gallimard)
Mariátegui, José Carlos. 1979 [1928]. *7 ensayos de interpretación de la realidad Peruana* (Caracas: Biblioteca Ayacucho)
Martin, Gerald. 1989. *Journeys through the Labyrinth: Latin American Fiction in the Twentieth Century* (London: Verso)
McCann, John. 1996. 'To What is Mallarmé Referring?', *Neophilologus*, 80: 385–98
Medina Figueredo, Juan. 1997. *La terredad de Orfeo: Tensión constructiva del habla en la poesía de Eugenio Montejo* (Valencia: Ediciones del Gobierno de Carabobo)
Milton, John. 1983 [1638]. *Lycidas*, ed. C. T. Thomas (London: Sangam)
Nietzsche, Friedrich. 2000 [1967]. *Basic Writings of Nietzsche*, trans. and ed. Walter Kaufmann (New York: Modern Library)
Novalis. 1929 [1798]. *Fragmente* (Dresden: Wolfgang Jess)
Osorio T., Nelson. 1985. *La formación de la vanguardia literaria en Venezuela: antecedentes y documentos* (Caracas: Academia Nacional de Historia)
Otto, Rudolf. 1959 [1917]. *The Idea of the Holy*, trans. John W. Harvey (Harmondsworth: Penguin Books)
Pattison, George. 2000. *Routledge Philosophy Guidebook to the Later Heidegger* (London: Routledge)
Paz, Octavio. 1967. *El arco y la lira: el poema; la revelación poética; poesía e historia* (Mexico City: Fondo de Cultura Económica)
—— 1988. *Libertad bajo palabra* (Madrid: Cátedra)
Pegrum, Mark (1996). 'Stop All the Clocks: The Postmodern Assault on Time', *Mots pluriels*, 1: 1, at http://motspluriels.arts.uwa.edu.au/MP197zmpeg.html [accessed 1 January 2009]
Pérez Perdomo, Francisco. 1986. 'La poesía de Vicente Gerbasi', in Vicente Gerbasi, *Obra poética* (Caracas: Biblioteca Ayacucho), pp. ix–xxi
Pessoa, Fernando. 1966. *Páginas íntimas e de auto-interpretação* (Lisboa: Ática)
Plato, 1912. *Ion*, with introduction and notes by J. M. MacGregor (Cambridge: University Press)
Proust, Marcel. 1987–89 [1913–27]. *À la recherche du temps perdu*, 4 vols, ed. Jean-Yves Tadié (Paris: Gallimard)
Quevedo, Francisco de. 1995. *Poesía completa*, vol. 1, ed. and with a prologue by José Manuel Blecua (Madrid: Turner)
Rama, Ángel (ed.). 1987. *Antología de 'El Techo de la Ballena'* (Caracas: Fundarte)
Ramos Sucre, José Antonio. 1980. *Obra completa* (Caracas: Biblioteca Ayacucho)
Read, Kay. 1998. *Time and Sacrifice in the Aztec Cosmos* (Bloomington: IN University of Indiana Press)
Ridley, Hugh. 1996. 'Gottfried Benn's *Orpheus' Death*', *Classics Ireland*, 3 http://

www.ucd.ie/cai/classics-ireland/1996/Ridley96.html [accessed 30 December 2008]

Riegel, Garland. 1994. 'Cicada in Chinese Folklore', *Cultural Entomological Digest*, 4 (November 1994), at http://www.insects.org/ced3/cicada_chfolk. html [accessed 30 December 2009]

Rilke, Rainer Maria. 1992 [1922]. *Sonnets to Orpheus*, trans. M. D. Herter Norton (New York: W. W. Norton)

Rivera, Francisco. 1986. 'La poesía de Eugenio Montejo', in *Entre el silencio y la palabra* (Caracas: Monte Avila), pp. 39–58

Roberts, Nicholas. 2004. 'Inhabiting the Poetic in the Work of Eugenio Montejo', *Romance Studies*, 22: 51–62

—— 2006. 'De ruiseñor a cigarra: la poética venezolana de Eugenio Montejo', *Ærea: anuario hispanoamericano de poesía*, 9: ccxcviii-cccii

——2007. '*Caballos y café*: Poetic Responses to Death in the Poetry of Eugenio Montejo', *Bulletin of Spanish Studies*, 84: 1043–64

Rodríguez Silva, Aníbal. 2005a. 'Presentación', in *Eugenio Montejo: Aproximaciones a su obra poética* (see Szinetar (2005) above), pp. 9–12

—— 2005b. 'Poesía y poética: la escritura en espejo', in *Eugenio Montejo: Aproximaciones a su obra poética* (see Szinetar (2005) above), pp. 71–81

Rosario Chacón Ortega, María del. 2000. 'Eugenio Montejo: La magia del alfabeto más allá del horizonte de la página', *Espéculo. Revista de estudios literarios*, 6: 15, at http://www.ucm.es/info/especulo/numero15/montejo.html [accessed 1 January 2009]

Seabra, José Agosto. 1974. *Fernando Pessoa ou o poetodrama* (São Paulo: Editora Perspectiva)

Segal, Charles. 1993 [1989]. *Orpheus: The Myth of the Poet* (Baltimore: Johns Hopkins University Press)

Silver, Philip. 1995 [1972]. *Luis Cernuda: el poeta en su leyenda* (Madrid: Editorial Castalia)

Sucre, Guillermo. 1985. 'La metáfora del silencio', in *La máscara, la transparencia*, 2nd ed. (Mexico: Fondo de Cultura Económica), pp. 293–319

Taylor, Robert. 1829. *The Diegesis: Being a discovery of the origin, evidences, and early history of Christianity, etc.* (London: E. Truelove)

The Bible. 1995. *The Holy Bible: New Revised Standard Version, Anglicized Edition* (Oxford: Oxford University Press)

Tillich, Paul. 1952. *The Courage to Be* (London: Nisbet and Co.)

Valéry, Paul. 1957. *Œuvres*, ed. Jean Hytier (Paris: Gallimard)

Vallejo, César. 1971. *César Vallejo: Cartas a Pablo Abril* (Buenos Aires: R. Alonso)

—— 1988. *Obra poética*, critical edition coordinated by América Ferrari, Colección Archivos, 4 (Madrid: CSIC)

Vallenilla Lanz, Laureano. 1961 [1919]. *Cesarismo democrático: estudios sobre las bases sociológicas de la constitución efectiva de Venezuela* (Caracas: Tipografía Garrido)

Wilson, Jason. 1979. *Octavio Paz: A Study of his Poetics* (Cambridge: Cambridge University Press)

Zimmerman, Michael E. 1983. 'Toward a Heideggerean *Ethos* for Radical Environmentalism', *Environmental Ethics*, 5: 99–131

FILMOGRAPHY

Le sang d'un poète. 1930. Dir. Jean Cocteau. Brandon Films.
Le testament d'Orphée. 1961. Dir. Jean Cocteau. Brandon Films.
Orphée. 1950. Dir. Jean Cocteau. Discina International.

INDEX

Vallenilla Lanz, Laureano, 3 n.5
Válvula, 2 n.3
Van Gogh, Vincent, 85–6, 97
Venezuela
    industralisation and urbanisation of, 4,
        8, 23, 42, 110, 130
    journeying/distance from, 160, 162–6,
        169–71, 172, 173, 178
    language of, 5–6, 11–12, 109, 183, 211
    nature (*paisajes*, flora, fauna) of, 4–5,
        6, 157, 163–4, 171–80, 181, 184,
        209, 210, 211
    ontology of, 102–4, 106, 167–71, 175,
        176–7, 186–7

    sun/light of, 174–7, 180, 184, 195,
        196, 204, 214
    see also poetry, and place; stones, of
        Venezuela
Viernes, 4 n.6
Villalba, Jóvito, 2 n.3
Virgil, 12
'Viva Venezuela', *see* Un Solo Pueblo
von Humboldt, Alejandro, 156–7
von Humboldt, Wilhelm, 156–7, 190 n.22

Wilson, Jason, 55 n.19